Power and Politics at the Seaside

Power and Politics at the Seaside is the first book of its kind to trace the development of the seaside tourism industry throughout the whole of the twentieth century. Drawing on rich local, regional and national sources, the book contests that politics and power relations are central to the development of the modern seaside resort. The main focus of the book is a case study of Devon's seaside resorts—England's most popular domestic holiday destinations—which demonstrates how ideology, class and power collided with landscape and place.

> *'This is a very useful venture... the authors are pushing at an open door in recommending closer interaction between a Tourism Studies which should become more emancipated from its core of very orthodox economics, and a tourism/leisure history which takes too little account of debates on contemporary issues and of the approaches used in them. I like the focus on recurring or enduring themes and conflicts, on power, on local government and on the Devon case-study.'*
>
> John K. Walton,
> Professor of Modern Social History at the
> University of Lancaster

Nigel J. Morgan is principal lecturer and Director of Graduate Studies in the School of Hospitality, Leisure and Tourism at the University of Wales, Cardiff. He was previously Tourism Development Officer for the Vale of Glamorgan Borough Council.

Annette Pritchard is a senior lecturer in the School of Hospitality, Leisure and Tourism at the University of Wales, Cardiff. She was previously Senior Research Officer for the Wales Tourist Board and is editor of *The Leisure Monitor*.

EXETER MARITIME STUDIES

General Editors: Michael Duffy and David J. Starkey

British Privateering Enterprise in the Eighteenth Century
by David J. Starkey (1990)

Parameters of British Naval Power 1650–1850
edited by Michael Duffy (1992)

The Rise of the Devon Seaside Resorts, 1750–1900
by John Travis (1993)

Man and the Maritime Environment
edited by Stephen Fisher (1994)

Manila Ransomed: The British Assault on Manila in the Seven Years War
by Nicholas Tracy (1995)

Trawling: The Rise and Fall of the British Trawl Fishery
by Robb Robinson (1996)

Pirates and Privateers: New Perspectives on the War on Trade in the Eighteenth and Nineteenth Centuries
edited by David J. Starkey, E.S. van Eyck van Heslinga and
J.A. de Moor (1997)

Cockburn and the British Navy in Transition: Admiral Sir George Cockburn, 1772–1853
by Roger Morriss (1997)

Recreation and the Sea
edited by Stephen Fisher (1997)

Exploiting the Sea: Aspects of Britain's Maritime Economy since 1870
edited by David J. Starkey and Alan G. Jamieson (1998)

Shipping Movements in the Ports of the United Kingdom 1871–1913
edited by David J. Starkey with Richard Gorski, Sue Milward and
Tony Pawlyn (1999)

Power and Politics at the Seaside

The Development of Devon's Resorts in the Twentieth Century

Nigel J. Morgan and Annette Pritchard
University of Wales Institute, Cardiff

UNIVERSITY
of
EXETER
PRESS

First published in 1999 by
University of Exeter Press
Reed Hall, Streatham Drive
Exeter EX4 4QR
UK
www.ex.ac.uk/uep/

British Library Cataloguing in Publication Data
A catalogue record for this book is available
from the British Library.

Paperback ISBN 0 85989 572 6
Hardback ISBN 0 85989 571 8

Typeset in 12/14 pt Garamond
by XL Publishing Services, Tiverton

Printed in Great Britain by Short Run Press Ltd, Exeter

Contents

List of figures   vi

List of tables   vii

List of maps   viii

Acknowledgements   ix

1   Introduction   1

2   Tourism, Power and the Historical Perspective   10

3   The British Seaside in the Twentieth Century   31

4   Resorts, Communities and Social Tone in Devon   62

5   Creating the Seaside Image   100

6   Planning Resort Entertainment   142

7   Power and Politics at the Seaside   179

Notes   191

Bibliography   219

Index   237

Figures

4.1   Ilfracombe Charabanc Trip, 1919   73

4.2   Ilfracombe Pavilion, *c*. 1890   83

4.3   Ilfracombe Town and Harbour, *c*. 1900   93

5.1   The 1928 Torquay Guide Cover   116

5.2   The 1960 Torquay Guide Cover   133

5.3   The 1968 Torbay Guide Cover   135

5.4   The 1988 Torbay Guide Cover   138

5.5   The 1985 Torbay Guide Cover   139

6.1   Ilfracombe Pavilion and Pleasure Grounds, *c*. 1922   164

6.2   Ilfracombe Pavilion Theatre, *c*. 1925   165

6.3   Ilfracombe Pavilion Interior, *c*. 1900   167

Tables

3.1   Holiday-taking by British Tourists, 1951–1975   39

3.2   Investment in England's Tourism Infrastructure,
       1986–1988   57

4.1   Defining Characteristics of Devon's Key Resorts   67

4.2   Tourism Businesses in Devon Resorts as a Percentage
       of Commercial Directory Entries, 1910–1939   69

4.3   Visitor Populations of Devon Resorts, 1921   70

4.4   Rail Passenger Traffic at Selected South Devon
       Stations, 1903–1934   71

4.5   Population Change in Devon Seaside Resorts, 1901–1981   81

5.1   Torquay and Sidmouth Advertisements in *The Times*,
       1911–1931   119

6.1   Entertainment Facilities in Torquay and Ilfracombe,
       1910–1939   147

7.1   Resorts Forming the Core of the British Seaside
       Industry in the 1990s   184

Maps

3.1 Key Twentieth-Century British Seaside Resorts   34
4.1 Devon and its Seaside Resorts   66

Acknowledgements

There are a number of people to whom we are very grateful for their help and support in producing this book. We would especially like to thank Dr Eleri Jones of the University of Wales Institute, Cardiff, for her thought-provoking comments and for reading the entire draft— *unwaith eto diolch yn fawr*! We would also like to thank Professor John Walton of the University of Central Lancashire, Dr Andrew Thorpe of the History Department at Exeter University and Tim Gale of UWIC's School of Hospitality, Leisure and Tourism for their extremely useful suggestions on the draft. The responsibility for any flaws in the final product, of course, rests with the authors. Sue Reardon's hard work on the departmental scanner also deserves a special mention, as do the staff at the University of Exeter Press, who have been great to work with throughout the project—especially Anna Henderson, Richard Willis, Genevieve Davey and Simon Baker. We are also grateful to Ilfracombe Museum and to Torbay Council for their kind permission to reproduce prints and photographs from their various collections.

Finally, it is important for us to express once more our gratitude to our respective families for their continuing help and encouragement. Without their earlier sacrifices we would never have been given an opportunity to write and we would like to dedicate this book to them. '*Hen a wyr, ifanc a dybia.*'

Nigel J. Morgan and Annette Pritchard
School of Hospitality, Leisure and Tourism
University of Wales Institute, Cardiff, July 1998

1

Introduction

All forms of leisure have become commercialised, endless
devices are offered to the idle person, each to be enjoyed only
on condition that he has the money to pay. Without money he
is condemned, unable to share in the pleasure and pastimes which
press on him from all sides. But commercialisation does not
merely erect a gate through which only those with the necessary
fee can pass. It has a profound effect on the nature of the fare
offered.

H. Durant, *The Problem of Leisure*[1]

The rise of the British seaside resort often receives a passing mention
in tourism textbooks and increasingly merits attention in leisure
histories, but far too often these references are over-generalisations
and, particularly in the former, often highly anachronistic. In both,
discussions rarely do justice to what was one of the earliest 'modern'
mass tourism sites. The main aim of this book is to provide a more
holistic treatment of the development of the British seaside in the
twentieth century, attempting to borrow ideas and synthesise work
from a range of disciplines to achieve what could be described as a
post-disciplinary analysis of the topic. We see it as a study that
examines tourism development in various ways—historically, socially
and culturally—rather than as an economic and social history that
takes tourism as its subject. It is likely that the book will raise at least
as many questions as it answers by taking such an approach, but the
time is long overdue when the gulf between social and economic
history, cultural studies and the various branches of geography is
bridged in tourism studies.

1

Why Focus on the Seaside?

Unfortunately, the growth and development of British seaside resorts are not sufficiently analysed by tourism texts, other than to locate tourism within a very broad historical context, often stretching from the Greeks and Romans to beyond the industrial revolution in a sweeping overview. In many ways this oversight is the result of the nature of the study of tourism. Often located within largely business or economic frameworks, tourism studies have tended to centre around investigations of the immediate impacts of the contemporary industry. Seaside resorts, if they are studied at all, tend to be analysed as cases of environments in decline and the scope of such studies is severely limited by both the processes and time-frames investigated. This approach to the study of tourism can leave the reader with the distinct impression that tourism is largely a phenomenon of the second half of the twentieth century, with earlier developments blurring into broad generalisations. As such, the development of the industry in the first half of the century has been marginalised within tourism studies by the lack of detailed investigation and specialist study.

These approaches have done no justice to the importance of the role of the seaside resort as a space for early 'mass' entertainment in the evolution of the tourism phenomenon. Developing from its eighteenth-century origins in England, by the later nineteenth century the seaside resort had become a significant type of urban settlement across Western Europe and the United States, with some even appearing in Eastern Europe before the First World War.[2] Since the Second World War, and particularly since the 1970s, however, the coastal resort has become a truly global phenomenon.[3] Yet as a site of consumption rather than production, and an activity often reliant on fragmented, small-scale enterprises, seaside tourism has been doubly disadvantaged as an arena of academic study. That researchers have been drawn more to the study of the economic impacts of tourism, to analyses of the activities of large, multinational corporations and to discussions of 'exotic' rather than 'mundane' tourism says more about what the dominant ideology deems to be important, than about the cultural, economic and historical significance of the

British seaside resort. The pursuit of academic knowledge is never neutral or objective but is closely related to prevailing power structures. Knowledge is a product of the social distribution of power, channelling and constructing meaning and providing us with definitions of 'appropriate' and 'worthy' subjects for study. The fact that the seaside industry is dominated by small-scale investment in the tourism infrastructure, is defined by the activities and motivations of small- to medium-sized operators, and (possibly most significantly, in terms of its perceived 'importance') is dominated by a seasonal, part-time, female workforce, probably goes a long way to explain its marginalisation within tourism studies.

Where the British seaside has formed the focus of study, it has largely been historians and geographers—not tourism researchers—who have investigated its development, with a few notable exceptions.[4] Indeed, the most recent text on the seaside resort—*The Rise and Fall of the British Coastal Resort,* which appeared in 1997—is dominated by contributions from geographers and historians.[5] Yet one cannot write about the development of tourism as we understand it today without discussing the evolution of the British coastal resort. Arguably, it is synonymous with tourism—as Walton has commented, the seaside resort has, in the long term, been 'as pervasive a [British] cultural export as football'.[6] As a site for tourism consumption, the fortunes of the *British* seaside product may well be in a state of flux and decline but the seaside resort's pre-eminence on the global stage cannot be challenged. If we are truly to understand the interplay between social relations and tourism processes, we must move towards a more integrated approach, one that clearly demands a historical appreciation of the development of tourism. Without this our understanding will be severely limited, obscuring the similarities of resort experience across the twentieth century.

In its exploration of key themes in the development of resorts—including the role of local government in seaside development, resort marketing, the planning of the resort infrastructure, and the provision of entertainment—our analysis will show that these processes and activities display remarkable longevity. In no way are techniques such as market segmentation and destination marketing pure inventions of the 1960s and 1970s. Some aspects of these themes will be covered

3

in greater detail than others, and, as others before us (notably John Walton's overview *The English Seaside Resort*), our analysis will be drawn heavily from case studies of selected resorts.[7] Yet, despite access to detailed case studies (often in thesis form), some important topics and geographical areas have had to be neglected for want of accessible material. In saying this, it is important to comment that the research map of resort studies is an interesting topic for question in itself: those resorts which have been seen as important have been studied, but some of the more politically peripheral regions have received rather less attention.

Despite the fact, for example, that Wales is the second most important area for seaside tourism in the UK, it has received scant attention, often its most important resorts are merely mentioned in passing in studies which largely focus on the English experience. Indeed, despite the work of researchers such as Durie in Scotland and Davies and Heuston in Ireland,[8] so little detailed work has been done on the resorts of Wales, Scotland and Ireland that it is as yet impossible to talk of a UK or British Isles resort experience and these countries deserve much more attention—particularly at case study level—in their own right. Interestingly, recent work by Morgan and Pritchard points to a later twentieth-century Welsh experience which is somewhat different from that of England.[9] Similarly, work commissioned by the Wales Tourist Board indicates that the Welsh resorts have not suffered the same scale and degree of decline associated with their English counterparts in the last quarter of the twentieth century, but this is rarely acknowledged in discussions of British resorts.[10] In view of the dearth of *British* literature, whilst this book deals with issues which are common to the twentieth-century British experience, it is the *English* experience which continues to dominate and a key focus is on Devon—generally regarded as Britain's most popular seaside tourism area. This book, therefore, does not attempt to be the definitive guide to the history of the British seaside in this century, but what it does try to do is to draw more attention to the importance of the seaside throughout this period and to the processes which characterised its development.

Why Politics and Power?

The inherent tensions within tourism destinations—amongst local
politicians, planners, residents and the tourism trade—over the
mutually conflicting needs of different groups of residents and
tourists are a key thread which runs throughout this book. It
underpins much of our discussion of the organisation, development
and marketing policies that have shaped the seaside resort environment. Such tensions and conflicts are by no means peculiar to the
seaside nor specific to any historical period. Indeed, the same issues
remain current and can be seen today in tourism across the globe,
from the conflicts between residents, small operators and multinational all-inclusive resorts in Jamaica, to the disputes over native
American sites under visitor pressure in the USA. Tourism is clearly
an arena in which we can legitimately observe conflicts and study the
dynamics of political and power relationships. As Enloe has said, the
fact that the tourism industry has been dismissed by conventional
political commentators as less important than, say, the arms or oil
industries, reveals more about 'the ideological construction of "seri-
ousness" than about the politics of tourism'.[11] Tourism in the
twentieth century, 'linked as it is with transnational corporations,
ruling elites and political hegemonies',[12] is not simply about power
relationships between societies, but also within them. Tourism
processes parallel the pre-existing socio-economic processes which
animate a society; they do not exist outside of them.[13]

Researchers have begun to tackle the interplay between the politics
of gender and race and tourism processes, and there are a handful of
writers who have examined the relationships between sexuality, space
and tourism.[14] Gender and race are clearly two of the key determinants of power relations and their interplay creates new dimensions
to inequalities as space has different implications for women and men
and for different races, even of the same social class. We have investigated the wielding of power in and through the tourism industry via
the experiences of different races, genders and sexes elsewhere in
Tourism Promotion and Power.[15] In that study we argued that contemporary touristic representations portray and reinforce existing power
structures and reflect a white, bourgeois, masculine, heterosexual and

5

Western perspective. In this book, however, we turn specifically to the relationship between tourism space and social class—a key determinant of power which remains surprisingly neglected in the tourism literature.

Shields has argued that places inherently 'express ... social divisions' and that they are much more than geographical locations since place and space have certain meanings and associations.[16] Any examination which involves place—in our case the seaside—therefore also necessitates an exploration of its 'emotional' geography.[17] In fact, just as cultural forms have been divided into 'high' and 'low', Shields describes how spaces have been mapped as 'systems of "centres and peripheries"'.[18] Marginal places are those which have been '"left behind" in the modern race for progress ... not necessarily on geographical peripheries but ... on the periphery of cultural systems of space in which places are ranked relative to each other'.[19] Arguably, the contemporary British seaside resort is one such peripheral place—a leisure site that has shifted from the centre to the margin. Once the symbol of high cultural and geographical capital, the British seaside lost its 'high' social tone in the twentieth century as its wealthier visitors responded to the influx of working-class visitors by seeking more exclusive leisure sites elsewhere. As such, the seaside reflects 'the development of cultural marginality [which] occurs only through a complex process of social activity and cultural work'.[20]

This book attempts to contribute to an examination of the processes described by Shields. In particular we seek to analyse the efforts of certain groups in resorts to resist social marginalisation by preserving 'high' cultural status and discouraging less 'desirable' or 'fashionable' clientele. Such an examination of the historical intersections of space, power and social and economic status can hardly fail to contribute to our understanding of modern tourism processes. The following chapter therefore provides a relatively detailed analysis of the relationships between tourism, leisure and power. It critically reviews developments within tourism and leisure theory, encompassing not only the debates surrounding the meaning of the tourism experience but also arguments within leisure theory. In doing so it contends that leisure and tourism are inherently intertwined with the dimensions of power which have structured and continued to structure twentieth-century British society. In other words, despite the tendency to present tourism as free time, its study leads the researcher not to the periphery but to the centre of society's power structures. Tourism thus reflects and reinforces divisions rooted outside the experience itself. Within tourism, the seaside is an arena where middle-class manipulations of access to resorts and the policing of working-class tourism behaviour can be identified and investigated. In particular, access to the seaside was controlled by a variety of factors, including the development of strategies by local elites to maintain resort 'social tone'. This tone was the result of interaction— and frequently conflict—between powerful groups within the local population and tourists. As we shall see, some of the more up-market British resorts were able to maintain a high social tone by pursuing deliberate policies of exclusion until well into the twentieth century.

Before we examine such policies, however, Chapter 3 provides an overview of the development of the British seaside in the twentieth century. In order to contextualise the evolution of the resort product the chapter divides into distinct halves. The first half of the chapter documents the chronological development of the seaside, whilst the second half draws out the remarkably consistent themes which have characterised this evolution. These themes include the significance of social gradation within and between resorts, the roles played by central and local government and the private sector in resort development, and the impact of cultural change on the seaside.

Chapter 4 moves the discussion beyond the general to the specific by examining the relationship between resorts, communities and social tone in Devon. In doing so it demonstrates that tourist spaces were arenas for conflict and that the control and usage of such space was continually contested by various factions in the resorts, principally residents' groups and local tourism operators. Critically, it reveals how resorts sought to attract 'desirable' visitors (those who were affluent and up-market) and exclude those working-class tourists who were much less desirable. The chapter begins, however, by introducing Devon and tracing the development of its resorts to provide the contextual foundation for our subsequent discussion of resort conflicts.

Chapters 5 and 6 examine the advertising and marketing of resorts and the development of resort entertainment facilities. In practical terms, Chapter 5 illustrates how local authority resort promotion was critical to the evolution of an advertising philosophy within the tourism industry itself. In suggesting this, we argue that the tendency to describe place marketing as a relatively recent phenomenon obscures the long tradition of resort advertising and underestimates the sophistication of even the earliest marketing strategies. Chapter 6 discusses the range of policies pursued by resorts in their provision of tourism facilities and entertainment. It highlights the internal mechanisms which underpinned the implementation of resort enter-tainment policies and the critical role played by local authorities in resort infrastructural development. More significantly, however, it demonstrates that the nature of the attractions that were deemed to be acceptable were instrumental in the maintenance of resort social tone. Both chapters thus examine not only the tourism strategies pursued by local authorities, but also reveal how marketing and enter-tainment articulated the social and cultural divisions which animated resort communities—divisions between residents, the tourism operators and the tourists themselves.

This book therefore explores the development of the seaside resort in Britain since 1900: it examines the spatial and temporal dynamics of resort tourism and investigates the local politics and patterns of holiday-making as an example of how leisure power relations operate on the micro-scale. It concludes that the development of the seaside in the twentieth century reveals the inherent conflict between those seeking to control leisure space and time and those seeking to utilise them. Above all, the following chapters demonstrate the durability of the concept of resort social tone. As historical analyses of seaside resort development, they identify those influences and power relations that shaped resort development and isolate some of the factors that determined the success or failure of particular seaside resorts. As such, the book clearly reveals that, although times may have changed enormously over the twentieth century, the parallels between success and failure are remarkably constant. Given that many mainstream tourism texts devote very little space to any detailed analysis of the historical processes which influence the development

8

of tourism, these parallels may well be obscured. In terms of the evolution of a 'stock' of historical knowledge of tourism, such a tendency has serious implications for the ability of tourism to develop as a field. Without a fuller exploration of this historical dimension, -analyses of contemporary tourism processes will remain at best partial and at worst misleading and inaccurate.

2

Tourism, Power and the
Historical Perspective

The 'charas' go rolling out and across the moors for the sea…
But rarely far from one another, because they know their part of
the town and their bit of beach, where they feel at home. At
Scarborough [for instance] they leave the north side to the lower
middle classes who come for a week or two…

R. Hoggart, *The Uses of Literacy*[1]

Power, and the processes that structure its influence, have been relatively peripheral to the discussion of tourism to date. However, there
is a developing body of theory which argues that power and politics
are central to analyses of tourism and it is the one which will structure
our analysis of seaside resorts.[2] In doing this we will be drawing on
Foucauldian ideas to contend that tourism space is inherently politicised and that tourism processes are processes of power.
Underpinning this emerging perspective is the belief that 'ideas,
cultures, and histories cannot seriously be understood or studied
without … their configurations of power, also being studied'.[3]
Hitherto, tourism has been variously seen as play, the opposite to
work, as the sacred rather than the profane, or as the strange in
contrast to the familiar.[4] These are concepts which support and reflect
varying interpretations of society but which are not grounded in
power—ignoring that 'Tourism is as much ideology as physical
movement'.[5] Concepts of alienation and authenticity which inform
such perspectives are rooted in modern, industrial societies and social

very — not concerned with power

structures, yet, despite this, there appears to be a reluctance to address the factors which shape those ideologies. This failure to observe properly the power configurations which inform and structure tourism has led to, at best, a partial study of the phenomenon, and, at worst, an obfuscation of the forces which underpin this global industry. On this basis, the following discussion will demonstrate that tourism is a cultural arena in which hegemonic ideas of superiority and inferiority are continuously played out.

Once regarded as unsuitable subjects for academic interest, the fields of leisure and tourism have begun to enjoy higher profiles, with the former having so far developed the stronger theoretical base. Leisure some time ago became a highly politicised field[6] and, in fact, the concept of the inherent freedom of leisure has been undermined to such an extent that it has been argued that it is no longer an

> efficient means of articulating pluralist assumptions of the status quo. [Indeed,] the image of leisure as a realm of freedom outside capitalism, as a desirable goal and a justification for the unpleasantness of work is now less credible... In short leisure is becoming politicised as its seeming self-containedness and implicit autonomy diminishes.[7]

The same connection between tourism, politics and power is less well developed, although some authors—from Enloe to Selwyn—have begun to address the cultural significance of tourism.[8] Within this slowly evolving theoretical arena particular power interests are seen to compete and examples can be found of work which looks at power, including Dann's work on the language of tourism[9] and Morgan and Pritchard's work on tourism imagery.[10] However, despite this emergent body of work, the interaction between tourism processes and power still merits further attention, particularly as, when it is recognised, it is all too often discussed as being specific to destinations of the developing world. A number of commentators have discussed a global system in which the economic and political forces that underpin the wealth of the first world are largely maintained by the underdevelopment of the third world—a world where some participate in tourism whilst others do not.[11] Much of the tourism infrastructure is supported by, and indeed is reliant upon, armies of

11

poorly paid workers servicing the needs of relatively affluent tourists. It has also been recognised that tourism 'involves processes which are constructed out of complex and varied social realities and relations are often hierarchical and unequal'.[12] Yet, in contrast to leisure studies, little work in tourism has focused on the inequalities which exist in the first world, particularly those which spring from class issues.

In large part this gap in the tourism literature is traceable to a failure to examine fully the relationship between tourism and its wider context. Indeed, at the beginning of the 1990s John Urry wrote that 'the sociology of tourism is currently not keeping up with tourism's economic and social development',[13] and almost a decade later that scenario has changed little. It is a sign of tourism's theoretical immaturity that tourism sociologists still feel compelled to justify themselves by arguing that greater social understanding of tourism will lead to greater economic development. As Cara Aitchison recently summarised, 'one can't help but notice the uphill struggle that sociology has within a subject which is still dominated by economics'.[14] Thirty years after the emergence of tourism as a field of study there remains little cross-over between those taking an economic or business perspective and those pursuing a more sociological or historical perspective. In attempting to go some way towards bridging this divide, we believe that such shared knowledge will encourage a much more rounded analysis of tourism processes.

The Meaning of Leisure and Tourism

To provide a framework for the study of tourism it is essential to locate the industry in the wider social, economic and political systems that shape our world. These systems embody power relations which, as Foucault argued, concern 'our bodies, our lives, our day-to-day existence…. Between every point of a social body … there exists relations of power.'[15] Recognising this, we need to re-examine notions of power, culture and history if we are fully to understand tourism processes. We are arguing here that tourism processes *manifest power* as they mirror and reinforce the distribution of power in society, operating as mechanisms whereby inequalities are articulated and validated. Such views are slowly gaining acceptance, but tourism itself is just beginning to develop a putative theoretical base and a number of competing theories are only slowly evolving. This book does not tackle all the questions of power that need addressing, but it does seek to discuss how one key dimension (that of social class) has been articulated and reflected in the development of one particular kind of tourist site—seaside resorts—throughout this century. We will focus on the interrelationships that characterise the development of seaside resorts and that were fundamental in shaping the social hierarchy of resorts in the twentieth century—processes which, despite massive social changes, arguably remain intact and are still in evidence wherever tourists holiday today.

In pursuing this analysis, tourism can usefully learn from the debates that have animated leisure studies for some time. As a significant leisure experience, tourism should be included in such debates in any case since an understanding of leisure and the kinds of constraints and influences that frame leisure choices can only lead to a more insightful analysis of tourism. Leisure has been described by John Wilson as 'part of the struggle for the control of space and time in which social groups are continually engaged', a struggle in which dominant groups seek 'to legitimate, through statute and administrative fiat, … appropriate use of space and time, and the subordinate groups resist this control through individual rebellion and collective action'.[16] Such commentators have stripped leisure of its seeming neutrality and freedom from constraining forces, to such an extent that it is now seen as 'less a matter of individual choice than a concomitant of social position, less a means by which society is unified through a leisure-consuming democracy than divided by material and cultural inequality'.[17] This perspective argues that any equation of leisure with 'free time' directs attention away from the power structure in which it operates. Rojek and Wilson have both pointed out that the word leisure derives from the Latin word *licere*, meaning to be lawful or allowed.[18] However, license has a double meaning: it can imply liberty or official sanction. As Wilson notes, this dual definition 'indicates the complex of associations the word "leisure" has for us, suggesting both freedom and constraint. Regulation and control—in short, politics—is thus an inherent part of the meaning of leisure to us.'[19] On the etymological evidence, leisure therefore implies not free time but activity subject to constraints. Thus, 'the concept of "free time"', Rojek argues, 'has no intrinsic meaning. Rather, its meaning always depends on the social context in which it occurs.'[20] This contention is the key to understanding the nature of leisure and, by implication, tourism. The 'meaning' of leisure is historically and culturally specific, conveying different meanings to different peoples at different times. It can only be understood in the context of its relation to a specific historical and cultural situation. This means that any analyses of leisure that are framed by concepts such as choice, flexibility, spontaneity, and self-determination—such as those of Parker[21]—have a number of flaws which have been well highlighted by Rojek.[22] Most crucially, since concepts such as 'freedom' and 'choice' are multidimensional and subjective, their meanings are subject to a variety of cultural and sub-cultural contexts, which are, in turn, determined by socio-economic factors. Similarly, emphasis on the flexible and spontaneous nature of leisure shifts the focus of study towards the individual and away from the social realm.

Tourism, firmly located within leisure processes, is concerned with power relations at all levels within societies, and although those relations are subject to constant re-negotiation, inequality dictates the nature of the bargain. As Nancy Duncan writes: 'personal relationships are also power relationships ... everyone is implicated in the production and reproduction of power relations.... Although places may be more or less overtly politized, there are no politically neutral spaces.'[23] The perception of tourist spaces as neutral and tourism activities as 'free time', allowing maximum discretion over the disposal of non-work time, therefore emerges as something of an illusion. Marxist and neo-Marxist scholars have redefined our understanding of the leisure experience by focusing on its social and economic context, as have feminists by highlighting the impact of gender and sexuality.[24] Similarly, Foucault's emphasis on the 'micropolitics of power' enables us to see power at work in many diverse sites 'far removed from the materiality of the state and its ideology'.[25] As a result of the emergence of these perspectives, no new theoretical work on tourism should now overlook the constraints placed upon its operation by socio-economic class, gender, race, age, sexuality or abilism.[26] Similarly, none of these factors should be viewed in isolation

14

as they intersect at different points, combining to generate particular relations of power, privilege and disadvantage. In essence, therefore, the tourism industry reflects and reinforces the distribution of social and cultural power in individual societies and in the global community, power which springs from an assemblage of interconnected sources. Clarke and Critcher have said that in the first world's so-called 'leisure democracy, a substantial minority remain disenfranchised'.[27] This observation is even more relevant when the focus shifts historically and geographically and the 'minority' becomes the majority.

Leisure and tourism are, as a result, inherently bound up with the dimensions of power which have structured and continue to structure twentieth-century British society. As Kinnaird and Hall, two prominent tourism writers, have argued: 'since tourism-related activity has become an important process of development, the social, economic and political relations which result are part of overall issues of power and control'.[28] In such ways does tourism lead the researcher to the heart of social power structures. As sociologists and, increasingly, cultural geographers begin to explore the subject, tourism is beginning to be seen as an arena that articulates these power structures, just as leisure and leisure history have been regarded for some time.[29] Certainly, as the subject becomes less dominated by economics, it is beginning to be recognised that tourism simultaneously reflects and reinforces social, cultural and economic divisions ultimately rooted outside the tourism experience itself.

Exploring History, Leisure and Power

Before we look at historical perspectives on tourism in detail, we first need to consider briefly here the development and direction of power-oriented perspectives within leisure history. This is particularly important as it will provide the framework for our subsequent analysis of the seaside. The study of class and leisure has been considerably explored by those scholars writing in the Marxist tradition, notably those who have tried to apply some of the ideas of the Frankfurt school of critical theory to leisure.[30] Leisure is seen here as a central dynamic of capitalist society, and as such, is determined by the

15

relations of capitalist production. It is contended that the subordi-
nation of certain groups in society has been successfully presented as
a form of freedom, and that work—often having little intrinsic satisfaction—is endured to achieve the material resources necessary to
fulfil leisure time desires. Leisure, in contrast, is seen by workers as
providing opportunities for freedom and creativity: literally, time in
which to recreate one's self and escape from the drudgery of labour.
Yet, Marxists argue, this perception of leisure as 'free time'—allowing
maximum discretion over the disposal of non-work time—is an
illusion because of its location within a capitalist system. It is this
'compensatory function' of all forms of leisure which makes it a vital
component of modern Western culture.[31] For example, theorists such
as Jean-Marie Brohm, Paul Hoch and Gerhard Vinnai have argued
that sport is, in Hargreaves's words, 'a mirror or a microcosm of
modern capitalist society, an integral part of a system of class domination and exploitation'.[32] Within such perspectives, sport is seen to
create a docile labour force, instilled with the dominant ideology of
aggressive competition, chauvinism and nationalism, integrating
participant and spectator into a consumer-orientated society.

Such views of the relationship between leisure forms and class have
been substantially criticised and appear to be seriously flawed.[33] For
instance, if sport creates docility, why are traditionally politically
radical areas such as South Wales and Clydeside in the UK also centres
of popular sports? Gareth Williams, researching the relationships
between class, community and rugby in South Wales, concluded:
'Rugby … was never a sedative to tranquillize unruly proletarian
crowds any more than it quelled industrial militancy'.[34] This view is
endorsed by Stedman Jones, who points out that Glasgow was one
of the earliest centres of football as a mass spectator sport before
1914, yet during and after the First World War the city was one of
Britain's most radical and militant areas.[35] As Stephen Jones argues:

> The evidence suggests that leisure failed as a superstructural
> adjunct of capitalism. There was no question of the working class
> being programmed or conditioned in their leisure time.…
> Cultural and recreational forms were not simply a mode of
> Capitalist expression; true they were partly a reflection of the

16

dominant culture, but a dominant culture which included 'alternative' and 'oppositional' proletarian values and leanings.[36]

To regard leisure as some simplistic social control mechanism would thus be seriously to understate the role of negotiation and to minimise autonomy in power interactions. As Joyce has said of the second half of the nineteenth century: 'Instead of an overmastering, trans-historical tendency towards conflict—along classical Marxist lines—what is evident is the inter-dependence of capital and labour. The vested interest workers and employers have in co-operation is at least as great as any tendency toward conflict.'[37] Attractive though it might be, music halls, 'chara' trips to Blackpool and the football pools have not been responsible for thwarting class consciousness. Stedman Jones warned of the dangers of an analysis of leisure which regards it as diverting 'putative class consciousness' into 'some system-maintaining channel of chauvinism, sport or consumerism'. Such an analysis would assign a purely passive role to the masses, seeing them as 'simply a blank page upon which each successive stage of capitalism has successively imposed its imprint'.[38]

This criticism of classical Marxism does not undermine the importance of class as one of the determinants of the leisure experience. By raising questions over the social and economic context of the leisure experience, Marxist and neo-Marxist scholars have redefined the terms of the leisure debate: no new work on leisure can now afford to overlook the constraints placed upon its operation by socioeconomic forces. Rather than to dismiss the influence of class in leisure processes, what we need is a more sophisticated way of understanding the relationships between class and cultural power. In particular, we need to appreciate how power is manifested at a micro as well as at a macro level. For this, it is helpful to turn to the writings of Michel Foucault. One of the key contributions of Foucault to this debate has been his assertion that power relations are as much about the politics of everyday life as they are about the grand issues of politics and sovereign power.[39]

Foucault's conception of power is very radical since it sees power not as a monopoly commodity, but one which is 'exercised through a net like organisation'.[40] It is a more subtle analysis of power relations than Marxism which would explain power purely in the context of

17

class relations as it recognises that power bestrides social categories. Power permeates all levels of existence and operates in every social site, both public and private, and we are all involved in its circulation since power goes 'to the depths of society'.[41] Thus, rather than merely radiating from the centre or the top of society, power is seen as circulating throughout societies. A more appropriate metaphor for understanding the way that power operates within society is that of a spider's web—power permeates all aspects of the web and it is not merely negative, it is also productive.[42] This is because societies are characterised by the struggle for power as social groups, classes, races, sexes and genders are in competition at many levels and the struggles are not just within societies, but between them.

Unlike a view of power which is rather more crude and unilinear, this perspective does not deny the autonomy of the less powerful to negotiate with or to subvert those who dominate. It is important to recognise, however, that neither does Foucault deny the dominance of powerful groups in societies. Rather, he argues that there are many mechanisms that mediate and contribute to the exercise of power and hence influence and regulate appropriate behaviours. If one accepts our contention above that leisure both as a definition and as a concept is constructed, channelled and controlled largely by the society in which it operates, then it must follow that leisure thus simultaneously reflects and reinforces any power divisions ultimately rooted outside the leisure experience itself.

Over the last century leisure provision has increased in scale and in range, yet although this entailed a concomitant increase in leisure availability, it simultaneously increased its commercialisation. As we will discuss below, the emergence of mass consumer capitalism reconstructed the leisure experience in Britain: clearly defining leisure time and space and establishing leisure as an item of consumption. As a commodity which has to be purchased in the market place, leisure throughout the twentieth century has been available only to those with access to key resources: time and money, described by Cross as 'the great scarcities of modern life'.[43] This material aspect of the inequality of leisure opportunity was historically and is currently reinforced by the exercising of cultural power. Culture consists of socially conditioned patterns as well as mental processes, reflected in people's behaviour and interaction as well as their thoughts. Thus conflict can arise when different groups drawing on different cultural resources lay claim to the same leisure space. This is also complicated as the leisure patterns of a social group reflect not only its own perception of what is appropriate behaviour, but also the views of those who are external to the group but in a position to enforce their expectations. This can be seen in the way in which female leisure patterns are often influenced by male perceptions of 'acceptability'. It is also evident, as we shall see, in the middle-class manipulation of access to resorts and the policing of working-class behaviour at the seaside, and also in the role played by various groups and organisations (local authorities, the media and trade organisations) within those processes. The enforcement of social hierarchies at the seaside in the twentieth century was not simply imposed from above but was the product of diffused power relations.

Throughout the course of this book, we shall see that the development of the seaside in this century has been characterised by the continuance of resort hierarchies. By this we mean that resorts were defined by their clientele—more specifically the class of their clientele. We shall see that access to resorts was controlled by a variety of factors, including geographical distance from urban populations and, crucially, the development of strategies employed by local elites. In our case study of Devon some of the more 'select' resorts actively discouraged transportation improvements and almost all resorts disdained the 'popular' entertainments associated with working-class seaside products. Whilst such strategies were by no means unique, as a collection of resorts, those of Devon managed to retain a more middle-class flavour than those of many other areas in Britain throughout much of the twentieth century. As a result, they provide an interesting example of how power and politics operated at the seaside. In order to locate the development of the twentieth-century resort in its wider context, however, we first need to explore how elites have always been wary of the use of leisure time and space. A selective review of the leisure history literature illustrates that leisure has long been a contested area—the forum of struggles initiated both from above and below.

Leisure, History and the Question of Conflict

Since the late 1970s the trickle of historical studies of leisure and consumption has become a flood, with writers discussing everything from football and horse-racing to reading and holiday-making.[44] Many of these works highlight the area as one of conflict—of disputes over time, space and behaviour.[45] In his important article on class expression and social control, Stedman Jones raised some interesting points on this theme of conflict, warning of the dangers of over-politicising the subject and viewing leisure as a means of diverting class consciousness, leading to theories of incorporation in a misplaced attempt to explain why workers accepted the commodification and codification of leisure.[46] However, he mistakenly perceives leisure as a peripheral arena of class conflicts when he writes:

> The struggle in the factory is a struggle in the relations of production…. Struggles over leisure time do not have this *inherent antagonism* built into them. The primary point of a holiday is not political. It is to enjoy yourself, for tomorrow you must work.[47]

Whilst correctly arguing that leisure should not be studied in isolation, Stedman Jones falls into the trap of regarding leisure as a separate and separable sphere of society. In the study of any society, however, a holistic approach is vital; to corrupt Marx and Engels's famous phrase—'There is no history of politics, of law, of science etc., of art, of religion'—there is no history of leisure.[48] In other words, individual human activities cannot have their own history as they cannot be studied in isolation. Raymond Williams in his essay on 'Culture' made the point that if 'all cultural processes were initiated by humans themselves' then it follows that 'none of them could be clearly understood unless they were seen in the context of human activities as a whole'.[49]

By marginalising leisure we run the risk not of over- but rather of under-politicising it. Arguably, since the emergence of leisure in its modern form, it has become leisure time and not work time which gives meaning and vitality to life. As the Yeos have written:

> Thus, working people at the point of production tell historical and sociological observers … that the factory is *not* where it's all

20

at. When asked, they make it quite clear in consciousness and in action that any aspirations and creative practices and hopes reside elsewhere in their lives.[50]

Clearly these other activities, usually enjoyed in leisure time, are not perceived by people as either secondary or marginal within their lives; why then should they be peripheralised by those studying society? If workers consider leisure as important, as offering real or perceived opportunities for freedom and self-expression, then its study can lead to an equal, if not greater extent than the study of work, not to an irrelevant backwater, but 'to the centre of large, class questions and struggles'.[51]

Leisure is not, and never has been, uncontested territory, isolated or immune from the social forces which animate society. Although holidaying may not necessarily always be an overt political act, Reid's work on Saint Monday and Howkins's research on Whitsun illustrate how it can be the arena, if not the cause, of struggle and protests.[52] These two studies demonstrate how the imposition of factory work-discipline was resisted both in the newly created working week and at particular holiday celebrations. The first discusses how workers absented themselves from work on Mondays and the second analyses how the working class continued to indulge in leisure behaviour which was deemed as unacceptable to the social elites. Thus, struggles within leisure *do* reflect those 'inherent antagonisms' which Stedman Jones argues exist only in the 'authentic' class arena of the realm of production. Protest within leisure differed from protest within work in its form and location, but both sprang from the same sources. If points of production are foci of friction—of struggle arising from inequality—so are those points of consumption, leisure and holiday-making.

Conflict is written on every page of leisure history and historians have documented friction within leisure over the last four centuries, from Wrightson's work on seventeenth-century alehouses to Williams's on modern communications.[53] Ruling elites have always regarded unlicensed recreation with alarm. Whenever and wherever the so-called lower orders gathered together in numbers—at wakes, fairs, boxing and football matches, in pubs, clubs and societies or on the streets—the authorities have seen a threat to the existing social

21

order. Such working-class control of public places, especially if accompanied by alcohol and partisanship, have been regarded as, at best, a nuisance, and at worst, a potential opportunity for the destruction of property.

The 'modern' form of leisure—tourism—which is our focus of study differs in definition, perception and practice from historical leisure. We have already argued above that leisure derives its 'meaning' from its social, economic and cultural contexts. In this sense there is no 'absolute' experience of leisure which can be studied across chronologically and culturally separated societies: 'leisure' is simply the significance and meaning ascribed to defined activities at particular periods in specific societies. In Britain our present understanding of leisure is temporally specific. Whilst it is always dangerous to label any period as 'traditional', pre-industrial recreational patterns were significantly different—although linear notions of class, leisure and industrial development are untenable. Eighteenth- and early-nineteenth-century leisure had been, in Bailey's words, located in 'a robust and ritualistic popular culture rooted in the tightly knit, inward-looking world of the country village'. It was a society where:

> The material apparatus of recreation was rudimentary and for the most part freely available from the common resources of the community.... Popular leisure was public and gregarious, and both its great and small occasions were heavily bound by the prescriptive ties of communal custom reinforced by a powerful oral tradition.[54]

Since the eighteenth century, however, recreation has been subject to processes of rationalisation, reform and commercialisation. Although, as Stedman Jones notes, it is important to recognise that the 'authentic' popular culture of one period is the commercialism of an earlier era,[55] during the nineteenth and early twentieth century popular culture was substantially re-shaped as part of a 'fractured and ambiguous'[56] transformation of British society. Although writers such as Joyce have demonstrated that the fragmented and uneven development of new systems of production should be seen as a process of 'incorporation rather than the supercession of earlier forms of industrial organisation',[57] many leisure patterns were reshaped.

22

During the Victorian period middle-class reformers tried to rationalise leisure in an attempt to reconstruct it within the framework of the dominant bourgeois ideology. Regarding leisure as a dangerous zone where the removal of work-discipline led to idleness, immorality and revolt, they sought to 'forge more effective behavioural constraints in leisure'.[58] Operating through such groups as the Royal Society for the Prevention of Cruelty to Animals, the campaigns had an inherent class bias, highlighted, for instance, by Harrison's study of religion and recreation in the nineteenth century. Thus cockfighting and bear-baiting became unacceptable cruelties whilst fox-hunting, shooting and fishing remained as recognised 'gentlemanly' pursuits.[59]

Reform and repression were not alone in reconstructing working-class leisure as counter-attraction, absorption and commercialisation were equally, if not more, significant. Thus football became disciplined and institutionalised and working men's clubs sprang up under middle-class auspices. Yet, whilst such processes *changed* popular culture, it nevertheless remained *popular* culture, imbued with working-class and not middle-class values.[60] As Stephen Jones comments: 'miners' institutes, the working mens' club movement and labour organisations of all kinds were a sure sign of working-class autonomy in the cultural sphere'. Such evidence endorses our rejection of crude social control analyses of leisure which stress its controlling mechanism but pay little attention to the tensions and contradictions in society, analyses which, as Jones continues, leave 'very little room for working-class creativity and resistance to the ideology of the ruling elite'.[61] Indeed, whilst leisure has been subject to change initiated from above, as Cunningham concludes: 'the flow [has been] in both directions' with popular recreational forms often shaping high culture.[62]

Although much debate still surrounds the process, by the first quarter of the twentieth century various social, economic and cultural processes had transformed Britain into a 'modern', urban, industrial society. Older forms of leisure persisted, but the developments in technology and communications and the rise of advertising and consumer capitalism had created new recreations such as the cinema, professional league football and the seaside holiday—recreations

23

which quickly became so much a part of British culture that they were soon regarded as traditional. Such developments 'signalled a further phase in the history of leisure, when a virtual leisure industry emerged to service the mass culture of the twentieth century'.[63]

Having identified the emergence of this commercially orientated mass leisure market in the later nineteenth and early twentieth centuries, it is surprising that leisure historians remained for so long unconcerned to trace developments in leisure habits beyond 1914. The publication in 1986 of Jones's study of inter-war Britain, *Workers at Play*,[64] has gone some way towards filling this gap, but as it focuses on the years between 1918 and 1939, there still remains a real need for serious studies of the second half of the twentieth century. Whilst Gary Cross's *Time and Money*, a discussion of popular consumerism in twentieth-century America, Britain and France,[65] has redressed this to some extent, broad historical analysis of the twentieth century has by no means been exhaustive and there remains a pressing need for more study of recent leisure history.

Themes and Contentions at the British Seaside

Within the broad developments in leisure patterns, the evolution of the seaside holiday during the eighteenth and nineteenth centuries played an important role, one which has been well-documented elsewhere.[66] Emerging in the mid- to late eighteenth century in the same tradition of royal patronage and medicinal recommendation as the country's inland spa towns, the British coastal watering-places were divided along class lines from the outset. Although those without access to money and free time were excluded virtually completely, there still quickly developed social distinctions between and within resorts. First the middle and then the lower middle classes began to imitate the practices and places of upper-class leisure behaviour. This meant that the social elites were constantly forced to search for exclusivity, often in the more remote resorts which were prohibitively costly to reach for the middle and working classes. If resorts became plebeian—as in the case of those of Kent in south-east England— the upper classes had the option of moving beyond the effective travel range of their social inferiors. This pattern of social exclusivity—itself

24

an expression of the cultural and social power relationships inherent within leisure—can be seen in resort development throughout the nineteenth and early twentieth centuries. Even in the mid-twentieth century certain resorts in Devon regarded themselves (and were perceived by their clientele) as attractive because of their social exclusivity, preserved by the area's physical remoteness and local tourism policies.

An Overview of the Seaside Literature

Of the general works on the subject, the starting point for any researcher working on a historical view of seaside tourism must be Pimlott's *The Englishman's Holiday*, important as the first serious treatment of this issue, and still insightful despite its age.[67] A similar attempt at a broad general survey, covering a longer period (from the mid-eighteenth to the later twentieth century), is Hern's *The Seaside Holiday*—heavily criticised as an inadequate revision of Pimlott, yet containing some interesting comments, especially on the class conflict over holiday-making provision and practice.[68] The next important texts of this type were written in the late 1970s and early 1980s when Walton and Walvin turned their attention to seaside tourism. Of the several overviews produced by these historians, the most thorough is Walton's *The English Seaside Resort*, which concentrates on the topographical and municipal development of the resorts.[69] This work, as many others, however, concentrates on the resorts' initial phase of expansion and does not cover the 1920s to 1940s when the British resort industry matured nor the period after the 1960s when it began to stagnate. Thus, there are still relatively few studies of British resorts which examine the mid- to later twentieth century, those of Alastair Durie, Laura Chase, Julian Dimetriadi and Sheila Agarwal being notable exceptions.[70]

As well as these overviews and case studies of individual resorts and regions, specific themes in seaside tourism have attracted attention. Two of particular interest to us are the questions of 'social tone' and the role of municipal government in shaping the character of the resorts. Perkin's work in the mid-1970s on the Victorian seaside resorts of north-west England provided the initial focus of the 'social

25

tone' debate. He suggested that the social structure and community development of resorts were largely traceable to their land-ownership patterns and leasing policies, as powerful aristocratic landlords were able to dictate both the type and the pace of building development.[71] This contention, whilst still useful, has been shown to need qualification as Mike Huggins, examining resort development around the mouth of the River Tees in north-east England, has demonstrated that the nature of the resorts' hinterlands was also important. His comparison between the North West and the North East of England illustrates how the latter's heavy industry and large population of unskilled workers was reflected in the low social tone of the North East resorts.[72]

Resorts often had to weigh up competing claims for access to their amenities and although leading influence groups of residents (often retired) and local authorities were usually able to exert a significant and even decisive influence on the pattern of resort development, the range of policies available was constrained by the pattern of demand in their key catchment areas. Thus, the development of individual resorts along divergent paths was dictated by 'the holiday expectations of a widening range of social and cultural groups' seeking 'expression and satisfaction in styles which were often mutually conflicting'.[73] As we shall see with inter-war Ilfracombe—linked to the depressed industries of South Wales—resorts could do little to swim against the tide of their key catchment areas.

Lowerson and Myerscough in their *Time to Spare in Victorian England* further undermined Perkin's emphasis on the central role of land-ownership patterns, demonstrating that whilst resorts with concentrated land-ownership patterns (such as Eastbourne under the unitary ownership of the Duke of Devonshire) were often more 'respectable', others (such as the far-from-respectable Bungalow Town on Shoreham Beach) likewise had unitary landholding.[74] Clearly the thesis needs moderation; land-owners were important as shapers of resorts, but other factors, notably catchment areas and accessibility, also deserve consideration.

The role of local government was also particularly critical in shaping resort development and here again the work of Walton is important. Exploring the relationship between municipal government and the holiday industry in Blackpool during 1876–1914, he demonstrated how the local authority—dominated by representatives of the construction and tourism industries—made Blackpool Britain's most successful working-class resort in the late nineteenth century.[75] Another useful contribution to this topic is Roberts's research on the municipal provision of entertainment in middle-class Bournemouth during the Victorian and Edwardian periods. Roberts emphasises the importance of the local council's efforts to enhance the holiday facilities and improve the resort's high social tone by the introduction of stringent by-laws, banning 'undesirable' behaviour.[76]

The social tone debate has thus largely focused on what Chase describes as 'the economic and political base of the seaside town's images and the importance of land ownership, political power structures, location and access'.[77] In this book, we take as our premise the contention that the gradations of resort 'social tone', accepted by seaside historians as still valid in the early twentieth century, continued well into the twentieth century, maintained by various factors, particularly geographical remoteness and local tourism policies. The social tone of resorts, whether they were 'select' or 'popular', was determined by the type of visitor attracted. There are obvious problems in differentiating between 'middle-class' and 'working-class' resorts as such rigid divisions are rather crude and clumsy—often resorts such as Scarborough were internally zoned, or perhaps a middle-class resort developed alongside a more popular resort, as St Annes did at Blackpool in the north-west, Hove at Brighton in the South and Clacton alongside Frinton on the eastern English coast. Moreover, as Joyce has argued, class as a historical and sociological concept must be carefully handled in that writers should take account of 'the actual terms in which contemporaries talked about the social order'.[78] Clearly, class, just as much as leisure itself, is less an objective reality and more 'a social construct, created differently by different historical actors.'[79]

Despite these reservations, however, distinctions between resorts can be clearly made on the basis of social divisions, and resorts catering for a working-class clientele can be identified by certain criteria, such as their reliance on small businesses with low overheads and small profit margins and their concentration on cheap accom-

27

modation, particularly guest houses often catering for those desiring a 'homely' atmosphere.[80] In contrast, more middle-class dominated resorts were characterised by a higher proportion of hotels to boarding houses, with high rateable and property values, tighter by-laws to control perceived 'nuisances', and a larger number of servants and laundry workers.[81]

Resort social tone thus was, and is, the result of interaction between the local population and the visitors and a balance was often achieved only after conflict, both between the residents and the visitors and within the local community itself. There were numerous debates in resorts throughout the century over whether to try to attract working- or middle-class visitors: the attraction of the former meant more holiday-makers but brought more disruption and lowered resort 'tone', whilst the middle-class visitors were fewer in number but spent more per head in the resorts.[82] Indeed, far from being unique to British resorts, this issue continues to preoccupy resort communities throughout the world.

The dilemma faced by British resorts over which visitors to attract can be traced in their local authority records. The discussions over the provision of public sector tourism amenities and the scope and direction of advertising activities are two areas of local government policy which we will investigate in some depth later. Resorts developed along clearly defined paths mapped in line with the wishes of a broad range of interests within them, but the direction of this development was frequently disputed. As we will see, the internal politics of the two major Devon resorts, Torquay and Ilfracombe, reveal an inherent friction between the 'holiday interest' (often led by the Hoteliers' Associations and the Chambers of Commerce) and the 'residential interest' (often dominated by those advocating a high social tone and drawing support from the substantial retired popula-tions). The struggle between these various groupings—in short, politics and power—will be a key theme throughout this book.

In the context of this exploration, the type of holiday-maker visiting the resorts is important. This is the most interesting and yet the most obscure aspect of seaside resort studies as detailed surveys are not common before the 1960s. It is, however, a vital area if the seaside is to be investigated as a microcosm of social relations. During the

28

twentieth century there have been major changes in society and in leisure, changes which affect the interaction of leisure, class and culture. If, as Walton has said, 'The seaside undoubtedly expressed class and cultural differences, the insoluble problem is how to show it *influenced* them'.[83] Edwardian commentators thought that seaside holiday-making fostered class cohesion in Britain for they felt it entailed a mixing of the classes. Whilst such mixing did occur, it is interesting that in the 1930s town-planners assumed that the social and recreational needs of holiday-makers from different classes were dissimilar and mutually conflicting, a point echoed in the 1950s in Richard Hoggart's study of working-class leisure.[84] More obviously, the view that the seaside witnessed class cohesion is seriously challenged by the continuance of resort social hierarchies throughout the twentieth century. However, if holiday-making expresses class then it has to express it differently over time to reflect the changing reality of society and arguably it does, as social tone at today's seaside resorts such as Majorca and Saint Lucia is merely an echo of earlier experiences at resorts such as Torquay and St Tropez.

Overlying the issues of local government activity and facility and entertainment provision is the question of the power context of tourism and the social relationships which animate the seaside, as all leisure sites. We shall argue, as Walton has for the nineteenth century, that the twentieth-century resort was also a 'crucible of conflict between classes and lifestyles',[85] as status-conscious visitors and residents competed with working-class tourists for access to leisure time and space. He went on to comment that 'The seaside brought mutually incompatible modes of recreation and enjoyment into close proximity in ways which seldom happened inland'.[86] As a result of the work of a generation of historians, this has become a central tenet of research on nineteenth-century seaside resorts. What we hope to demonstrate in the following chapters is that such incompatibility— of lifestyles, behaviour and tastes—finds strong echoes in twentieth-century British resorts.

The examination of the tourism policies of Devon's resorts will prove interesting in the context of the social tone debate, furnishing information on the social politics of leisure. Devon provides some fascinating insights into this issue: having entered the 'mass' holiday

29

market late, its experiences are somewhat different from those of the resorts of Lancashire or Kent as described as by Walton, Parry and Whyman, since the policies of exclusion can be seen operating well into the twentieth century.[87] Now that we have outlined the book's theoretical and historiographic context, it is time to examine that broader development of seaside tourism in Britain over the twentieth century, before we turn to a detailed analysis of Devon, its most popular tourism region since the late 1950s.

3

The British Seaside in the Twentieth Century

The reasons why one resort prospers and another is in crisis is due to the complex interaction of global and national shifts in culture and the economics of the tourism industry, and the way that these interact with the local dimensions of culture, class images, the built environment created by previous rounds of investment, and the capacity of both the local state and private investors to adapt to change.

A. Williams and G. Shaw, 'Riding the big dipper[1]

The rise of the British coastal resort phenomenon was very much a product of the prevailing socio-economic and cultural contexts within which it developed, as indeed has been its much vaunted decline in the latter decades of the twentieth century. The reasons for the growth of the British seaside product in the eighteenth and nineteenth centuries have been well-documented elsewhere (as we mentioned above) and we do not intend to rehearse these discussions here—we are primarily concerned with its development in the much less researched twentieth century. It should be noted, however, that the resort phenomenon was inextricably linked to Britain's experience of the industrial revolution, which effected rapid social, economic and cultural change. In particular, it entailed the concentration of large populations into urban centres and the regimentation of people's lives so vital to a capitalist factory-based economy. The relationship between Britain's seaside and its industrial centres has characterised

31

and structured the experience of resorts in much of the twentieth century—the one providing pre-eminent leisure sites, the other providing key markets.

In order to contextualize the evolution of resorts over this century, the first half of this chapter adopts a chronological approach, documenting the key changes which influenced their development. The second half of the chapter is more concerned to draw out the remarkably consistent themes which have characterised the seaside product for over a hundred years. These themes are: the continuance of social graduation between and zoning within seaside resorts; the contrasting attitudes of central and local government to resort development; the fluctuating patterns of investment; and the cultural changes which have combined to undermine the fashionability of the seaside product.

Tracing the Development of the Seaside

In the twentieth century its seaside resorts emerged as an evocative icon of Britain at play, as the holiday became what Gary Cross has described as 'a perfect "metaphor" of the consumer moment'.[2] Between 1870 and 1940 the domestic seaside resorts reached their maturity,[3] advancing in the post-war years into a period of consolidation before lack of investment, the challenge of Continental destinations and the oil-crisis-induced slump forced the industry into a 1970s and early 1980s decline.[4] In the later 1980s some of the more progressive resorts (such as Torquay and Blackpool) emerged from a process of re-orientation and re-structuring to mount an effective challenge for the business of the new more discerning consumer of the 1990s, but many of the smaller and medium-sized seaside resorts (such as Barry Island and Porthcawl in Southeastern Wales) face an uncertain future in the new millennium.

1900–1945: The Burgeoning of the Seaside Industry

By the early twentieth century the majority of towns which were to dominate the country's tourism trade throughout the century (Map 3.1) were already recognised resorts, in contrast to Europe where many resorts did not evolve until after the First World War. Of the modern British resorts, only Felixstowe, Newquay and Skegness in England and Prestatyn in Wales were little more than villages at the time of the 1911 census.[5] The period 1900–45 saw far-reaching changes in British society, changes which were reflected in its holiday industry and which created fresh challenges for the seaside resorts. The First World War and its aftermath brought radical social transformation to Europe, and in the 'Roaring Twenties' people indulged in the modern forms of leisure on a hitherto unprecedented scale. Social changes, particularly in the position of women in society, brought fashion and attitudinal shifts which led in turn to the re-emergence of the craze for bathing and a new enthusiasm for sunbathing—both trends which favoured the seaside resorts.[6] Although the two World Wars were obviously major interruptions, as Durie has shown in detail for the Scottish resorts,[7] the conflicts had relatively little long-term impact on British resorts and these decades witnessed the consolidation of the British seaside industry and the rise of recognisably 'modern' resort activities. In the inter-war years many facilities—from cinemas and amusement arcades to swimming pools and pavilions—sprang up, and whilst very few new grand hotels were built, family hotels prospered. At the same time, as increased motor transport began to enable visitors to travel between resorts—rather than simply staying in one for the duration of their holiday—the rivalry between resorts increased and advertising became an important sphere of resort activity.[8]

The increasing prevalence of the car among the British middle classes also accelerated the trend from the lodging-house single-centre holiday to the increased mobility offered by motoring holidays, although the accommodation still tended to be seaside resort-based.[9] Some evidence suggests that, as early as the 1930s, the market for traditional seaside holidays languished in the larger, more popular resorts such as Blackpool, where Parry has suggested the numbers of seaside landladies stagnated and the building of new boarding houses ceased.[10] Nevertheless, patterns of British holiday-making remained unaltered throughout most of the century, especially amongst the working class where visitors often returned each year to the same resort, even to the same guest house, spending their leisure time amongst neighbours and workmates.[11]

33

Map 3.1: *Key Twentieth-Century British Seaside Resorts*

1930

Context of inter war leisure growth

The British leisure industry as a whole hugely expanded in the inter-war years. The growth rate in the mass entertainment sector between 1931 and 1939 was 49 per cent, a figure far exceeding those in other economic sectors. Indeed, of all the sectors, sport and entertainment experienced the third greatest increase in employment between 1931 and 1937.[12] These figures support Walton's contention that the inter-war period saw counter-cyclical investment in the holiday industry—and even during economic downturns investment in this sector continued.[13] At Rhyl, for instance, the period saw major infra-structural projects and a significant expansion in the range of resort entertainment amenities, including the building of a new theatre, three cinemas, a bowls pavilion and a new open air swimming pool.[14] In many resorts such improvements to the infrastructure and amenities were often designed as unemployment relief schemes—in the resorts of Ilfracombe in Devon and Barry Island in South Wales promenades and swimming pools were built specifically to provide work for the local unemployed. Thus, whilst other sectors of the economy flagged, Britain's seaside resorts boomed, spending an estimated £3–4 million annually on seafront improvements in the 1930s. Blackpool, which alone spent £3 million on improvements to its parks, promenade and Winter Gardens in these years, was merely the most prominent example of a trend to be seen all around the British coast.[15]

Counter cyclical investment

These years also saw tremendous social and cultural changes which impacted on leisure behaviour and resort development and marketing, particularly the rise of 'modernity' highlighted by Chase.[16] Writing in 1940, Graves and Hodge identified the years immediately following the First World War as a period of tremendous advance in women's struggle for equality, years when new fashions and mores allowed them greater physical, social, intellectual and legal freedom.[17] In 1932 Delisle Burns wrote: 'Recent changes in the amount of leisure and its uses have caused social tendencies towards … equality and towards "movements" which aim at modifying the traditional position of women ….'[18] Related to this greater freedom for women was the emergence of a significant cultural trend which was to char-acterise much of the remainder of the century and which was to exert a strong influence on the development of the seaside product. The designer Coco Chanel's popularisation of the suntan—an icon of the

35

twentieth century, a symbol of wealth and the ability to afford a holiday—made it a social 'must' rather than a social stigma associated with manual work. The arrival of sunbathing enhanced the value of resorts with sunny, sandy beaches. It also signalled significant shifts in social behaviour which reinforced 'notions of the beach as a liminal zone where behaviour which elsewhere transgressed norms of approved conduct became acceptable and expected'[19]—a theme we will revisit at the end of this chapter.

The seaside expansion was also encouraged by legislative moves which stimulated municipal promotional enterprise and introduced paid holidays. The Health and Pleasure Resorts Act of 1921 for the first time allowed local authorities to fund resort advertising via revenue from deck chairs, beach tents and bathing machines and from admission charges to municipal attractions.[20] This was a major innovation, one which we will explore in more detail later. The other significant piece of inter-war legislation was the 1938 Paid Holidays Act. Contemporary surveys, notably Elizabeth Brunner's conducted to inform post-war reconstruction, suggest that the Act had little immediate effect. The year 1938 proved to be a peak for holiday bookings, after which railways and hotels reported a decrease in bookings, probably a combination of a time-lagged response to the 1937 economic downturn and to pre-war instability. After the Second World War, however, the legislation was to have a profound effect.[21]

It is difficult to contextualize the extent either of resort growth or of holiday-makers' numbers in this period because of the paucity of information in the form of surveys or market research.[22] The figures which do exist therefore need to be treated with a considerable degree of caution given that they are largely estimates. Working from contemporary 'guesstimates', Walton has suggested that in the mid-1930s Blackpool was Britain's largest resort, attracting around 7 million annual visitors, followed by Southend, attracting 5.5 million, Hastings attracting 3 million, Rhyl 2.5 million and Bournemouth, Southport and Redcar each attracting 2 million.[23] These resorts were simply the most prominent examples of what was clearly already a huge seaside industry—one which in the coming decades was to reach a zenith never later matched.

1945–1974: From Maturity to Stagnation

Resorts around the British coast were transformed in the Second World War—beaches were mined and enclosed with barbed wire, promenades were dominated by gun emplacements and piers were closed or partially dismantled.[24] In many resorts hotels and boarding houses were also used to accommodate evacuees and military personnel.[25] Resorts across Britain accommodated thousands of evacuees, many of them children, who had been moved from the large urban centres and ports vulnerable to bombing. By the spring of 1941 over 2,000 unaccompanied children and several thousand adults were living in Ilfracombe, placing pressure on accommodation and public utilities and creating a great deal of tension with the residents.[26] As late as 1954 the resort still housed many families in requisitioned accommodation,[27] indeed the de-requisitioning of seaside hotels and boarding houses around the country was extremely protracted despite intensive lobbying by the Urban District Councils' Association, the Travel Association of Great Britain and the resorts' MPs in the late 1940s.[28]

The Second World War and its aftermath brought major difficulties to the tourism industry which to a large extent was not yet perceived as a significant economic sector by central government. The suspension of the tourist trade for six years and the neglect of amenities presented many resorts, particularly those on the east and south coasts of England, with an urgent requirement for investment. It was not just the resort accommodation which was affected by wartime measures long after the conflict had ended. At many resorts beaches, parks and pleasure grounds remained closed and mined—cordoned off by barbed wire—even in the late 1940s,[29] whilst at others the wartime use of parks and gardens for agriculture meant that many open spaces were in disrepair at a time when there was no funding available for renovation.[30] But, whilst central government did regard tourism as a depressed industry, little aid was forthcoming in an age of austerity.[31] This post-war financial stringency was exacerbated by petrol rationing throughout the late 1940s and the situation was particularly difficult in 1948 when a ban on foreign holidays was lifted—allowing travel abroad—whilst the basic petrol ration was cut

37

as an austerity measure.[32] Even when the petrol ration was restored later that year, allowing about 90 miles of travel each month, the more remote British resorts 'remained inaccessible to many private motorists.'[33]

Although such constraints and restrictions did nothing actively to encourage domestic tourism from the mid-1940s to the mid-1950s, the tourism trade was relatively buoyant. The seasons of 1945–47 were particularly successful as 'holiday-makers ... inspired to a great extent by the first enthusiastic flush of demobilisation accompanied by gratuity money ... enjoyed their first real holiday for several years.'[34] Somewhat ironically, however, in view of the problems discussed above, Britain's seaside resorts were ill-prepared for the holiday rush which accompanied peace—a rush which, whilst it was not as spectacular as that of 1919–20—was still substantial. Resort accommodation and facilities were inadequate, food shortages and petrol rationing imposed considerable restrictions on tourists and high rail fares and overcharging undermined the emergent travel boom. In the resorts themselves cuts in expenditure and shortages of skilled labour were also major problems. Yet, despite such difficulties there was also an optimism in the coastal communities, reflected in inflated seaside resort property prices which were often treble the pre-war figures— especially in the towns of Eastbourne, Bournemouth, Torquay and Paignton.[35] There was also a bright side to austerity for the seaside resorts, most notably the curbing of foreign travel in the late 1940s and early 1950s, a restriction which contributed to a 50 per cent increase in the volume of domestic British tourism between 1939 and 1951.[36]

This post-war domestic travel boom was achieved by private and municipal enterprise, often in spite of blocks on public-sector investment as resorts across the country lobbied the government in vain for aid.[37] Attempts by resorts to renovate wartime infrastructural damage were consistently frustrated by a central government whose priorities were urban regeneration and the revival of manufacturing industries. For example, Ilfracombe Council lobbied the Departments of Health and Transport for permission to renovate its tourism infrastructure for almost ten years without success.[38] In 1948 the Ministry of Health, which had to approve local government

38

tourism-related loans, refused to sanction one for £12,000 to £15,000 for a scheme in Ilfracombe to construct a promenade, new bathing huts and access to the beach as it was for 'purely amenity purposes', and it was not until 1953 that a loan to enable the desperately needed pier repairs was granted by the Department of Transport.[39]

It was thus with little central government financial support or planning that the British tourism industry expanded into one of huge significance in the 1950s—becoming a major foreign currency earner.[40] By 1949 tourism was worth £60 million—almost double the nation's shipbuilding industry—while between 1951 and 1960 domestic tourism spending increased from £380 to £550 million as the industry became Britain's fourth most important foreign currency earner.[41] In particular, the numbers of domestic holidays exploded over this period. Whereas before the Second World War 15 million people took holidays, by the early 1950s total numbers of holidays exceeded 21 million, topping 60 million holidays (encompassing almost 30 per cent of the population) in 1960. Moreover, less than 4 per cent of these holidays were spent abroad.[42] In the early 1950s almost 70 per cent of domestic holidays were spent at the seaside, with the South West of England the most popular destination, accounting for 14 per cent of domestic holidays.[43]

During this period, and especially between 1960 and 1978, there was a considerable expansion in domestic tourism, as table 3.1 shows.

Table 3.1: Holiday-taking by British Tourists, 1951–75 (4+ nights), in millions (£)

	1951	1955	1965	1969	1970	1973	1975
Domestic	25.00	25.00	30.00	30.50	34.50	40.50	40.00
Overseas	1.50	2.00	5.00	5.75	5.75	8.25	8.00
Total	26.50	27.00	35.00	36.25	40.25	48.75	48.00

Source: British National Tourism Survey 1951–75, quoted in Demetriadi J. (1997) 'The golden years: English seaside resorts 1950–74', 49–78 in Shaw G. and Williams A. (eds) *The Rise and Fall of British Coastal Resorts. Cultural and Economic Perspectives*, Cassell, London: 53.

Increasing almost continuously during the 1950s, 1960s and 1970s, the numbers of domestic tourists increased as incomes rose, although much of the growth in the latter period reflected an increasing tendency to take second or third holidays.[44] Holidays spent abroad also recorded a significant increase in this period, with much of this growth recorded in the 1960s and 1970s. Tourist numbers peaked in the early 1970s before the first international oil crisis and its impact on disposable incomes temporarily checked the expansion. Growth stabilised during the remainder of the decade until a further decline in the late 1970s and early 1980s induced by recession.[45]

Several factors combined to create the tourism boom of the three post-war decades. These years were characterised by rising disposable income, the delayed impact of paid holidays, increasing leisure time, more car-owning households and an improving road network. Increased leisure time was the result of shorter working weeks and changes in holiday entitlement. For example, whereas in 1968 no manual worker had an entitlement of four weeks, by 1978 over a third had at least this amount.[46] The increase in car ownership also played a vital role in the development of tourism. The democratisation of the car only occurred outside the USA in the 1950s but during this decade car-borne tourism increased dramatically in Britain, rising from 21 to 47 per cent of holiday-makers between 1951 and 1960.[47] The numbers of private cars in Britain grew from just over 2 million to almost 4 million during 1950–6, rising by a further 4 million by 1960 and topping 11 million in 1970. By 1980 there were 14 million cars on the road, with 60 per cent of households owning at least one car.[48]

In spite of foreign and domestic competition, the seaside resorts of Britain remained 'remarkably dynamic' during the 1940s and 1950s and indeed, Walton has commented that 'enough towns managed to combine traditional attributes with openness to innovation to ensure that most established resorts did more than survive: they prospered.'[49] Although there were substantial shifts in holidaying patterns between the 1950s and the 1970s—encompassing changes in accommodation and facility provision, and in tourists' expectations—it is interesting that holiday-making behaviour retained much of its pre-war character. In the 1950s the 'traditional boarding house seaside holiday,

40

based on a railway journey to an individual resort, still held sway ... as it had in 1900'.[50] Despite the increasingly dominant motorcar and the emergence of bed and breakfast establishments and campsites which focused investment outside the resorts, the traditional patterns -of holiday-making remained remarkably constant. Even in the late 1970s: 'it would seem that the British holidaymaker [was] "tied" either by tradition or institutional factors such as "wakes weeks" to the week or fortnight holiday period'.[51] These so-called 'wakes weeks' or 'stop fortnights'—such as the coal miners' fortnight in Barry Island—saw the workers (and their families) of whole factories, coal mines etc. decamp to seaside resorts for their annual holiday.

miners' fortnight

Beneath the expansion of the self-catering sector and the seemingly uninterrupted growth in the British tourist industry during 1945–73, this period also held the seeds of the late 1970s decline of the domestic seaside industry. The tourism boom of the 1960s and early 1970s masked the need to improve and update the British holiday product. In many ways, this period could be described as one of lost opportunities and although 'A lot of money was made ... little was ploughed back. Facilities became jaded and standards were assumed to be high enough. Heads were buried in the golden sand.'[52] This failure made the British tourism industry, vulnerable to the rivalry of sunny foreign beaches, easy prey to such competition and between 1951 and 1965 the numbers of Britons holidaying abroad increased from 1.5 million to 5 million.[53]

Lost opportunities during the boom

It would be fair to point out, however, that whilst the general trend in overseas holidays was upwards, this was not a period of uninterrupted growth in foreign travel. Holidays abroad were affected by a variety of factors, including the adverse publicity surrounding the overseas industry; the fear of the unknown (especially of flying and unfamiliar foods); and, not least, the Middle East oil crisis. Indeed, Demetriadi argues that it was not until the end of the 1960s 'that overseas mass tourism began to burgeon at a level to markedly affect the domestic seaside trade'.[54] However, the flight of the more affluent abroad was beginning to be reflected in a fall both in the average income of domestic holidaymakers and in their average level of expenditure in the 1960s.[55] Resorts were particularly affected by shortages in quality accommodation: the numbers of large seaside hotels (those

41

with between 100 and 200 rooms) declined by 40 per cent in the 1960s and the costs of refurbishment proved to be too expensive for many, both large and small. As a result, there was a 'gradual erosion of higher income, upper- and middle-class support for the resorts, with the notable exceptions of middle class bastions such as Torquay, Bournemouth and Eastbourne, where the accommodation tended to match the clientele'.[56]

1974–2000: An Industry on Shifting Sands

The virtually continuous expansion of the 1960s and early to mid-1970s was followed in the later 1970s and 1980s by a sharp slump at the seaside. Domestic holidays declined in the face of foreign competition, increasing personal mobility, higher expectations of facilities and amenities, and a gradual change in the appeal of the traditional seaside holiday as fashions changed and tourists sought more diverse and exotic experiences. Reaching a 1970s peak in 1972–3, the volume of domestic tourism fell in 1974 with the first international oil crisis and remained relatively depressed until the late 1980s. Between 1979 and 1982 domestic tourism was particularly hard hit by the recession which struck the UK economy, a downturn exacerbated by a succession of poor summers. Between 1975 and 1985 major holidays taken in Britain fell from 27 to 20 million, whilst those taken overseas leapt from 12 to 22 million—a trend reflected in the expenditure on holidays at home and overseas. In 1974 spending on main holidays was 61 per cent on the domestic market and 39 per cent on overseas market; by 1981 the proportions had changed to 45 and 55 per cent, although half the domestic tourism remained seaside-based.[57]

In addition to the loss of luxury accommodation which had begun in the 1960s, there were other threats to the resorts' infrastructure which began to be increasingly obvious in the 1970s. These decades were years of short-sighted local planning decisions which allowed the removal of many attractions, whilst granting permission to modernist architectural developments which visually degraded resort environments. The small resort of Mumbles, near Swansea, lost the world's first passenger railway (and thus a significant potential tourist attraction) whilst scores of resorts, from Rhyl to Penarth and Torquay

42

saw unsightly multi-storey car parks built on prime seafront sites. In many resorts (such as Rhyl and Ilfracombe) major entertainment facilities—particularly theatres and concert venues with high overheads—were closed or converted to other functions without being replaced by facilities of an adequate standard.[58]

At the same time much of the seaside accommodation around Britain was closed or turned over to other uses, often becoming student accommodation, nursing homes, housing shelters, hostels or low-quality rented accommodation. Unlike the seasonal tourist trade, these uses provided owners and landlords with year-round income but the trend had a highly damaging long-term impact on the image of many resorts and on their abilities to service the needs of the holiday consumer. Moreover, whilst the seaside accommodation base was declining in both quantity and quality, resorts also faced the challenge of newly emergent forms of domestic tourism. Particularly significant amongst these was the growth in urban tourism as much of the new hotel investment since the 1980s has tended to occur in cities where trade is both year-round and multi-dimensional (often encompassing business and conference-based tourism). This shift of hotel investment to cities has also been exacerbated by the internationalisation and rationalisation processes occurring within large hotel groups which have exhibited an increasing preference for major urban sites rather than coastal locations.[59]

In spite of these deep-seated problems and the early 1980s recession, tourism remained hugely important, and although holiday tourism nights fell from 76 to 72 million during 1977–81, tourism expenditure increased from £365 to £635 million.[60] At the beginning of the 1980s Britons were spending almost £5 billion on 48.7 million domestic holidays[61] and by the middle of the decade tourism accounted for 1.4 million jobs and contributed £12.5 billion to the UK economy.[62] The British seaside industry responded to the early 1980s crisis by turning to 'newer' areas of tourism such as activity holidays, conferences, language schools and the overseas market, although the numbers of resorts able to develop new markets successfully was limited by the shortage of quality accommodation, the size of hotel stock and the ability to provide new conference facilities.

Other major growth areas for resorts in the late 1970s and 1980s were second holidays and weekend breaks. Indeed, spending on short holidays increased by 32 per cent in real terms between 1974 and 1982, reflecting an increase from 28 to 37 million holidays.[63] Rather than painting a picture of absolute decline in the popularity of the British tourism product, it is thus more accurate to refer to an *overall* stagnation of activity, within which there are some areas of *growth* and others of *decline*. In the mid-1990s domestic tourism in the UK continued to be an important area of economic activity, worth £8.5 billion in annual spending. Almost half of this spending occurred at the seaside which remains the UK's pre-eminent tourism site, although it is more significant in some parts of the UK than others. Thus, whilst in Scotland the seaside accounts for just over a quarter of domestic holiday spending, in Wales it accounts for nearly 60 per cent, and in Northern Ireland and England it accounts for almost a half, with the West Country being 'by far the biggest region destination for long holidays' in England.[64]

Key Themes at the Seaside

As we have seen so far in this chapter, the social and economic changes which stimulated the growth of the British seaside phenomenon have also been responsible for its stagnation. What is perhaps most surprising, however, is the underlying continuity in the tourism patterns and behaviour at the seaside over the century. There are several key themes which can be discerned in tracing the development of the British seaside and those we will focus on in the remainder of this chapter are: resort hierarchies; the roles of the central and local state; investment patterns; and cultural change. Whilst each phase in the development of the global seaside phenomenon has seen its geographic focus shift, the underlying principles which have driven or fuelled its development remain remarkably constant and despite its relative decline the seaside remains the pre-eminent tourism site— in Britain and the world. The most constant factor in its development for those concerned with issues of power and politics is that, just as the seaside product within Britain developed within a hierarchical framework defined by social tone, so too have its global successors. As Shaw and Williams have pointed out, the foreign holiday—'no matter how tightly packaged and culturally sanitized—has become an indicator of style, fashion and status ... stratified by class'.[65] It is this articulation of class within tourism spaces which we will now explore.

Social Class, Resort Zoning and Hierarchies

One of the most remarkable features both of twentieth-century British society at large and its experience of the tourism industry in particular, is the enduring and consistent nature of class divisions—however they are defined. Whilst there have obviously been significant changes within and between classes, these have had little impact on the distribution of wealth between classes. Indeed, as we will see, the gulf between the rich and poor has widened in Britain in recent years. Social divisions have been visible at the British seaside since its emergence as a tourism site. As Walton has commented:

> Seaside resorts were often crucibles of conflict over lifestyles, as visitors from differing and sometimes incompatible backgrounds with divergent expectations about holiday enjoyments and environments competed for access to and use of valued space within resorts, although by the early twentieth century sophisticated patterns of social segregation between and within resorts had emerged to mitigate these tensions.[66]

In the parliamentary debate of 1938 on the Holidays With Pay Bill, Roland Robinson (MP for the resort of Blackpool) boasted that 'The summer holiday, so recently a privilege of a minority has become the prerogative of the million'.[67] This progressive extension of tourism opportunities to large numbers of the population by a process of diffusion from above is often presented as paralleling the extension of democracy to the masses, 'as an integral part of the evolution and emergence of a pluralist society in which the significance of social class has diminished.'[68] Certainly changes in both the supply and the demand sides of tourism have increased holiday-making opportunities. On the demand side significant changes include: paid holidays and increased leisure time, rising real income and living standards, increasing levels of car ownership and a cultural change in attitudes towards holidays. Consequently, the century has witnessed a huge expansion of the UK tourism industry and although early figures are unavailable, it is notable that while in 1937 15 million tourists took holidays of a week or more, by 1974 114 million domestic holidays were taken in Britain.[69]

At the same, however, it is crucial to recognise that this huge increase in holiday-making masks an underlying pattern of exclusion from the tourism market which has remained constant. Whilst the century is often described as witnessing the rise of 'mass' holiday-taking, it is also true that many people have been and remain unable to take an annual holiday—at the seaside or anywhere else. The so-called democratisation of holiday-taking has been grossly exaggerated. As Walvin warns:

> there is a deceptively uniform pattern, of more and more working people enjoying visits to the coast. But beneath it … lay a complexity of economic forces which determined the individual's ability or inability to enjoy a seaside break—or any other form of costly leisure.[70]

As we argued in Chapter 2, leisure activity has always reflected the material and cultural resources of the participating group and low income levels significantly shape leisure behaviour. For instance, in her study of working-class lifestyles in Lambeth in the early years of the century, Maud Pember Reeves painted a picture of appalling poverty. In households where a third of the income was devoted to paying the rent, people were deprived not only of material prerequisites but also of privacy and leisure. Poverty also led to ill-health, which deprived people of the physical ability to enjoy certain activities.[71] Later, in the inter-war depression, mass unemployment meant 'the erosion of life's little pleasures' for millions of households, and far from affording holidays, many people could not enjoy such everyday leisure as going to the pub, the cinema or to football matches.[72] The Amulree Report of 1938 highlighted the importance in certain regions of Britain of powerful local patterns of regular holiday savings centring around the workplace, the pub, the corner-shop and the 'club-man'. Wage levels and regular employment apart, it was also this ability to save which facilitated the working-class holiday.[73] Yet, at the outbreak of war in 1939—after the worst of the depression was over—it was estimated that at £10 the minimum cost of a week's holiday for a family of four at the seaside was too expensive for the 13 million workers and their families who earned less than £4 a week.[74]

The post-war extension of paid holidays, the increases in leisure time and the growth of dual income households (prompted by the mass entry of women into the workforce) did little to narrow such economic divisions between the classes within Britain. Throughout the 1950s, 1960s and 1970s holidays were still unavailable to many, in the 1970s 50 per cent of the UK's lowest socio-economic group did not take a holiday away from home and surveys from the middle of that decade reveal that 8 million people had had no holiday away from home in the previous five years. At the end of the 1970s 40 per cent of the UK population did not go away on holiday—a proportion which had remained remarkably constant over the century and shows no signs of changing as it draws to a close.[75] At the end of the twentieth century, it remains the case that just under half of all semi- and unskilled workers take no holiday whatsoever, and of those that do only 15 per cent holiday abroad.[76] This contention is supported by recent surveys into the holiday-making habits of the British population, which suggest that increased tourism figures are the result of the higher social classes taking more and more holidays rather than any extension of a holiday-making democracy.[77]

At the end of the 1990s consumption and lifestyle still reflect those class divisions which have underpinned British society since the First World War. As Hudson and Williams have recently argued, in our much heralded leisure democracy it is largely the middle classes who are able to enjoy rich and varied leisure experiences and holiday-making opportunities, whilst the affluent working class have access to annual holidays abroad to destinations such as the Mediterranean. For the semi- and unskilled and those dependent on benefits, holidays are often a distant dream.[78] As we have discussed elsewhere, the distribution of income has become increasingly unequal in recent years in the UK.[79] In 1979 the bottom 40 per cent of its households accounted for 24 per cent of the country's expenditure, but by 1995 that figure had fallen to 12 per cent.[80] Moreover, basic essentials account for over half of their spending whilst the richest households devote almost 60 per cent of their spending to luxuries—particularly travel and leisure activities.[81]

Social class thus emerges as a vital determinant of tourism as of all leisure activity. Moreover, its impact also exacerbates other vectors of inequality such as family structure and gender. For example, the family life cycle, a factor affecting the holiday behaviour of all classes, has always had a greater impact on those families on a tighter budget. Family structure has intersected with economic position throughout the century so that working-class people have been more likely to be able to afford a holiday when they were young and childless or between the time when their offspring left home and their own retirement.[82] In 1949 a survey revealed that 75 per cent of families with more than three children were unable to take a holiday.[83] Similarly, discussing the mid-1950s, Walvin notes that holiday-makers were more common in the 16–24 age group than the 25–39 age group, reflecting the fact that the latter were more likely to have young children. Tourist numbers increased again after the age of 40, but fell again amongst the retired population with only one in three pensioners holidaying.[84] Class, intersecting with family structure and gender, has also not only dictated access to holidays, but also the nature of holidays. For instance, in 1949 a survey for *News Review* showed that married women preferred inclusive to self-catering holidays as the former provided them with more of an escape from their domestic role.[85] Interestingly, these concerns were echoed in a study by the Wales Tourist Board which examined holiday-making patterns in the mid-1990s.[86]

What are extremely interesting in the context of this discussion are the holiday aspirations of many of those unable to afford holidays or the kind of holiday they would like. The Mass Observation survey of 1949 revealed that 75 per cent of those interviewed wanted to go abroad on holiday; furthermore, only a small percentage of those who holidayed in 1948 and who planned to do so again in 1949 would have repeated the holiday if an alternative had been available. That so many did repeat their holiday year after year illustrates the powerful economic and cultural constraints in operation at the time.[87] Certainly, for the greater part of this century working-class tourists often holidayed in the same resort every year with their own neighbours and work-mates from home, frequently staying in the same boarding house year after year. Such traditions were firmly rooted in working-class culture as the communal life of the factories, streets and houses, dictated by poverty and a lack of privacy, found reflection in working-class holiday patterns. Even as late as the 1970s Halsey (a leading sociologist) could define traditional working-class holiday behaviour as characterised by a 'high degree of organisation, collective orientation and passivity'.[88] As Walton has written: 'Once it had taken hold, the working-class holiday habit took on a cosy conservatism which lasted beyond the Second World War and has only recently come under serious attack'.[89]

Not surprisingly, the holiday habits of different classes have impacted on the experiences of the seaside resorts of Britain throughout the twentieth century. For example, the more middle-class resorts such as Bournemouth, Torquay and Sidmouth have been more insulated from decline than working-class resorts such as Morecambe, Barry Island or Rhyl. Perhaps the clearest articulation of class at the seaside has been through the differentiation of tourism spaces along class lines (which we explore in detail in Chapter 4). Conflicts within resort communities did not exist merely because of the divisions between visitors or between visitors and a monolithic resident population, there were also notable rifts within the communities themselves. In particular, retirees and commuters began to exert significant power and influence within the local government of resort towns as early as the 1920s and 1930s. As became increasingly evident as the century progressed, their interests frequently conflicted with those who wanted to develop the resort infrastructure and, as we will discuss in Chapter 4, this divergence of opinion was highly significant in the erosion of the resort ethos in many seaside towns.

Population growth at the seaside in the twentieth century was, in fact, largely dependent on these two groups, the retirees and commuters. The development of seaside resorts as retirement centres or, more disparagingly, 'Costa Geriatricas', was well established during the first half of the twentieth century and gained even further momentum in its second half. Similarly, the development of resorts as commuter dormitories for the leading urban centres was also signif-

49

icant and seaside commuting was a widespread factor in resort growth in the inter-war years. Indeed, the four top resorts—Brighton, Southend, Blackpool and Bournemouth—which remained far ahead of the others in terms of population all had large and growing commuter populations by the 1951 census.[90] The very accessibility of certain resorts therefore was, ironically, responsible both for their continued growth and later for their decline as entertainment sites— as the influence of commuters (just like retirees) diluted the resort ethos in these communities. This ethos was further undermined by these groups' desires to keep local taxes low and their disapproval of local government spending on the holiday industry which disrupted their way of life. This is not to say that their impact was always wholly negative as retirement and commuter communities boosted ailing resort economies. In doing so, however, they clearly shifted the focus of political life in these towns from tourism to residential concerns— a trend which in the latter end of the twentieth century has been one of the fundamental factors affecting the resorts' prospects for revival.

Resorts and the Response of Central Government

The stagnation in many resorts in the later twentieth century was compounded by the failure of central government to recognise and address the very real problems affecting the British tourism industry. Such problems may well have been temporarily obscured by rising visitor numbers and rising tourism expenditure in the 1950s, 1960s and 1970s but their deep-seated nature became increasingly apparent in the second half of the century. Yet, despite the economic signifi-cance of the tourism industry, central government has consistently failed to involve itself in resort regeneration, leaving that responsi-bility to quasi-non-governmental organisations and to local authorities (for whom tourism is a non-statutory and therefore non-essential responsibility).

This lack of government action is in no small part due to tourism's 'candy floss' image, as throughout the century a tourism job has been regarded as, at best, a second- or even third-rate job, and certainly one which could not compare with the jobs offered by the manu-facturing industries.[91] The weakness of central state activity in tourism

50

in Britain is heightened when a comparison is drawn with many other European countries, notably France and Spain—a point made by Shaw and Williams. The 1950s hotel building boom in Spain and Portugal was partly state-funded, whilst the opening up of western Cyprus, Madeira and the Costa del Sol to tourism was facilitated by state airport investment.[92]

The activities of the non-governmental organisations—notably the four national tourist boards which have been charged with the development and marketing of tourism in the UK since the 1969 Development of Tourism Act—have also been severely hampered. In particular, they have been constrained by insufficient funding and by political imperatives which have often worked against the effective development of the tourism industry, including the seaside resort. As we have contended elsewhere in relation to Wales, political consid-erations have led to a tendency to spread what little resources are available rather too evenly and thinly across resorts.[93] The end result has been a product characterised by mediocrity as resorts have been brought up to a lowest common denominator in terms of public investment and development. This is a worrying sign and it seems as though resorts in the future will further exhibit this politically induced uniform mediocrity given the increasing need to demonstrate that investment is being distributed fairly and equally. In England, the withdrawal of grant-aiding powers from the English Tourist Board in the early 1990s is also likely to have far-reaching long-term impli-cations for the English seaside product.

The Intervention of Local Government

Whilst it is apparent that central government has consistently failed to address the issues affecting the British tourism industry, by contrast the local state has displayed a significant commitment to seaside development and revitalisation. As Agarwarl has pointed out, given that tourism is to a large extent a local-resource based industry, the 'role and involvement of the public sector in planning for renewal within coastal resorts … is of critical importance'.[94] Indeed, dynamic local authorities such as Blackpool and Torquay have been key agents in the creation of a seaside product which could compete not only in the heyday of the resort but also in the more demanding years since the late 1970s. The activities of local government have usually focused on marketing and product investment, from environmental improvements designed to stimulate private sector investment, to the building of marinas and facilities such as conference centres and theatres. Despite the interventionist role of local government, however, resort authorities have faced two key challenges over the century: firstly, they have often been financially constrained, and secondly, their communities have been frequently divided by vociferous interest groups.

Local authorities were already pursuing interventionist activities at the seaside in the late nineteenth century, moving into recreational and entertainment provision, as well as developing the resort environment by building and maintaining promenades, parks and gardens. Authorities at the seaside were also more likely to operate utilities such as gas, water and electricity works than those inland, and efforts were beginning to be made to become active in resort marketing, although it was not until the Health Resorts and Watering Places Act of 1921 that this developed in earnest.[95] Such local government policies were not pursued by left-wing councils, but were operated mainly by Conservative local government bodies to provide support services for the small entrepreneurs who dominated resort economies and electorates. Later labelled 'municipal Conservatism',[96] these policies were aimed at advancing the interests of the resort as 'a business collective, in competition with rivals at home and abroad, and needing public provision and operation of activities and amenities which would not have attracted private investment or for which private enterprise was seen as unsuitable in the context'.[97]

The influence of local government increased significantly in the inter-war period, particularly in resorts that witnessed a decline in the role of landed estates and in the larger, more resourced resorts. In such towns, local government pursued highly interventionist strategies designed to provide the resort infrastructure (such as parks, promenades and theatres) and the resort superstructure (such as entertainments and orchestras and, of course, resort advertising). The 1920s and 1930s were the high point of local authority investment in seaside amenities, with the public sector providing everything from promenades, parks, pavilions and swimming pools to sun-terraces and sea defences. Seaside resorts accounted for eight of the eleven highest *per capita* spending County Boroughs in England and Wales between 1919 and 1939 as far as parks and open spaces expenditure was concerned.[98] Authorities also provided amenities which reflected the new open-air athletic and sporting fashions in holidaying, and golf courses and tennis courts were popular additions to many resort seafronts. This was a period when the local state advanced and complemented the interests of the business communities in the resorts and social welfare considerations (such as municipal housing) were often sidelined in the drive towards 'municipal capitalism'— unless tourism-related schemes served as unemployment relief projects.[99]

It would obviously be a mistake to assume that this municipal drive was universally welcomed in all resorts and, particularly in the financially stringent early 1930s, there was sustained opposition to high spending and alleged mismanagement of public facilities from increasingly powerful and vocal residents, especially those who had retired to the resorts. It is also important to point out that no clear relationship between municipal enterprise and resort success could be established in the inter-war period. Scarborough and Hastings, for instance, were at the forefront of innovation in many areas, but did not see their efforts reflected in population growth.[100] Despite this lack of clear evidence for a causal link, however, the local state re-emerged as the key agent for change in resorts in the post-war period.

For many resorts the post-war decades were ones characterised by a superficial prosperity which masked a failure to keep pace with changing holiday patterns, although there were periods of significant investment (the sharpest peak of activity being the 1974 reorganisation of local government). This mid-1970s redrawing of local political boundaries created a frenetic round of spending as surplus capital was channelled by both outgoing and incoming authorities into schemes designed on the one hand as 'legacies' and on the other as 'statements of ambition'. For those resorts which were able to develop their facilities and reposition their images, it was largely their local authorities (in the 1980s and 1990s often in partnership with regional or national tourist boards) which initiated, encouraged and supported resort development.[101] An active local authority could not guarantee regeneration in the face of external change—as in the case of Barry Island in the late 1980s [102]—but many rejuvenated resorts such as Tenby and Torquay have had highly interventionist councils prepared to invest in tourism.

Investment Patterns at the Seaside

The pattern of public-sector involvement in the seaside is reasonably well researched, but only provides a partial view of investment and an understanding of private-sector investment is critical to any analysis of the development of the seaside product. One of Agarwarl's conclusions in her study of resort policy is that 'the nature of the relationship between the local state and the private commercial operator more often than not determined policy outcome. Co-operation and close collaboration between the two … is … an essential pre-requisite to local economic regeneration.'[103] Despite its importance, however, the private sector has received relatively little attention amongst tourism scholars. Shaw and Williams—two writers who have devoted attention to this topic—have pointed out that: 'tourism research has largely bypassed the study of entrepreneurial activity and nowhere is this more evident than in the studies of the resort cycle itself which assumes largely mechanistic and somewhat predictable responses by the private sector'.[104]

There are many factors which have contributed to this failure, not least the very nature of the subject matter. Financial details of any business can be difficult to investigate and this is a problem which is compounded as one moves from large- to small-scale businesses. As a result, it is necessary to examine the sources of information which do exist and attempt, where appropriate, to extrapolate to the wider context. As a starting point, it is undoubtedly true that the problems associated with an ageing resort product have been exacerbated by the evident failure of both the private and public sectors to renew and develop its infrastructure. In part, some of this failure can be related to the lack of market intelligence data available to resort operators and strategists. The paucity of information collected before the 1970s makes it very difficult to quantify trends, resort strengths

54

and weaknesses and changes in holiday-making patterns.

As we shall explore in more depth in later chapters, this failure to invest was not a phenomenon of modern construction; instead it was well rooted in the 1950s, the period popularly fashioned as the heyday of the seaside resort. In more recent years it has continued to inhibit the revitalisation of many resorts dominated by small-scale, independent operators whose businesses are characterised by marginal investments and profitability, resulting in stagnation, declining profitability and little in the way of prospects for the future.[105] The industry has long been dominated by owner-controlled family businesses whose responses to external change have been slow.[106] Many of these problems exhibited by the operators of tourism businesses in seaside resorts are clearly associated with their small size, a problem accentuated since the 1970s by the withdrawal of the larger operators, as in the case of Butlins in Barry Island and First Leisure in Rhyl. Many operators have little previous experience in the industry and many were motivated by a variety of reasons for entering the industry, often bearing little relevance to tourism itself: everything from a desire to escape from another lifestyle, to a desire to gain independence or fulfil a dream. As a result, they display a strong tendency to migrate toward the resort areas they themselves previously visited on holiday.[107] Given the diverse reasons for entering the tourism business, it should come as no surprise that few operators appear to be concerned with 'making money'.[108] This lack of a business culture, industry experience and an entrepreneurial base, however, holds severe implications for the industry. Many resorts have been, and remain, characterised by marginal businesses, often owned by the semi-retired or 'dream-seekers' who have used their personal capital to finance their operations. The continuance of such investment patterns will further marginalise the resort product and undermine its future prospects.

In the inter-war period, our above emphasis on public-sector investment should not obscure the continuing importance of private enterprise in development—most obviously in hotel building—particularly in evidence in Torquay.[109] There was also continuing investment in large-scale entertainment complexes, with Blackpool's Pleasure Beach[110] and Margate's Dreamland[111] at the leading edge. The problem, as noted by Walton, is that whilst it may seem that private

investment in entertainment and amenities was drawn dispropor-
tionally to the fastest-growing resorts in the inter-war years, more
research is needed to test this area of resort development.[112] One fact
is clear from the evidence which does exist, and that is the consistent
failure to invest in the seaside product throughout the post-war
decades. In addition, even where investment did occur, it took the
form of consolidation rather than innovation—upgrading existing
amenities rather than creating new tourism environments.[113] The
investment patterns experienced by the seaside resorts in Britain are
in direct contrast to those of their closest rivals—the resorts of the
Mediterranean—a fact which largely explains the decline in quality
of the British product. Those of Spain, for instance, have demonstrated an enviable ability to reinvest and reinvent their products to
deliver the new environments and infrastructures which appeal to
contemporary tourists.[114] Such adaptability is likely to become much
more important in the future as shifts in fashion and popular culture
accelerate.

In the post-war decades the evidence is much more clear that
seaside investment has been inadequate and, where it has occurred,
it has been drawn to the larger resorts. Few large hotels were built in
Devon between 1945 and the late 1970s and those which were
constructed were small establishments. England's largest resort area
was therefore not immune to the trend to invest in tourism accommodation in urban areas instead of seaside resorts. In 1970 almost
half of the county's hotels with less than 20 rooms had been built
since 1960 whilst 90 per cent of the large hotels had been built before
1950, the majority of them in the nineteenth century.[115] Research
conducted by the English Tourist Board in the mid-1980s confirms
the continuance of such patterns, suggesting that 'hotel investment
has been particularly poor in many resorts, certainly when compared
with other parts of the tourist economy.'[116]

In many ways this trend is a result of the very nature of the resorts'
serviced accommodation sector, dominated as it is by small-scale
independent operators with varying management or strategic abilities.
Table 3.2 reveals the huge disparities in investment levels (both
completed or proposed) between resorts and other rival sectors in
the late 1980s. This is a major problem for the resorts, particularly

56

when one remembers that then—as now—they accounted for around a half of all holiday-taking. The figures also indicate that such investment trends continue to compound the problems of small- to medium-sized resorts. Investment in attractions in the latter is extremely limited as investment which has occurred has tended to focus on the larger resorts—which are themselves dominated by Blackpool. Small- to medium-sized resorts thus tend to suffer from an infrastructure which is fragmented, small-scale and, in the case of attractions, frequently subsidised by local authorities.

Table 3.2: Investment in England's Tourism Environments, 1986–88, in millions (£)

Sector	1986 Resorts	1986 Others	1988 Resorts	1988 Others
Hotels	41.9	716.3	32.7	1342.8
Self-catering	12.2	125.6	41.4	211.1
Attractions*	21.0	109.0	32.0	611.9
Conference facilities	18.1	57.6	17.8	466.7
Total	93.2	1008.5	123.9	2632.5

*includes visitor facilities and excludes marinas.
Source: English Tourist Board: Investment Monitors, 1986 and 1988, English Tourist Board, London.

The prospects for these smaller resorts appear to be bleak, particularly when this investment pattern is set against the dominance of their larger rivals. In fact, smaller resorts have lost at least 50 per cent of their visitors in the last 20 years and during the peak season they accommodate fewer than 2,000 staying visitors per week.[117] Only eight resorts—Blackpool, Scarborough, Great Yarmouth, Brighton, Isle of Wight, Bournemouth, Torbay and Newquay—accounted for at least 75 per cent of the volume and value of seaside tourism in England at the end of the 1980s.[118] It is these resorts which continue to dominate the development and marketing of the resort product in

England, and in Wales the same pattern emerges with the dominance of Rhyl, Llandudno and Tenby.[119]

Cultural Change, Identity and the Seaside

This century has witnessed the enormous growth of Britain's seaside resorts, followed by their subsequent stagnation and in many cases decline. Much of our discussion to date has centred on discussions of policies and investment patterns, yet the stagnation of the traditional British seaside resort is not solely attributable to economic restructuring. Indeed, these economic and social patterns themselves 'cannot be fully understood without the consideration of culture, a factor that is … integrally involved in the process of urban and regional change'.[120] Arguably, it is these cultural changes which have had the most significant long-term impact on our love affair with the seaside.[121] In fact, some commentators, notably John Urry, would argue that such cultural changes have been so sweeping that the seaside has lost its automatic association with the word holiday.

The crux of Urry's thesis is that seaside resorts are the 'victims of the "cultural wars" of the service class'.[122] It is the arts and the cultural mores of this group which have triumphed over those of others and which have condemned the seaside resort as 'vulgar and basic—the very negation of culture'.[123] Thus, they have become entities which people of good taste—the new 'ethical tourist'—would rarely contemplate to visit.[124] Urry argues that it is these ethical tourists who determine much of what is desirable and acceptable for today's holiday consumer. He suggests that their cultural capital is such that they extend far beyond their immediate sphere of influence, permeating the holiday preferences of the many as opposed to the few. He goes on to argue that these sophisticated tourists' preferences for natural (holistic, unspoilt and 'real') holiday experiences, for out-of-the-way exclusive destinations, and for specialist products and operators are in direct conflict with the attributes of the traditional seaside resort.

Whilst there can be little doubt about the *existence* of the types of tourists described by Urry, their *dominance* of holiday tastes is open to question. Given that half of all domestic British holidays are still taken

58

at the coast, we would contend that the seaside *per se* remains synonymous with holidays. It is simply that many contemporary tourists have expanded their vacation horizons to encompass more 'exotic' seaside locales, whether they be the main or an add-on element of the holiday. Many overseas holiday packages are marketed in conjunction with a stay at a coastal resort, and for every tourist who takes a cultural or a themed holiday, there are many more who devote their holidays to sun, sand and sea destinations in the Mediterranean, the Caribbean and in Southeast Asia. Moreover, if a much broader geographical view is taken and one looks at emerging tourism patterns in post-Communist Eastern Europe, Hall has suggested that another phase in the mass rush to the sun, sand and sea product is only just beginning along the Adriatic and Black Sea coasts.[125] As such, it is arguable that far too much attention has been paid to the 'new' tourism which, by definition, occupies a niche within a vast and varied global industry. Conceivably the emergence of the ethical tourist is yet another incarnation of the phenomenon of social zoning, dividing the elites from the masses—culturally and spatially. Too great an emphasis on the 'vulgarity' of the British seaside also tends to disguise the very diverse nature of the domestic seaside product. Whilst it is undoubtedly true that many resorts were founded on entertainments such as funfairs, bathing beauty contests and amusement arcades, it is also true that many resorts eschewed such developments in their desire to maintain social exclusivity, as we will see in Chapter 4.

Notwithstanding this discussion over the extent of the impact of cultural change, it cannot be denied that trends and fashions in popular culture have helped to shape and fashion the development of resorts throughout this century. The popularisation of the suntan, mentioned above, is probably the most prominent and obvious of these. It would also be foolish to try to deny the increasing sophistication and variety demanded by tourists throughout this century. Indeed, the continuing need to cater for the 'pleasures of the new, the fickle, the unexpected'[126] is likely to define the future development of the British seaside resorts. At the end of the twentieth century, however, it would be too simplistic to talk about the entire British seaside as a product in terminal decline. The upgrading of facilities, the improvement of standards and more aggressive marketing has done much to reposition the domestic product in the 1990s. Certain types of resorts have been and remain successful products. As Williams and Shaw comment: 'the largest tourist resorts—Great Yarmouth, Brighton, Torbay, ... Blackpool ...—have been able to restructure relatively effectively through large class investments in conference centres, ... [whilst] smaller resorts with a distinctive heritage or niche market have also prospered'.[127] Those resorts which have suffered most have tended to be those small and medium-sized resorts (such as Clacton, Colwyn Bay, Aberystwyth and Ilfracombe) which lack any product distinctiveness or do not have the required resources or political determination to initiate effective regeneration.

Throughout the century the British seaside resort has been a distinct and distinctive entity—'a liminal zone, transitional between land and sea'[128]—and, despite the cultural changes described by Urry, that uniqueness is still evident today, reflected in resort demographics, politics, environment and aesthetics. The seaside resort has always been an intriguing social and cultural space: on the one hand it is where people have been able to eschew the constraints of social *mores*, whilst on the other hand, it has also been an arena where strong and sustained attempts were made to control social behaviour, both in terms of who was allowed access and which entertainments were sanctioned. This is apparent in Shields's examination of how Brighton on the English south coast 'came to be associated with pleasure, with the liminal and with the carnivalesque' and how it developed 'from Regency pleasure and healing centre to the gay Victorian resort to "dirty weekend" destination and Bank Holiday riots on the beach'.[129] He argues that whilst the seaside was a place for play, industrial Britain was perceived to be 'productive', London (with the legislature) to be 'serious' and rural Britain to be 'innocent'.[130] In Britain, as elsewhere, the seaside thus 'became the topos of a set of connected discourses on pleasure and pleasurable activities'.[131] As Walton has commented, the seaside certainly exhibited a distinctive seaside architecture (from Brighton to Miami Beach), and celebrated a peculiar interpretation of the carnivalesque (from Blackpool to Coney Island and Atlantic City). Here, social rules 'were more generously defined and flexibly imposed in the self-consciously different environment of seaside and holiday, for the relaxation of *mores* was not just about the liminal

60

qualities of the seaside environment: it was also about the annual liber-
ation from labour discipline and all that went with it'.[132]

Much of the distinctiveness of this entertainment culture of excess
has undoubtedly been eroded and is no longer peculiar to the seaside
(witness the spectacle of the leisure sites of Las Vegas, Reno and, to
a lesser extent, Sun City in South Africa). Similarly, the dramatic shifts
in the social *mores* which govern contemporary public (and especially
'private') behaviour have diluted much of the impact of seaside entertainment which focused on 'caricature, inversion, "otherness,"
transgression, indignity, absurdity and the carnivalesque'.[133] Yet,
despite such cultural change, the seaside can still lay claim to 'distinctive environmental, governmental, aesthetic and cultural identities',[134]
and, again in the words of Walton, the holiday beach 'as distinctive,
relaxed landscape with figures' remains 'firmly implanted in the
popular imagination'.[135]

In the first half of the twentieth century Britain's seaside resorts
were more likely to have a high proportion of their population in the
over-65 age groups and a low proportion in the under-15 age groups.
They had considerable surpluses of women over men, especially in
the retirement resorts (such as those of the south coast). They also
had low birth rates, but some had among the highest illegitimacy rates
(reflecting maybe the 'anonymity' of the summer season and transient
labour markets) and high concentrations in professional and service
occupations.[136] Seaside towns were also socially and politically conservative and difficult places for labour to organise. Despite high
seasonal unemployment and high poverty levels, neither trade unions
nor left-wing views flourished in these communities. Arguably, these
generic qualities of seaside resorts, which to a large extent gave them
a collective identity, remain today and are typical of communities such
as Blackpool. Despite the massive social, economic and cultural
changes which we have outlined in this chapter, the 'prime concerns
of resorts' rulers' throughout the century have been (and are today)
the 'protection of an image of consensual respectability'.[137] As we shall
now explore in Chapter 4, resort social tone—articulated in local
politics—defined the experience of many resort communities
throughout the century.

4

Resorts, Communities and Social Tone in Devon

In most aspects of the tourist trade there is a sharp difference of interests between the rich and the poor and between those who cater for the one and those who cater for the other. The rich want exclusiveness. Thus those who cater for them try to keep away the normal holiday-maker, the tripper, the motor coach and the holiday camp; they even attempt to have an all round season …. Those who cater for the poor, on the other hand, want widespread publicity, communal services, holiday camps, day excursions, low prices and little or no rise in prices during the season…. In fact every town in Devon aims at catching certain types of visitor and claims certain attributes in itself which others have not.

Nuffield College Social Reconstruction Survey, 1944:
The Devon Tourist Trade

Forming part of the peninsula which is the far South West of England, Devon is a highly peripheral area which is characterised by a poorly developed infrastructure and limited economic activity. It is also one of the most naturally beautiful areas of Britain, boasting two National Parks, three Areas of Outstanding Natural Beauty and a coastline of high scenic quality, most of which is designated as Heritage Coast or a Coastal Preservation Area.[1] This impressive coastline, set against the backdrop of a rugged moorland hinterland, has played a key role in making Devon Britain's leading holiday area in this century. Perhaps the key factor in *shaping* its tourism industry, however, has been the relative physical isolation of the county, enabling many of its resorts to maintain their social exclusivity well into the twentieth century. So pervasive was this desire to maintain a high social tone that in 1932 the official guide of Torquay could proclaim that:

> [Those] whose idea of a holiday is compounded of Big Wheels, paper caps, donkeys ... tin whistles, and generally a remorseless harlequinade, turn their backs on the town, and swarm to watering-places which cater for that sort of thing. The residue, the thoroughly normal, healthy and educated people who are the backbone of the nation, love Torquay as few other towns are loved, and it is they who throng its pleasant ways the long year round ...[2]

One of the main aims of this chapter is to examine the forces which underpinned such exclusivity. In particular, it demonstrates that tourist spaces were arenas for conflict and that the control and usage of such space was continually contested by various factions in the resorts, principally residents' groups and those who relied on tourism for a living. Generally speaking, resort communities in Devon were concerned to maintain their social exclusivity at the expense of encouraging popular mass tourism. To this end, their tourism policy-makers and the pressure groups which influenced them sought to attract 'desirable', affluent and fashionable visitors and to exclude the less advantaged lower middle and working classes.

Such tensions and conflicts over space have been and continue to be played out across tourism sites in Britain and beyond. As we discussed in the introduction, however, such contests have been largely marginalised in analyses of tourism. The body of work concerned with how public recreational space is contested and controlled is largely incipient and, although some examples can be found in tourism,[3] that which has emerged has tended to be drawn from cultural and feminist geography. Throughout this book, we are concerned to contribute to tourism's understanding of the contested nature of space by illuminating the class conflicts which dominated resort development in the twentieth century. In this analysis, this chapter is pivotal as it examines the meaning of 'social tone' and investigates its operation in Devon. Prior to this, however, the first half of the chapter briefly introduces Devon and traces the development of its resorts in order to contexualise the later discussion.

Devon and the Seaside Tourism Industry

The sea has been instrumental in shaping Devon's tourism industry. Indeed, the county's relative remoteness and inhospitable interior, combined with its lengthy coastline and numerous harbours, gives Devon a strong maritime orientation and the current recreational links with the sea continue an ancient tradition. Rare in having both a north and south seaboard, the county is unique in Britain in that each coastline has its own separate focus of trade and communications. Far from being a barrier to communication, the sea has brought the county into closer contact with the French, Irish and Welsh seaboards (as well as areas further afield), a factor which was to prove significant in the development of some of Devon's resorts in the nineteenth and twentieth centuries. In contrast, Devon's physical geography has long constrained its overland communication links with the rest of Britain. This geographical isolation was largely responsible for the character of Devon's economic development and its individual identity, imbuing it with a distinctive rural culture.[4] The internal geography of Devon has similarly determined development and, in effect, has created a divided county in which transport networks have always favoured the southern coastal settlements whilst those of the north have suffered from inadequate road and rail links.[5]

The sea, or rather the coastline, was critical in creating Devon's tourism industry. The county's coastal zone is rich in scenic features, including sandy spits, sand dunes and many gently sloping sandy beaches which have high aesthetic qualities, all of which enabled Devon to capitalise on the twentieth-century obsession with sunshine and suntans. In addition to gentle sands (including Goodrington Sands in the south and Woolacombe in the north) Devon's north coast is well endowed with coastal relief, a factor which has been described as 'one of the dominant influences on an individual's perception of coastal scenery'.[6] These precipitous cliffs have, however, restricted coastal development in the north and of the 15 settlements classified as resorts by Devon County Council in 1981, only five were on the north coast: Ilfracombe, Combe Martin, Lynmouth, Westward Ho! and Woolacombe (see Map 4.1).[7]

The physical environment alone does not explain the rise of Devon's tourism industry, for whilst tourists are attracted by the scenery, this beauty is also confirmed by the lack of heavy industry and high concentrations of urbanisation—both rooted in Devon's geographical remoteness.[8] The seaside tourism industry which rose to pre-eminence in the county was grafted onto pre-existing, essentially primary employment patterns, particularly agriculture, fishing, shipbuilding and coastal trading. Most of Devon's resorts began as fishing communities, which increasingly turned to tourism when the fishing and extractive industries declined in the industrial revolution.[9] Such was the extent of this realignment of employment patterns that by the early twentieth century Devon already had what could be termed a service economy—domestic service (including tourism-related service) had become its largest employment sector, followed by agriculture and transport.[10]

Tracing the Development of Devon's Resorts

In the twentieth century Devon became *the* major domestic holiday destination in Britain. Although figures for the first half of the century are scarce, it is clear that between the end of the First World War and the late 1970s the county experienced a huge increase in tourist numbers. By the mid-1960s Devon had captured 20 per cent of the British market and by the late 1970s the numbers of annual tourists holidaying in the county exceeded 3.4 million.[11] Expanding throughout the century, tourism assumed a huge importance to Devon's economy, indeed tourism and leisure enterprises (although often characterised by seasonal unemployment and low wages) have done much to offset the decline of Devon's traditional maritime and agricultural activities. By the late 1980s such was the annual volume of the tourism industry that tourism nights exceeded 30 million and expenditure £530 million—clearly Devon's most lucrative economic sector.[12]

The original siting of Devon's tourism industry was largely dictated

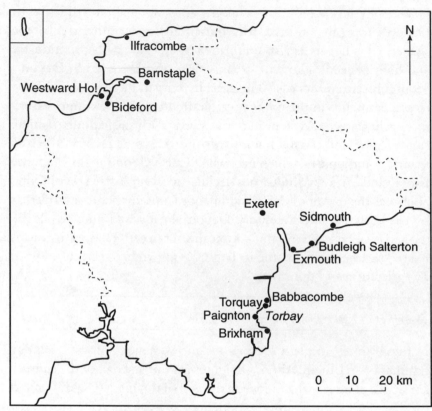

Map 4.1: *Devon and its Seaside Resorts*

by the nature of the coastline: on the southern coastline several estuaries fostered many resorts, but by contrast far fewer developed on the northern seaboard due to the constraining geography of its coastal cliffs. Accessible sandy beaches attract tourists and thus resort developments have concentrated at such locations (including Dawlish, Exmouth, Teignmouth, and the Torbay resorts in the south and at Woolacombe in the north). It is noticeable that, with no safe, sandy beaches between Budleigh Salterton and Lyme Regis in the south, the communities of Seaton, Sidmouth and Budleigh Salterton did not develop into traditional 'family' resorts but evolved into small holiday towns and retirement centres (Table 4.1).[13] Likewise, the wild coastline from Dartmouth to Plymouth in the South West, with no towns and few beaches, has not fostered resort development, although from Bigbury to Plymouth the more accessible coast has served local day-trippers since the inter-war years (see Map 4.1).[14]

Table 4.1: Defining Characteristics of Devon's Key Resorts

Resort	Defining Characteristics
Sidmouth	exclusive/residential visitors/retirement
Lynton/Lynmouth	exclusive/residential visitors/retirement
Seaton	exclusive/residential visitors/retirement
Budleigh Salterton	exclusive/residential visitors/retirement
Salcombe	exclusive/yachting centre
Dartmouth	exclusive/yachting centre
Torquay	fashionable/residential visitors/retirement
Ilfracombe	popular/residential visitors/day-tripper
Paignton	popular/family/beach
Teignmouth	popular/family/beach
Dawlish	popular/family/beach
Dawlish Warren	day-tripper/beach
Exmouth	day-tripper/beach

Whilst the emergence of the resorts pre-dates the coming of the railway age, the pattern of railway development was hugely influential in the evolution of the Devon seaside, even with the post-war dominance of the motorcar. Tourism accommodation has remained coastal and is largely concentrated in those resorts which were reached by the railways in the Victorian period. The enduring influence of the railways can be seen in the fact that, as no lines ever reached the south Devon coast west of Brixham, the coastal communities there never developed into 'traditional' resorts.[15] In contrast, where the railways went, new resorts developed or existing ones expanded, initially at Teignmouth and Torquay (opening in the mid-nineteenth century), followed by Exmouth, Seaton, Sidmouth and Budleigh Salterton in later decades. Thus, whilst the railways nurtured developments in the south, the lack of rail links constrained development in the northern resorts.[16] After the railways arrived in the north in the last quarter of the nineteenth century, however, these resorts boomed, especially that of Ilfracombe.[17] The development of Devon's seaside industry thus mirrored that of Britain as a whole, with the caveat that its relatively late entry into the market (largely due to its inaccessibility) enabled it to retain its exclusivity far beyond the experience of other British resort areas. Yet despite the fact that Devon's resorts have thus operated on a rather different timescale, tourism's domination of the Devon economy was reasonably well established by the early twentieth century. Indeed, by 1910 tourism-related activities accounted for between a quarter and a third of the commercial businesses in the county's resorts, rising to almost 70 per cent in Ilfracombe (see Table 4.2).

The years between 1900 and 1914 were very successful tourism seasons in Devon, despite industrial unrest and the outbreak of the First World War (which was to prove only a temporary disruption to resort ambitions in the county). After the war, although resorts such as Torquay and Ilfracombe had to cope with neglected facilities, slow de-requisitioning of hotels and public buildings and financial constraints, the rush to the seaside in 1919–20 was phenomenal. Torquay was already the premier resort in Devon, although others such as Ilfracombe were also rapidly developing and carving out niches in the British seaside industry. One such resort was Paignton,

Table 4.2: Tourism Businesses in Devon Resorts as a Percentage of Commercial Directory Entries, 1910–1939

	1910	1919	1930	1939
Budleigh Salterton	26	48	18	23
Dawlish	33	45	29	28
Exmouth	27	34	30	26
Ilfracombe	67	73	42	43
Lynton	56	42	38	37
Paignton	34	41	28	33
Seaton	35	17	35	18
Sidmouth	25	44	23	26
Teignmouth	36	44	35	31
Torquay	32	37	31	29

Note: all figures to nearest percentage.
Source: Kelly's Directories of Devonshire, 1910–39.

which established a reputation as a leading family resort in the inter-war period (see Table 4.1). Much of this success was due to its wide expanse of sandy beaches, but it was also a result of substantial local authority investment, notably a £54,000 programme of improvements including new cliff gardens, promenades, putting greens and a boating lake.[18] Exmouth was another of the few Devon resorts which encouraged 'mass' tourism, developing as a very popular resort attracting large numbers of day-trippers, many of them drawn from the nearby city of Exeter. Here in Exmouth, the local authority was also keen to encourage the tourist trade and the council financed municipal entertainments, bands, beach kiosks, bowling greens, tennis courts, mini-golf and a swimming pool in these years.[19]

The inter-war dominance of tourism in Devon's resorts can be seen in Table 4.3. Based on the 1921 census which was unusually taken in June, this presents what Walton and O'Neill have described as 'a very valuable window on the hidden demography of resort life at a key transitional point' in their development.[20] In resorts such as Ilfracombe and Lynton on the north coast visitors made up between approximately a quarter and over a third of their respective early summer populations—figures which represent a huge influx of tourists considering 'popular' resorts such as Ilfracombe would not have experienced their peak arrivals until August. In contrast, in resorts south of Teignmouth, visitors only accounted for between 13 and 16 per cent of their populations. The resorts closest to Exeter, the nearest urban catchment area of any size, had the lowest numbers of staying visitors, largely due to the dominance of day-trippers in resorts such as Exmouth and Dawlish Warren—visitors who would not be counted in the census.[21]

Table 4.3: Visitor Populations of Devon Resorts, 1921

	Total enumerated population	Numbers of visitors	Visitors as a percentage of total enumerated population
Budleigh Salterton	2,624	223	8.5
Dawlish	4,675	318	6.8
Exmouth	13,606	816	6.0
Ilfracombe	11,772	3,037	25.8
Lynton	2,587	882	34.1
Paignton	14,451	1,965	13.6
Seaton	2,295	450	19.6
Sidmouth	5,668	731	12.9
Teignmouth	10,970	1,722	15.7
Torquay	39,431	5,757	14.6

Source: Office of Population and Census Statistics, Census Report 1921.

With the exception of such figures which provide a valuable—yet still imprecise and tantalising—glimpse of the impact of tourism in the county, there is a severe lack of appropriate statistical indicators relating to resort development in this period.[22] One further 'snapshot' of the pattern of Devon's holiday trade and the growth of its south coast resorts comes from data detailing the volume of rail passenger traffic (Table 4.4). Although such figures do not solely relate to tourist arrivals (and reflect the growing commuter function of some resorts), the massive leap in the numbers of travellers in Devon between the First World War and the mid-1920s was largely due to increases in tourist numbers. Indeed, the throughput of rail passengers at each resort approximately doubled in that decade, peaking in 1923, before declining in the economic slump of 1930–2.[23]

Table 4.4: Rail Passenger Traffic at Selected South Devon Stations, 1903–1934

	Dawlish Warren	Dawlish	Teignmouth	Torquay	Paignton
1903	–	6,540	14,477	27,761	11,333
1913	565	7,424	17,053	30,484	17,625
1923	1,267	12,643	27,726	64,304	30,548
1929	1,410	13,068	24,668	66,253	33,396
1930	1,325	12,803	23,254	64,154	33,117
1931	1,275	11,371	21,329	56,074	30,870
1932	1,161	10,686	19,377	47,784	28,317
1933	1,217	10,699	19,122	42,183	28,971
1934	1,313	10,479	19,084	43,564	29,218

Source: Traffic at GWR stations, 1903–38, PRO Rail 266/45.

This expansion in the numbers of tourists did not, however, substantially alter the holiday-making patterns which had been established in the late nineteenth century. As Lewes has shown, even after the Second World War—when the numbers coming into Devon increased still further—growth continued to be channelled along familiar lines and traditional accommodation remained at the centre of the seaside resort experience. The expansion of the railways had created many of the seaside resorts and their dominance of the transport networks until the 1920s preserved the early pattern. Even with the maturity of road transport and the massive increase in the numbers of holiday-makers between the wars, new tourism development remained located mainly on the outskirts of existing resorts.

Although newer forms of accommodation (such as holidays camps) did begin to appear (Brixham and Seaton being among Devon's more popular sites with developers), these were also coastally based.[24]

Despite the continuing significance of the railway resorts, this is not to say that the motorcar was not a crucial agent of change in holiday-making patterns. Although the democratisation of this transport form came well after 1945, its impact was beginning to be apparent in the inter-war period.[25] The early years of the 1920s witnessed the emergence of motor vehicles as a major force in transport and in the years after the First World War motor coaches opened up much of Devon to working-class travellers. A major rail strike in 1919 first demonstrated the advantages of road transport (especially charabancs) and by 1920 newspapers were reporting that the railways 'regarded [with] some alarm the inroads made on their passenger traffic by this class of vehicle'.[26] With rail fares treble their pre-war prices, the West Country resorts benefited from the popular week-long motor coach-tours from London which, at between 14 and 18 guineas, included first-class hotel accommodation.[27] The arrival of these tours and of the cheaper 'charas' had a notable effect on Devon as they were increasingly able to reach the more remote areas of the county. By 1930 Britain's registered vehicles exceeded two million.[28]

By the outbreak of the Second World War Devon's resorts were firmly established, and although the war and its aftermath did bring difficulties to the county's tourism industry, they did not suffer as much as one might expect. Indeed, Devon's resorts were not hit by the conflict on the same scale as their eastern and southern counterparts and it could even be argued that they actually benefited in some respects from the upheavals of the war years. In fact, the Nuffield survey of 1944 concluded that the influx of evacuees, together with the relocated military and civilian personnel, meant that the county's 'Hotels, like the distributive trades, … suffered little from the War'.[29] In the post-war years, however, the resorts faced a difficult period (as they had after the First World War) as tourist demand boomed at a time when resort amenities required extensive renovation. In the aftermath of the war, Devon's resorts did confront and successfully overcome the obstacles presented by austerity and reconstruction to

72

Figure 4.1: *Ilfracombe Charabanc Trip, 1919*
The increasing democratisation of holiday-making. During the early inter-war years social and economic changes together with improvements in transport opened up previously inaccessible areas of Devon. This charabanc leaving Ilfracombe in 1919 was typical of many pressed into service to cope with the post-war holiday boom. (Reproduced by kind permission of the Ilfracombe Museum.)

73

remain in the forefront of the domestic market, although the financial strain of this undertaking should not be underestimated. After six years of neglect the resorts were ill-prepared for the holiday rush which accompanied peace and preparations were hampered by the continuance of wartime restrictions, slow de-requisitioning, rationing and a shortage of skilled labour.

Despite such problems, by 1951 the South West had emerged as the most popular British holiday-making region, accounting for 14 per cent of domestic tourism and edging out the North West with 13 per cent.[30] This share of domestic holidays rose to 20 per cent by 1965 and 23 per cent by 1973, representing an increase from 3.5 million to 8 million holidays over the period 1951–73.[31] As we saw in Chapter 3, there is little precise national or regional analytical data available on the tourism industry before the mid-1960s, although annual figures are available for Devon after 1960. By the late 1960s and early 1970s tourism expenditure in the South West as a whole totalled £230 million and in Devon expenditure increased from £50 to £99 million during 1969–73. The industry was also a significant employer in these decades, providing the equivalent of 27,000 full-time jobs at the end of the 1960s—increasing to 38,000 in the mid-1970s. Indeed, the continued domination of the holiday trades can be seen in the county's employment figures. Although there is no one source of tourism employment data, sectors such as the hotel and catering trades provide useful indicators. In 1969 the percentage of employees employed in the hotel and catering trades was 6.6 per cent in Devon, well above the 2.6 per cent national figure, rising to 20 per cent in Torquay and reaching a massive 35 per cent in Ilfracombe.[32]

At the beginning of the 1970s, Devon's seaside industry was thus seemingly well placed to capitalise on emerging trends in holiday-making. The increased leisure time in this decade (discussed in Chapter 3) created a demand for more holidays and weekend breaks—a trend which benefited the South West of England, which became a favoured short-break destination. The completion of the M5 motorway in the mid-1970s further enhanced the region's potential to cater for this type of visitor and brought an extra 18 million people within three-and-a-half hours' drive-time of Devon.[33] In fact, the social diffusion of car ownership since the 1960s led to the motorcar's final usurpation of the railways' dominance of Devon's tourism industry. By the end of the 1960s over 80 per cent of holidaymakers to Devon and Cornwall were arriving by car, a higher proportion than any other region in England, probably due to the area's suitability for car-centred holidays.[34] This pattern partly caused and partly cushioned the effects of the loss of rail links in the period (as a result of the Beeching report on railway rationalisation). In the early 1960s Seaton, Sidmouth and Budleigh Salterton all lost their connections, whilst the Ilfracombe station closed in 1970.[35]

Despite the recent almost total domination of the motorcar, the pattern of holiday-making in Devon has remained remarkably consistent throughout the century and those shifts in holiday-making which did occur during 1945–74 could be seen as simply the acceleration of previous trends in transport and accommodation provision.[36] The coastal resorts remained the focus of tourism and became even more dependent on the holiday industry after the Second World War. At the end of the 1960s, despite the growth in self-catering accommodation outside resorts, the bulk of the county's bedspaces remained in its major resorts. Of over 250,000 bedspaces, 85,000 were in Torbay and 27,000 in Ilfracombe alone. This concentration was even more marked in the serviced sector with almost 75 per cent of hotel and guest house bedspaces in the five resorts of Torbay, Exmouth, Sidmouth, Teignmouth and Ilfracombe. Almost half of these were in Torbay, which in 1971 boasted almost half of the county's hotels with over 50 rooms,[37] and by the end of the decade accommodated 1.4 million or 40 per cent of Devon's annual tourists.[38]

Despite the growth in domestic holiday-making in the 1960s and 1970s, there were already signs that resorts in Devon—as in Britain as a whole—were stagnating as the more affluent consumers turned to continental European destinations. The package holiday which was in its infancy in the 1950s became a real threat to the South West resorts in the 1960s. As the regional paper, the *Western Morning News,* pointed out in 1968, there were:

> seemingly eternal grumbles about poor access to the west, both
> by road and air, and the increasing competition of the foreign
> package type of holiday. However keen and cost-conscious a

Westcountry hotelier may be, he cannot compete with Majorca's sunshine figures.[39]

Although such concerns were real, whilst many resorts in Britain lost their more up-market visitors, Devon actually continued to compete quite successfully in the luxury end of the market and, per capita, tourism expenditure in the county remained high relative to other regions. In 1969 tourism expenditure at £24 per person per holiday trip compared favourably with the national average of £19 and Devon continued to attract a greater proportion of tourists from the higher socio-economic groups, as it had done throughout the century.[40] However, notwithstanding the region's continued ability to attract the luxury segment of the domestic market, the British Travel Association nevertheless urged the South West not to rest on its laurels, suggesting that it place less emphasis on passive sun-oriented holidays and concentrate on raising standards of accommodation and facilities to sustain its competitiveness with foreign destinations.[41]

As we highlighted in our key themes at the end of the previous chapter, the investment issue was a major concern for all British seaside resorts during this period. What investment there was, however, took the form of consolidation rather than innovation, and although there was more investment in certain Devon resorts in the 1970s (including Torquay), the evidence suggests that the smaller resorts could not sustain units large enough to cover capital costs.[42] In Ilfracombe, for example, key amenities—notably the town's main theatre and its bandstand—were closed without being replaced by facilities of an adequate standard. Even resilient Torquay suffered and its change of fortunes plunged the town's commercial heart into decline. 'Ugly amusement arcades, charmless souvenir shops and garish fast-food places' opened up near its harbour, while cheap bed and breakfast establishments sprang up to cater for the growing market of Midlands holiday-makers able to reach the resort as a result of the new M5.[43]

During the late 1970s and early 1980s Devon's tourism industry failed to develop at a pace that kept up with changing tourist demands. Although £70 million was invested in accommodation between 1978 and 1982, it was not enough to stave off an erosion of the seaside accommodation base through the conversion of former holiday accommodation to other uses.[44] Between 1982 and 1987 there was a 10 per cent loss of accommodation units as (with the exception of Torbay) all the major resorts experienced a decline in bedspace capacity, whilst the smaller resorts and the non-resort sector gained units.[45] This trend directly conflicted with the County Council's commitment 'to maintain and develop the role of holiday resorts as the mainstays of the holiday industry', allowing 'Large-scale development of holiday accommodation and facilities ... only in the larger holiday resorts and only in cases where such developments will not harm their character.'[46]

Despite such warning signs for its resorts, the Devon tourism industry was still responsible for over 30,000 full-time jobs in the mid-1970s. In the mid-1980s the South West region as a whole still attracted a quarter of all long domestic trips and it was the most popular off-peak destination, whilst in Devon itself tourism spending increased from £250 to £370 million between 1980 and 1987.[47] Yet, although Devon was pre-eminent in the domestic industry, this could not insulate it from the slump in tourism as a result of the recession. Annual visitors to the county fell from a 1978 peak of 3.5 million to under 3 million in 1982, a decline in tourism nights of over 16 per cent.[48] Perhaps not surprisingly, given the changes in holiday habits, the seaside resorts were hardest hit—their hotels and guest houses suffered more than rural self-catering establishments and guest numbers fell by 10 per cent over 1979–80. This accelerated the shift from the traditional to the self-catering sector: in the 20 years prior to 1987 the former's share had fallen from 55 to 43 per cent and by this date only Sidmouth of the east Devon coastal towns had more bedspaces in serviced than non-serviced accommodation.[49] The county-wide shift of visitors away from the resorts hit Torbay, Teignmouth and Dawlish in the south hardest. By contrast, north Devon, with its large stock of self-catering accommodation, increased its county share in the 1960s and 1970s—rising from 22 to 26 per cent during 1975–80. However, although the north coast still remained the second most popular Devon district in the 1980s, this trend began to reverse when improved marketing re-asserted the popularity of Torbay's traditional accommodation in the early 1980s.[50]

At the close of the twentieth century, therefore, despite all the social, economic and cultural changes which have swept Britain, arguably the essence of Devon's tourism industry has changed little. Devon as a whole remains reliant on a relatively stable primary sector and an established tourism and public service sector, although these have been joined by a developing regional specialism in new, high technology firms.[51] The factors which facilitated Devon's early development as a tourism centre also continue to shape the contemporary direction of the county's economy. The region continues to suffer from remoteness and poor communications, with earnings well below the UK national average. The recessions of 1980–2 and 1989–91 caused particular damage to the Devon economy—like many other peripheral rural economies across Britain—and brought job losses in the construction, transport, agriculture and food industries. In the early 1980s the impact of such job losses had been offset by the growth in the public sector, which together with the income of retirees stabilised the Devon economy.[52] In the mid-1980s, however, a significant revival failed to materialise and in the 1990s further job losses occurred in the defence-related industries as a result of the post-Cold War peace dividend. In both these decades, despite its anticipated impact, tourism failed to deliver an economic renaissance, although its contribution to bolstering an economy in difficulty should not be underestimated.

Communities and Conflicts in Devon's Resorts

In Chapter 3 we saw that the expansion of the British holiday industry in the twentieth century also brought with it significant changes in the internal composition of resorts—changes which were to exert a substantial influence in the local political arena and on the priorities of resort authorities. Walton has pointed out that most seaside resorts in the first half of the twentieth century were characterised by impressive population growth, generally as the result of an increasing retirement or dormitory function.[53] The resorts which recorded the greatest rates of population growth—Blackpool, Southend, Bournemouth, Brighton and Hove—all acquired significant commuter populations, whilst resorts such as Southport, Torquay and Weston-Super-Mare expanded as a result of incoming retirees.

Significantly, however, of the two incoming groups, retirement communities were the more important in the social structure of resort communities as they were usually people of relatively substantial resources. As such, seaside retirement has been described as 'one of the most important components of resort growth in most English and Welsh regions ... [with] an even more far reaching expansion ... in the 1960s and 1970s'.[54] As we noted in Chapter 3, this shift in the social composition of resorts signalled a significant realignment in their priorities which was to have far-reaching implications for the development of seaside resorts throughout the century. In many resorts, the influence of retired migrants was substantial and the local political structures often reflected the views of this increasingly vocal and well-represented section of the community. Their interests, often dominated by a desire for low taxation and a resistance to expenditure on resort development, were frequently inimical to those of the local tourism industry. The power of such retired groups can be traced in many British resorts throughout the twentieth century, and in the following pages we examine their influence in those of Devon.

In the twentieth century Devon's demographics have been characterised by two trends: an ageing population and growth in the seaside resorts. As we have already indicated, the two trends were inextricably linked, creating significant implications for the development of the resort's tourism industries. By 1911 two-thirds of the Devon population lived in a few expanding towns and on the coastal belt, and in the next decade it was the latter which experienced the greatest growth, reflecting the importance of the holiday industry and the influx of retired individuals which these communities were already attracting.[55] The trend of an ageing population, traceable in the late nineteenth century, accelerated in the twentieth to become a prominent feature of the county's demography. In 1911 only 7 per cent of the Devon population was over 65, but this age group increased by a dramatic 39 per cent during 1931-51.[56] Thus whilst one in eight of the resort of Sidmouth's residents were retired in 1939, by 1958 this had increased to one in three.[57] This trend of an ageing population was exacerbated by the emigration of Devon's younger population as they searched for employment opportunities in other areas of Britain which were enjoying industrial expansion.

Growth was not uniform across the seaside resorts, however, and between 1921 and 1961 resorts experienced contrasting growth rates which reflected their diverging fortunes. Thus those enjoying rapid expansion included Torquay, Paignton and Brixham, whilst those stagnating included Ilfracombe on the north coast (see Table 4.6).[58] The success of Devon's seaside resorts brought a further round of expansion during 1961–71 as the influx of mature and retired workers into the county outstripped the natural decrease and the net outward migration of younger workers. This trend was typical of the South West region, where 60 per cent of the population increase during 1961–4 was attributable to immigration,[59] a third of migrants into Devon and Cornwall being of retirement age between 1961 and 1968.[60] It was the larger resorts which expanded most rapidly, accounting for over 12 per cent of all new dwellings built in the county in the decade 1965–75.[61] Between 1961 and 1976 the resorts of east Devon experienced the fastest growth rate when almost 30,000 migrants flooded into the area,[62] whilst throughout the 1960s and 1970s any population increases in the resorts of Ilfracombe, Torbay and Sidmouth were almost entirely due to their expanding retired populations.[63]

These demographic changes meant that by the beginning of the 1970s almost a fifth of the county population was over 65 years of age, a figure which topped a quarter in the new County Borough of Torbay.[64] Indeed, by the mid-1980s, of all the English regions, the South West had the lowest proportion of its population under five years old, whilst it had much the highest proportion over retirement age—nearly 21 per cent compared to a UK average of less than 18 per cent, with the highest proportion (31 per cent) being in east Devon with its resorts of Sidmouth and Budleigh Salterton.[65] In effect, the retired communities' grip on Devon's seaside was complete.

Residents and Resort Development

Such demographic patterns suggest that the success of Devon's seaside resorts was inextricably linked with their increased populations and superficially the two trends do appear to go hand-in-hand. However, this would be an over-simplification of what was a highly

Table 4.5: Population Change in Devon Seaside Resorts, 1901–1981

	1901	1911	1921	1931	1951	1961	1971	1981
Devon	662,196	699,703	709,614	732,968	796,621	822,699	898,404	958,745
Brixham	8,092	7,954	7,774	8,145	8,756	10,721	–	–
Budleigh Salterton	1,883	2,170	2,624	3,162	3,954	3,865	4,157	4,436
Dartmouth	6,579	7,005	7,219	6,708	5,831	5,758	5,707	6,298
Dawlish	4,003	4,099	4,675	4,580	7,508	7,803	9,519	10,755
Exmouth	10,485	11,962	13,606	14,591	17,222	19,753	25,827	28,775
Ilfracombe	8,557	8,935	11,772	9,175	9,228	8,696	9,859	10,133
Lynton/ Lynmouth	1,641	1,770	2,587	2,011	2,120	1,918	1,984	2,037
Paignton	8,385	11,241	14,451	18,414	25,553	30,292	–	–
Salcombe	1,710	2,032	2,199	2,384	2,579	2,549	2,496	2,374
Seaton	1,325	1,694	2,295	2,349	2,903	3,445	4,139	4,974
Sidmouth[1]	4,201	5,612	5,668	6,126	10,408	10,890	12,076	12,446
Teignmouth[2]	8,636	9,215	10,970	10,017	10,597	11,528	12,575	13,257
Torquay	33,625	38,771	39,431	46,165	53,281	54,046		
Torbay[3]							109,257	115,582

Notes:
1. includes Salcombe Regis and Sidbury
2. includes Shaldon
3. includes the old parishes of Brixton, Churston Ferrers, Cockington, St Marychurch, Paignton, Tormohun and Torquay.
Sources: Census Reports.

complex and multi-layered relationship. Ironically, the tourist traders in successful resorts triumphed in spite of the influx of retirees, not because of them. People retired to the seaside because of its attractiveness and each wave of migrants had as their priority the preservation of such attractions and the minimisation of disruptions which would be caused by new tourism developments.

Conflict between residents and tourism entrepreneurs erupted in Devon as long ago as the 1870s, as the experience of Ilfracombe illustrates. Even at this relatively early stage, the resort's municipal government was highly involved in the development of tourism facilities to enhance the town's attractions. One such scheme was the 1887–8 construction of the Victoria Pavilion modelled on the Palm House at Kew, which was to become the centrepiece of Ilfracombe's seafront facilities for many years. As in other resorts, this scheme met with stiff opposition as residential and trade interests clashed. Ilfracombe's Ratepayers' Protection Society, formed in the 1870s, was to exert substantial influence on local politics at key periods within the resort's development—usually at times of high municipal expenditure. It mounted a sustained campaign of opposition to developments such as the Pavilion, preferring municipal expenditure restraint to investment.[66]

Residential opposition to tourism development did not always take the form of clashes over expenditure, however. It was also manifested in more 'moral' philosophical clashes such as the debates over the sanctity of Sunday. The issue of whether Sundays should remain a day of rest or a day for more active leisure was particularly highlighted in Ilfracombe in the mid-1920s. In 1924 the town council introduced Sunday pier concerts in an attempt to promote the resort and attract visitors, a strategy which was so popular with tourists that the Southern Railway re-introduced Sunday trains and other operators launched Sunday charabanc trips. Despite the obvious success of this strategy, it was strongly resisted by local residents' groups and by the local clergy, the latter protesting against Sunday trips throughout 1924 and 1925. As one town councillor suggested, regardless of the impact on the town's tourism industry, 'There were a number of people in Ilfracombe who would like to see the old fashioned Sunday restored, with no Sunday concerts, no band and no boat trips.'[67]

Just as the focus for conflict over the extent of tourism development varied, so did the influence of the various factions in resorts like Ilfracombe over local government tourism policies. Sometimes the interests of residents' groups prevailed, whilst at other times it was the views of those who depended on the tourism industry for their livelihoods which succeeded. Interestingly, there does appear to be a strong correlation between the numbers of councillors representing the tourism industry's interests and the high-points of

Figure 4.2: *Ilfracombe Pavilion, c. 1890*
Victorian entertainment facility provision. Built in 1887–8 on Ropery Meadow, the Victoria Pavilion doubled as a concert hall and winter gardens and became one of Ilfracombe's premier attractions throughout the twentieth century. (Reproduced by kind permission of the Ilfracombe Museum.)

Ilfracombe council's tourism initiatives. Whilst it is sometimes difficult to ascertain the occupations of councillors from local government records, when it is possible, some interesting findings emerge. Over the period 1910–30 as a whole, around a third of Ilfracombe's councillors were involved in the tourism industry, but between 1919 and 1925—years of intensive investment in the resort—this increased to almost a half. The presence of this group on the council was instrumental in securing policies designed to promote resort development. During 1919–20 rates were increased by 20 percent to fund tourism investment and a professional director of entertainments was appointed. The enhancement of the tourism environment was also a priority in these years and expenditure tripled to over £1,000 in 1920, whilst the Victoria Pavilion was also re-modelled during this period.[68]

These schemes were by no means universally welcomed, however, and generated substantial controversy despite the pro-development group's 'serious effort to convince inhabitants that it was in their interest to follow out a more progressive policy in … the town'.[69] Indeed, within five years there emerged a sustained ratepayer and residential campaign to oppose expenditure on resort facilities and in the 1930s a proposal to develop Ilfracombe's wet weather amenities at a cost of £21,000 provoked heated and antagonistic discussions. Despite the fact that the lack of such facilities was a serious gap in the resort's product mix, the proposal was vehemently attacked by the Ratepayers' Association and even by the town's Chamber of Commerce. At the heart of the debate was the question posed in many British resorts in these years: whether to spend or save—expenditure versus economy. Those resorts such as Bournemouth that invested (providing new facilities at a cost of £750,000 in 1933) were better equipped to attract and retain visitors than those that did not.[70]

Such bitter divisions of opinion were by no means unique to Ilfracombe and also characterised the development of inter-war Torquay. In fact, this period was a time of intense political activity in the town as the debates over the extent of municipal investment in tourism exacerbated existing divisions. Although it would be simplistic to suggest that there were coherent and stable groupings voting in concert on the local authority, there were clear factions in the council, divided primarily on the issue of Torquay's development as a tourist resort. The most vocal factions were the 'forward development' campaigners (often labelled the 'hotel group') who were keen to popularise Torquay with summer and winter visitors; the Labour group which favoured the direct provision and operation of municipal facilities; and the residential interests who advocated low rates, which included both moderate and conservative elements and which often co-operated with the Citizens' League which had been formed in 1930 to combat the perceived extravagance of the local authority. The divisions in the resort between such groupings were substantial and engendered what one mayor described in 1931 as 'an atmosphere of unrest and suspicion, one faction suspecting and distrusting another which is to the serious detriment of the town as a whole, and certainly in my opinion has retarded progress'.[1]

Just as in Ilfracombe, the strife within Torquay's 'political nation' in the 1920s was caused by conflicts arising from the financing of tourism-related projects. In 1926 the Hoteliers' Association chairman warned that the town's progress must not be 'retarded by economy fanatics', as:

> Visitors of the type Torquay requires, must have amusements and diversion elsewhere than those provided by the hotels.... Unless Torquay is kept up to date, made smart and attractive, and with an atmosphere of progress ... it will recede.[2]

Whilst the strength of these arguments won the tourism case on council in the 1920s and the authority continued its investment in the resort product—acquiring open spaces and building tennis courts, mini-golf and bowling greens—conflicts re-emerged in the 1930s against a backdrop of slump, financial crises and demands for economy. The Hoteliers' Association found itself confronted by residential interests and the Citizens' League which constantly opposed development, urging the preservation of Torquay as a 'select' resort. Adopting the motto 'Efficiency with Economy', the League vigorously opposed (what it termed) 'squandamania' on projects such as the widening of the town's main seafront road and the building of a new seafront band enclosure. It was highly successful in these activities, securing major triumphs in the local elections of the early and mid-1930s and delaying many of the moves to develop further the resort's tourism infrastructure.

Those who advocated economy over investment in the late 1930s briefly re-emerged as a major force in resort politics after the Second World War. Indeed, in the late 1940s local government in resorts such as Torquay and Ilfracombe was dogged by a lack of co-ordination and co-operation and the activities of the residential groups were to prove inimical to resort success. In Ilfracombe, the president of the Chamber of Trade and a prominent hotelier echoed those sentiments which had been expressed in the 1920s when he said:

> Progress is disappointingly slow. Ilfracombe's need is for co-operation and that seems difficult to find.... I hope that with the coming year ... all townsfolk will realise how we depend on visitors for our livelihood. To get them here we ... [need] modern entertainments. These entertainments must not make Ilfracombe cheap, they must be designed with vision to fit into our beautiful land, whilst providing the amenities visitors need.[3]

However, the post-war competition between British resorts was fierce and, as we shall see in Chapter 5, increasing importance was attached to effective resort promotion. In many ways, these issues of resort promotion and development became pivotal in the development of municipal unity during this period. Unlike in the inter-war and immediate post-war years (when opposition to tourism expenditure was strongly articulated), in the 1950s municipal authorities embarked on initiatives which were often hampered by a lack of resources but which were largely supported by their communities as the influence of residential organisations was limited by apathy, financial constraints and by popular concern over the well-being of resort economies.

Although there were such periods when their influence waned, the influence of retired residents nevertheless remained significant in seaside resorts throughout the post-war period. Indeed, so critical has their role been that they have been identified in the 1980s and 1990s as critical to the future of resorts.[4] The experience of resorts remains tightly bound up in the local political relationships between the tourism industry and resort residents, many of the more proactive being retired incomers. The fundamentally oppositional nature of this latter group—based around issues of expenditure or economy—has had a serious impact on resort fortunes in many instances. Moreover, in addition to opposing the increased rate burden which such developments would entail, many of these elderly residents have a strong interest in maintaining resorts as they were when they first moved there and oppose developments to improve resorts' tourist appeal precisely because of the threats these pose to resort characters.

Following the pattern of local political relations experienced in the 1930s, the 1960s witnessed a return to the politics of division in Devon as the tourism industry clashed once more with residential—in particular retirees'—interests. Grass-roots organisations such as the Torquay Development Protection Group and the Torquay Ratepayers' Association mobilised to oppose development initiatives. Seeking to prevent Torquay becoming a 'glorified Monte Carlo', the Association (like its inter-war forerunner) was successful in the local elections, seeing victories in the mid-1960s by groups urging the Council: 'to abandon all schemes either in hand, accepted as Council policy, or approved in principle ... or any other schemes designed for the attraction of visitors, unless a guarantee can be given ... that no part of the asset of such schemes will fall to be met by the ratepayers in any way'.[75] So bitter were the disputes that some councillors suggested that a wedge was being driven between the holiday interest and the residents, particularly the retired population which dominated the Ratepayers' Association. As the Chairman of the Torquay Ratepayers' Association commented about tourism development schemes in 1970: 'The only people who are going to benefit are the hoteliers and a few trades. Everything is geared to their welfare, and the ratepayers foot the bill.'[76]

These disagreements over the resorts' priorities were exacerbated by changes in their local government structures, particularly the 1974 local government reorganisation which merged many British resorts with residential, industrial or rural hinterlands. Tourism priorities were thus further diluted and elected representatives inherited ailing resort infrastructures which they were ill-equipped to improve. In Ilfracombe its Chamber of Commerce noted (with some prescience) that, as a result of the reorganisation:

It is possible that less consideration will ... be given to the needs of Ilfracombe's holiday industry. Certainly it is unlikely that the large scale attempts to provide the modern entertainment facilities needed to keep Ilfracombe as the centre of tourism in North Devon will be undertaken.[77]

The divisions over tourism policies in the mid-1970s came at a time when resorts across Britain were beginning to realise the consequences of their failure to invest. By the 1970s, a third of Britons were holidaying abroad whilst at home there was much concern about the status of the British seaside. Various newspapers commented on 'the tone of the British seaside' which was described as 'shifting, turning rougher and less friendly'.[78] Residents, many of them retired, voiced concern over the tone of resorts troubled by drugs, drink, and crime, whilst local newspapers were worried about the direction resorts were taking with bouncers, drunkenness and violence being endemic.[79]

Such anecdotal complaints were more clearly articulated in a 1978 survey which revealed the problematic nature of the tourism industry in Devon. In describing tourism's parasitic qualities and problems, the report commented 'there is clear evidence ... that throughout the county tourism is disliked for what it is doing to "the quality of life"'.[80] Similarly, in a survey conducted in Torbay in the late 1970s, apart from noise and disturbance, other tourism-related problems identified by residents included high suicide and pregnancy rates, an above average incidence of drug-taking, the more familiar problems of traffic and environmental pressures, and a low winter house occupancy—with 40 per cent of Paignton's houses empty in winter.[81] Although in the 1980s and 1990s Devon County Council has been committed to 'reconcile the needs of residents with the enjoyment of holidaymakers', this task has proved difficult given the inherently conflictual nature of this relationship.[82]

Devon Resorts and Social Tone

Residential conflicts over the control of the public spaces in resorts were an integral element in debates regarding the social tone of resorts. Studies of resort development in the nineteenth century illustrate how the wealthy residents of resort towns attempted to maintain their exclusivity by opposing infrastructural developments such as harbour improvements which would popularise the facilities available for tourist consumption.[83] Similarly, the work of May and Travis has shown how relative remoteness from the large urban centres of potential working-class day-trippers, together with local residential opposition to increased rail and steamer traffic, enabled Devon's resorts to maintain their social exclusivity well into the twentieth century.[84] By contrast, much less attention has been paid to the post-1914 period: in 1914 all the Devon resorts were 'select' and 'respectable' and although social gradations did exist they ranged only from middle-class Ilfracombe to the more genteel Torquay.[85] The extent of the struggles to maintain social tone and their degree of success over the twentieth century is the focus of the remainder of this chapter.

The social tone of a resort was inextricably linked to its social exclusivity. High degrees of social exclusivity—resulting from the patronage of up-market visitors—conferred a high social tone. In addition, not only was the presence of elites significant, so too was the resort's accessibility, the quality of its hotels and the type of entertainments it provided. As holiday-making developed into something approaching a 'mass' phenomenon, relatively inaccessible resorts continued to offer exclusivity to their patrons, precisely because of the difficulties and expenses involved in travelling there. Thus, in Walton's words, 'remoteness also meant selectness'.[86] As he continues: 'In a less concentrated and less assertive way, "better-class" demand also expressed itself in the colonization by discerning, quiet-seeking visitors of the remoter coasts of west Wales, the West Country and East Anglia'.[87] In this way, the desirable attributes sought by relatively exclusive consumers included peace and quiet, natural and nature-oriented pursuits and 'genteel' sports such as golf, tennis, sailing, horse-racing and cycling.[88] In contrast, resorts catering for lower-middle and working-class tourists provided the newer forms of 'mass' entertainments. There are thus significant parallels between the exclusive resorts' visitors of the nineteenth and earlier twentieth centuries and Urry's contemporary 'ethical' tourist we described in Chapter 3.

The remoteness and selectness of Devon's resorts were challenged by the introduction of mass forms of transport such as the railway in the second half of the nineteenth century and the charabancs in the early twentieth. It would be a mistake to assume, however, that the arrival of the railways necessarily meant the erosion of social exclusivity and the arrival of the masses. At the turn of the century, despite their railroad links, Devon's resorts remained exclusive. Torquay, Devon's major resort with a population of 30,000, still attracted titled visitors, especially in the winter season, and the other Devon resorts were attracting a broad section of the middle classes whilst still resisting large-scale working-class influxes.[89] Even Ilfracombe, despite drawing steamer-borne day-trippers from the industrial centres of South Wales and Bristol, catered principally for a middle-class market, and Exmouth (attracting more trippers than any other south Devon resort) only drew about 4,000 each year—a tenth the tripper trade of the Bristol Channel resort of Weston-Super-Mare.[90]

Working-class trippers were discouraged from frequenting Devon despite the rail access by a number of factors, particularly distance. As Travis has concluded:

> The difficulty of access far outweighed all internal factors ... Even in late Victorian times distance was still the main force at work filtering out the lower classes, although by then some of the wealthy visitors had become residents and had formed a social elite which in turn helped to defend the select character of the resorts.[91]

Few tourists outside the middle classes had the material resources to reach its resorts, none of which provided amusements designed to attract this market in any case. Thus the operation of distance, combined with the absence of centres of working-class populations, ensured that those resorts with a controlling interest favouring a select clientele were able to pursue exclusionist policies until well beyond the inter-war period.

Resorts which drew most of their clientele from the day-tripper market (like Weston-Super-Mare slightly up the Bristol Channel from Devon) were perceived to exhibit an undesirable and low social tone in the eyes of the social elites of resorts like Torquay. Where day-trippers and residential visitors coincided, therefore, the interests of the latter tended to be defended against those of the former because of their perceived greater desirability. Woolacombe in north Devon, for instance, was definite in its desire to remain select and in the mid-1930s its local paper commented that it did not want to 'see Woolacombe turned into another Blackpool ... the tripper and the residential visitors do not mix and what we want ... is the residential visitor'.[92]

In spite of the massive social and economic changes of the twentieth century—including increased accessibility due to improved transport networks and larger tourist numbers as a consequence of rising living standards and legislation—the basic spatial pattern of the Devon industry and the select nature of its resorts remained unaltered. Distance and power enabled sections of society within the seaside towns effectively to control working-class access to leisure resources. However, resort social tone is the result of interactions between residents and visitors and is thus never constant. Tone fluctuates as previously fashionable resorts struggle to maintain their exclusivity, and in Devon today resorts vary from the slightly faded Ilfracombe to fashionable Torquay to the still relatively exclusive Sidmouth.

In the late Victorian era, however, Ilfracombe was the epitome of a respectable seaside town and the period 1880–1914 was very much its heyday. Indeed, it could be argued that during these years Ilfracombe successfully managed to retain its upper- and upper-middle-class appeal whilst also attracting a broader tourist population. Thus, wealthy individuals, middle-class visitors and working-class day trippers holidayed together relatively happily.[93] Nevertheless, it would be a misrepresentation of the situation to suggest that this was a large-scale phenomenon in Ilfracombe—never mind the majority of British resorts.

Ilfracombe's working-class visitors were relatively small in number and stayed for only a short period of time, many of them Welsh trippers attracted by the bars of the cross-Channel steamers. Yet, although their impact was limited spatially and temporally, this influx of lower-middle- and working-class visitors from the coalfields and factories of South Wales resulted in many of Ilfracombe's aristocratic patrons leaving the resort for elsewhere.[94] Ilfracombe's diverse market appeal therefore meant that this relatively small and confined resort was forced to cater for the co-existence of different types of visitors, often with conflicting interests and demands. This was a difficult balancing act to achieve primarily because Ilfracombe's pre-eminent concern was 'to secure visitors of good social standing and well filled purses' which meant that 'the tone of the resort must be maintained'.[95] At the same time, however, the downturn in Ilfracombe's fortunes meant that any custom—including that of potentially rowdy working class Welsh miners—was welcome, a situation which demanded the provision of 'something more definitely attractive to all classes of visitor, something for those who want to dance and other amusements for those who want something more highbrow'.[96]

At the other extreme in resort exclusivity—and also of municipal involvement in tourism development—were Devon resorts such as Sidmouth and Budleigh Salterton (see Table 4.1). Sidmouth, in particular, provides an excellent example of a resort where the controlling groups within the community consciously pursued policies designed to exclude certain types of tourist—policies which achieved a high degree of success. A sizeable resort with a population just over half that of Ilfracombe, Sidmouth differed significantly from the north coast resort. In the inter-war period its Bank Holiday day-tripper trade was minimal and the average number of staying visitors was kept down—in the words of the town clerk—'by supreme effort' to about 3,000 at any one time. This policy of exclusion, maintained by the local authority and the town's tourism pressure groups, can be clearly seen in operation in 1933. Here, the local authority used town boundary changes to secure powers preventing 'nuisances' such as touting and street advertising and, more significantly, to block plans for a holiday camp development at nearby Salcombe Regis.[97] Whilst the local authority did invest in some tourism-related facilities— opening a new esplanade in 1926 and the Connaught Pleasure Gardens in 1934—municipal involvement in tourism development was limited.[98] Moreover, during the inter-war period Sidmouth Council did not organise or fund any tourism entertainment— unthinkable in resorts such as Ilfracombe and Torquay—and spent minimal sums on resort promotion, preferring to rely on the activities of the town's score or so high-class hotels.[99]

Figure 4.3: *Ilfracombe Town and Harbour, c. 1900*
The cross-channel steamer traffic was critical in shaping Ilfracombe's social tone. (Reproduced by kind permission of the Ilfracombe Museum.)

By contrast, Torquay's local authority was highly active both in facility and entertainment provision and, as we shall see in Chapter 5, in resort advertising. Torquay's initial rise to prominence occurred between the 1840s and 1860s when the resort attracted aristocratic and royal guests who built prestigious villas and created what was to become the resort's enduring reputation for fashionability. The 1860s also saw the construction of a series of fashionable sea-front hotels (the Imperial, the Torbay and the Belgrave), establishments which were to remain in the front-rank of British hotels for much of the twentieth century. In the decade before the First World War Torquay, already an exclusive winter resort, developed into a year-round holiday town as its summer season increased in popularity. Throughout this period, Torquay remained unquestionably 'select', patronised by an upper-middle- and upper-class clientele attracted by the society life of the town: the promenading on the Strand and Victoria Parade, the balls at the town's Baths and its many hotels, and the annual Regatta and review of the fleet.[100]

Despite this, even in the pre-war decade, Torquay also witnessed the increasing influx of a different type of visitor—often drawn from the working classes of the northern manufacturing towns—on day or weekend trips. Such visitors were not universally welcomed in the resort and vociferous interest groups emerged which flinched at the prospect of working-class holiday-makers and, by implication, working-class entertainments. This debate was highlighted by a visitor's letter to the *Torquay Times* in 1910 which compared Torquay with Bournemouth 'where everything possible is done to make the place popular', in contrast to the former where 'there are certain people ... who do not want it to be a popular place and want to keep it as select ... as possible'.[101] Yet, although there were constant concerns raised about the influx of less fashionable visitors, such fears were by no means universal, particularly amongst those who advocated pro-development policies, notably in the Chamber of Commerce. As one local writer commented in 1910: 'I have no patience with those who turn up their noses and sneer about the coming of trippers. Some of these sneerers almost owe their positions to the prosperous summer seasons which we are having.'[102]

Although such sentiments were not uncommon, it was the views of those who opposed the 'trippers' which prevailed, for whilst the ensuing decades witnessed a broadening of its clientele, Torquay retained its extremely select character before the Second World War. Before 1914 visitors' lists in the local press reveal that they were invariably middle- and upper-class and that French and military visitors were particularly prominent. In spite of this, conflict raged over the pace of development within Torquay between the holiday trade interest and its more conservative elements who were opposed to the influx of less fashionable visitors. Events in the 1920s and 1930s were to bring this conflict over Torquay's social tone into even sharper relief as it was during this period that Torquay's winter season declined—a development symptomatic of the changing nature of its tourist trade. More and more affluent working class visitors began to frequent the hitherto middle- and upper-class dominated resort: as the *Western Times* (one of the local papers) noted in 1920, 'Torquay's connection with the Midlands is of great and growing importance'.[103]

As the resort wrestled with social and economic changes which threatened its social tone, there was friction between those who sought to retain the more select trade and those who urged moving with the times. The former, at this time supported by the local paper, were concerned not to '"Brightonise" Torquay'. One of its editorials in 1923 commented that:

> There is, we fear, a tendency on the part of certain officials and others to introduce into Torquay a class of attractions which, however laudable the motive, will not conduce to the popularity of the town. Torquay is not Brighton, neither is it Blackpool. It stands upon a different plane to these watering places, a higher one, if we venture to make this assertion.[104]

The latter were more prepared to adapt to changing circumstances and advocated a completely different strategy, arguing that:

> Before the war, the people who mostly patronised Torquay were the middle class ... For the last few years, these people have not been coming here because they cannot afford it ... the people who have been coming here recently are those who circumstances have improved during the war, such as clerks, railway

95

employees, shopkeepers and artizans of various trades…. We have not the money to be independent, so why not realise and face the facts? *We must cater for the multitude* and if necessary become another Blackpool…. Times have altered, and we must alter accordingly.[105]

Such an extreme view was not, however, very representative of the interests in the town and whilst some echoed these sentiments, the majority of the more conservative residential elements were keen to see it retain its select approach. The *Torquay Times*, in an editorial in 1929, typified the disquiet engendered by increasing numbers of day-trippers when it advised that:

> unless we cater for a more permanent class of visitor the other ten months of the year will be a very lean time. In other words, we must not vulgarise Torquay for the tripper element. These people are welcome here in their own season, but we must not alter the town to suit their tastes for the short period they remain here.[106]

Despite these changes in the composition of visitors to Torquay, it nevertheless remained a very fashionable resort in the 1920s and 1930s. Even the pressures of increased tourist numbers failed to threaten this reputation and in the 1930s Torquay enhanced its position as a fashionable resort, attracting much of the considerable inter-war capital investment in Britain's seaside tourism industry.[107] Much of this was due to its continued popularity with the middle classes who sought seclusion, having been driven out of the more popular and populous resorts elsewhere in Britain by working-class tourists.[108] Despite its role as a middle-class 'refuge', this period did begin to see the demise of Torquay's 'gentry' era—the end of its existence as a select watering-place and the beginning of its rise as a modern resort. The pace of social change was slow, however, and whilst the inter-war period established Torquay as one of the most progressive British resorts and a leading destination for domestic holiday-makers, the resort managed to retain its relatively high social tone.

In the later 1930s, Torquay in fact developed (due to its communications networks, its diversity of functions and the policies of the local authority) a 'popular fashionability' which rejected both extremes of the exclusivity of Sidmouth and the popularity of resorts such as Blackpool, Brighton and, in Devon, Paignton. In fact, it developed into one of Europe's premier resorts, a position it did not lose until its fashionability began to evaporate in the late 1950s. Drawing its clientele from a broad economic and geographic range, but concentrating on prosperous regions with rising real incomes (such as the South East and the Midlands), the resort was able to weather the vicissitudes of the inter-war depression. In spite of the profitability of this trade, however, some in the resort continued to consider such development detrimental, as one letter to the town's local paper put it:

> oil and water will not mix ... despite democracy social 'classes' still exist; and so long as this is so they will have to be catered for in different ways ... Torquay was never intended by her situation or the grandeur of her coastline to become a playground for the masses.[109]

Indeed, even after the Second World War, the overriding concern in Torquay remained the protection of its status as a select resort. This desire was manifested during the late 1940s and 1950s in the refusal of the local authority to grant planning permission for casinos and for seafront kiosks and in its banning of donkeys and ponies from the resort's beaches. The reality of the importance of social tone in the post-war decades is epitomised by the *Torquay Times'* comment on the use of beach loud-speakers in 1947:

> Torquay is fast becoming raucous and loud and those well-meaning souls who for years have shouted 'we must not be "Blackpoolised"', have very nearly had it. The rot has set in ... If Torquay wants to become a town of fish and chips, orange peel, fruit machines, and more and more noise, a natural process of evolution will provide it by 1948.[110]

This prediction was rather premature as even in the mid-1950s Torquay could still boast a fashionable reputation, although the coming decades increasingly betrayed the reality beneath this image. Torquay rapidly lost its more wealthy clientele and by the end of the

1970s it had acquired a 'shabby' air. In essence, the tourism slump of the later 1970s stripped away the veneer of prosperity to expose the stagnation gripping Torquay.

Significantly, however, just as the social tone of resorts like Torquay seemed irrevocably damaged and their local communities permanently divided over their desire for a tourist industry, some British resorts have managed to re-emerge reinvigorated in the later 1980s and 1990s. As we indicated in Chapter 3, resorts such as Blackpool and, of particular interest to us here, Torquay have emerged from the trough of the early 1980s to become models for other resorts seeking to reposition themselves within the domestic tourist industry. Strategies were developed to encourage not only the retention of summer and conference markets but also to develop the off-peak season and the overseas markets. In the case of Torquay, the English Tourist Board's strategy recommended that 'special emphasis should be placed on attracting newcomers from the younger age groups, people in the higher social groups, and residents of the Midlands and South East of England'.[111]

Key to such repositionings have been image-building campaigns and the enhancement of public- and private-sector tourism facilities. Torquay was reborn in an artful blend of the traditional and modern, its advertising suggesting that it is a sophisticated resort capable of offering old-fashioned service and elegance together with modern facilities. New developments such a marina—specifically designed to attract foreign visitors—and up-market shopping centres have been supplemented by a multi-million pound conference, exhibition and leisure facility in the English Riviera Centre. The revitalisation of the resort has also witnessed a revival of its social tone, and the success of the Imperial Hotel (one of Torquay's leading establishments since it opened in 1867) bears witness to the resilience of the resort. The lines of Jaguars and Rolls-Royces in its car park and its insistence on male diners wearing a jacket and tie suggests that people do not holiday there because they cannot afford to go abroad. For two decades this five-star hotel maintained its standards whilst Torquay became somewhat shabby. Now a revival beckons, as the *Independent* predicted in 1989: 'Torquay's brave new future is to be built not on deck chairs, buckets and spades or candy floss—but on shopping malls, a conference centre and a marina'.[112]

Just as image campaigns and the enhancement of tourism facilities have been crucial in this revival, so these two areas of resort activity have played key roles in resort development throughout the twentieth century. As we shall now explore in Chapters 5 and 6, these areas also articulated the social and cultural divisions which animated resort communities—divisions between residents, the tourism traders and the tourists themselves

5

Creating the Seaside Image

I do not suggest we should make Ilfracombe like Blackpool, but I do suggest to the Joint Advertising Committee that they will have to think in a much bigger way. It seems we are content to go on year after year in the same old way…. Let us go forward and do bigger things. We want money for advertising and we must get it. We could do a lot more if our funds were bigger. We cannot exist on the beauty of our hills …
Councillor Bennetto, Ilfracombe Urban District Council, 1948[1]

The focus of this chapter is local government resort promotion, an area which was central to UK resort development in the twentieth century and therefore critical to the evolution of an advertising philosophy within the tourism industry itself. The discussion is also central to our focus on power and politics at the seaside, since, as Chase has commented, attempts to shape coastal resort social tone were articulated in the nature and choice of resort advertising imagery. Indeed, the uses of such imagery provide valuable insights into 'the interplay of changing social attitudes, political conflict, physical growth, and economic interests'[2] at the seaside. Our analysis here will demonstrate that advertising assumed a vital role in the tourism activities of British seaside municipalities over the twentieth century and that the evolution of their resort publicity services went hand in hand with the development of their holiday industries and reflected their social tones. As an examination of the historical development of tourism destination advertising, the chapter therefore argues that the tendency to describe place marketing as a relatively recent phenomena obscures the long tradition of resort advertising in Britain and seriously under-estimates the sophistication of the early marketing strategies.[3]

The Seaside and Tourism Promotion

The marketing of destinations is becoming a well-explored subject and it is not our intention to rehearse here the range and implementation of place marketing techniques since there are a number of excellent works on the subject to which the reader can refer.[4] What interests us in this chapter is to trace the *historical* development of British seaside resort promotional activities in this century by examining a number of case study resorts. It was not until the later nineteenth century that British seaside resorts began promotional activities in earnest, for it was only when the middle classes (rather than merely the upper classes) began to frequent the seaside that the resorts were forced to compete for trade on a truly national basis. Prior to this, marketing had not been a major concern since all the resorts had been fashionable and what advertising did exist merely emphasised their salubrious qualities.[5] Until the turn of the century most resorts were ill-equipped for the new challenge this competition presented as they lacked both the necessary administrative and organisational structures and the financial resources. Thus promotion operated on an *ad hoc* basis in most British resorts before the First World War, although a few of the more dynamic resorts had begun concerted promotional activities earlier. Blackpool, in the forefront of this trend, began advertising in earnest in the 1870s and by 1914 its domestic and overseas advertising campaigns (financed from a £4,000 publicity budget) placed it far ahead of other British seaside resorts.[6] Yet, although Blackpool may have set the pace, other resorts also advanced rapidly in the years before the First World War, establishing publicity associations and advertising committees which published official guides and placed press advertisements.[7]

The period 1870–1940 has been identified as the time when most resort images (whether fashionable or popular) were established—most of which have proved remarkably enduring.[8] It was during 1905–13 for instance, that the Devon resorts of Torquay and Ilfracombe established their publicity organisations and the period

1919–29 which witnessed the consolidation of these efforts, culminating in the high quality advertising material of the 1930s. In the area of advertising policies there was a clear difference between those resorts which sought to attract 'exclusive', 'semi-exclusive' and 'popular' markets—differences which began to be clearly articulated during the inter-war period and were subsequently to exert significant influences on the future directions of resorts.

In our discussions we concentrate on the strategies adopted by the Devon resorts to illustrate resort promotional practice, and specifically to illustrate how social tone was (and is) formed via resort advertising. Sidmouth, Torquay and Ilfracombe will provide the case studies of resorts which were, respectively: exclusive, semi-exclusive and popular. As we saw in Chapter 4, Sidmouth's town council rigorously pursued policies designed to maintain resort exclusivity. Whereas in most instances these policies were reactive and implemented opportunistically, in the resort's advertising strategies we can clearly see its determination to maintain a high social tone. Despite changes in the composition of the council, a consistent strategy of exclusion emerges from the council minutes and from the advertising literature. Moreover, far from being confined to the earlier decades of the century, such attitudes and policies continued to underpin council activities in the 1960s, 1970s and beyond: throughout the twentieth century Sidmouth has projected itself as a haven of genteel respectability for the discriminating visitor in search of seclusion.

It is largely in the marketing messages rather than in the marketing techniques that Sidmouth differed from most Devon resorts, and indeed from many small- to medium-sized British seaside resorts, although, as we shall see, there are strong parallels with other 'select' resorts such as Frinton on the south-east coast which also shunned advertising and maintained its inter-war image by featuring in the fashion and sports pages of newspapers.[9] Often working in collaboration with the railway companies, resort councils have throughout the century advertised in the national and provincial press, published brochures for distribution by the railways, travel agents and their own publicity departments, and produced posters for nation-wide display. In these areas there has been little to distinguish Sidmouth Council from other resort local authorities, but what is unusual is its low-key

102

approach, which provides a stark contrast to the activities of more 'popular' resorts such as Torquay and Ilfracombe. These different approaches reflect the differing aims of the resorts over the decades. Ilfracombe and, to a lesser extent, Torquay pursued policies designed to attract larger numbers of visitors, whereas, in Pimlott's words, 'Sidmouth succeeded in the opposite aim of excluding the masses.'[10]

Whilst before the Second World War, the publicity and entertainment committees of Torquay and Ilfracombe met regularly to discuss marketing, the relevant committees in Sidmouth met very infrequently, particularly during 1928–39 when it was convened only a handful of times a year.[11] Furthermore, business at these meetings was generally confined to discussions of press advertising, guide production and railway schemes, a well defined but (by comparison to those of other resorts) very limited and unimaginative agenda. Thus, whilst the Torquay and Ilfracombe publicity and entertainment committees enjoyed high profiles and were often chaired by prominent councillors, the equivalent Sidmouth committee met too infrequently to acquire any real influence. Perhaps not surprisingly, given the resort's desire to remain exclusive, marketing was never accorded a high priority by Sidmouth Council and its advertising was produced on a much less professional basis. This was a policy which had much in common with that which had been pursued by other resorts in the late nineteenth century, as Sidmouth relied on the promotion generated by the town's relatively large cache of luxury hotels to attract the appropriate clientele.

In contrast, as a large and fashionable resort of national and international repute, Torquay has long had a highly sophisticated approach to publicity. Underpinned by substantial financial resources and enjoying a special relationship with the Great Western Railway Company (GWR), until the nationalisation of the British railways in 1947, Torquay has always been at the forefront of British resort advertising, both in its organisational framework and in the quality of its literature which has consistently been of the highest standard. Ilfracombe also boasts an impressive record of resort promotion initiatives, although, as we shall see, this was largely confined to the first half of the century as by the 1960s this once-fashionable resort had atrophied and its economic fortunes were clearly reflected in

103

advertising that became stagnant and lacking in dynamism in the 1970s and 1980s.

Municipal Advertising Established

In the late nineteenth century advertising activities in most resorts were dominated by the private sector, often co-ordinated by various *ad hoc* advertising committees financed by public subscription and fund-raising events.[12] Yet, effective though many of these individual schemes undoubtedly were, they were piecemeal and it was only with the increasing involvement of local authorities in the decade immediately before the First World War that more concerted advertising activity emerged. Some of these very early joint public–private sector schemes included those between the Torquay Chamber of Commerce and the town's council, which established an information bureau, produced pictorial advertising posters and advertised the resort in the principal European hotels frequented by American tourists.[13]

The Intervention of Local Government in Resort Promotion

Building on the early public–private sector partnerships, the real breakthrough for promotion in Torquay came in 1905–6 with the formation of an advertising fund administered by a joint committee drawn from the local authority and the town's Chamber of Commerce, a breakthrough achieved largely by the efforts of the Chamber of Commerce and endorsed by the town's traders, hoteliers and boarding house keepers. Financed by public subscription and a local authority grant, the committee was able to run a poster campaign in towns and key railway stations in the Midlands and northern England, placed daily press advertisements and produced pamphlets with a 10,000 print-run. The scheme was a great success and the 1906 annual report of the Torquay Chamber of Commerce announced that the 'outstanding feature of the year's work has been the inauguration of the Combined Advertising Fund'.[14] This joint advertising committee (JAC) was to prove an effective and enduring body, forming the cornerstone of the town's publicity activities in the coming decades, particularly whilst central government refused to allow local authorities to subsidise resort advertising directly.

Ilfracombe also witnessed a similar public sector intervention in marketing, although a few years later than Torquay. The vital move came in March 1910 with the formation of a JAC which during 1911–12 assumed responsibility for Ilfracombe's brochure and for its press advertising, placing advertisements in railway brochures and in London newspapers.[15] In 1913 the JAC was placed on a firmer financial and organisational footing, resourced by an annual grant from the council and composed of local authority, tourism operators' and ratepayers' representatives—a basic shape which remained unchanged for many years.[16] This financial commitment enabled the resort to advertise not just in leading British newspapers but also in the continental edition of the *Daily Mail*, in addition to exhibiting at an Earl's Court trade fair and advertising in carriages of the Metropolitan Railway[17]—activities which form the cornerstone of much destination marketing activity today.[18]

This local authority involvement was critical to the development of effective advertising philosophies within resorts and enabled such towns to expand their activities significantly both at home and abroad. In Torquay, for instance, there was a concerted move to attract overseas visitors and the town's JAC sent literature to the new Daily Mail Travel Bureau in Paris in 1910 and the following year advertised in *The Times of India* and the *Continental Daily Mail*. Meanwhile, the resort continued to broadcast its attractions at the national level via its London information bureau (established in 1911), through press advertisements in the *Daily Mail* and a dozen other national papers, and by one of the earliest ventures into promotional film which was shown in the Midlands and the North in 1913.[19]

While in retrospect it may seem so, it would be misleading to represent this increasing local authority involvement in resort marketing as seamless and uncontested. Much of the work of consolidating and expanding municipal marketing activity was often achieved in the face of vociferous opposition—especially from resort residents who did not want to see more and more tourists arriving in their towns. Divisions over the nature, quantity and cost of publicity were quite common in many resorts and one Torquay councillor's

105

outburst at a Council meeting in 1912 was typical of such opposition. Opposing further efforts to advertise Torquay, he argued that residents did not want day-trippers and that in any case Torquay's attractions were already widely promoted.[20] Such ideas were frequently expressed in the town before the First World War and after 1918 the opposition gained ground as the resort became increasingly 'popularised'. In Torquay the tourism industry was usually united in demanding more advertising and its views were often in the ascendant on the town council. As a result, after 1912 the Torquay JAC included representatives from the hoteliers' and the traders' associations—a recognition that these groups were key partners in resort advertising.[21] Its ability to mobilise public opinion behind demands for increased advertising spending varied over the years, but broadly speaking this pro-tourism lobby was very successful in defeating anti-holiday trade opposition.[22]

Although it was the public sector which played the pivotal role in resort advertising, private-sector organisations (notably hotels and transport companies) were equally critical to promotional initiatives, the latter being active from the 1860s.[23] Indeed, the railway companies were integral to the efficiency of resort promotion activities, as they had been to the development of the seaside product itself. The GWR was an especially vital partner in resort publicity and its partnership schemes were crucial components of many resorts' advertising strategies. Although the company (influenced by American precedents) had begun producing series of booklets on places of interest served by its lines as early as the late nineteenth century, it only began advertising in earnest in 1904 with the appearance of the new Cornish Riviera Express service and the introduction of a new guidebook. Two years later this guide became the famous *Holiday Haunts* which came to epitomise inter-war British tourism publicity and in 1908 the company adopted the slogan 'The Holiday Line'. Together with the 'Cornish Riviera' this phrase was to become synonymous with GWR advertising campaigns, being used on its brochures, posters and illustrated folders, the latter appearing in the years before the First World War.[24]

The extraordinary range of sophisticated techniques developed at this early stage of destination marketing in many ways seriously undermines any notion that contemporary marketing approaches are highly innovative. Whilst many refinements have been made to the earlier tools, the fundamental channels of communication remain largely unchanged today. This pattern of advertising established before the First World War set the scene for the development of resort marketing activities throughout the century. By the outbreak of that War, all the key elements of resort marketing were present: close partnerships with the private sector (particularly the transport operators serving the resorts), national press and poster advertising, public relations activities, the production of an annual brochure and, in some resorts, a recognition of the need to attract overseas visitors.[25]

The Emergence of Inter-War Professionalism

The inter-war years saw the emergence of new holidaymaking habits which, as we outlined in Chapter 3, brought new challenges and opportunities to the British resorts. The social changes of this period, particularly in the position of women, brought shifts in fashion which resort advertising was quick to seize on. The trends towards suntanned complexions (increasingly popular amongst women) and the social acceptance of briefer swimming costumes were reflected in the marketing of resorts. Thus, sunshine and sex became common advertising themes as brochures and posters made liberal use of photographs of bathing belles—a trend which accelerated during the physical fitness-obsessed 1930s.[26]

Promotional Partnerships Re-established

Despite such advertising opportunities, immediately after the war resort promotional activities were constrained by a lack of financial and material resources: for instance, Torquay had to postpone publication of a new illustrated booklet due to paper shortages in 1918.[27] A further obstacle was the continued state control of the railways (requisitioned in the war) which prevented joint advertising schemes and posed problems for resorts across Britain.[28] Yet, in spite of such difficulties resorts throughout Britain did manage to implement ambitious promotion schemes during 1918–19 in order to capitalise on the captive domestic market created by the restrictions on foreign travel.[29]

In the circumstances, not only were the years between 1919 and 1921 very busy ones for Britain's resorts but they were also a period of remarkable progress for those resort publicity organisations which responded to calls for concerted advertising campaigns. Typical of these was the *Torquay Times'* appeal in February 1920 for 'judicious advertising … which [will] appeal to the most desirable class of visitors'.[30] The advertising successes of 1920–1 were also partly due to renewed railway company participation in resort advertising. In 1921 Ilfracombe renewed its advertisements in the GWR's *Holiday Haunts* and that spring the GWR also embarked on an ambitious joint scheme with Torquay's town council, traders and hoteliers which included the production and distribution of 80,000 copies of a four-page folder.[31] Promotional frameworks in both resorts were thus re-established which integrated organisations such as the GWR, the hoteliers and traders and the local councils on committees with remits for press advertising and guide production—all funded by municipal contributions, money-raising concerts, and public subscriptions.[32]

Conflict over the 1921 Health and Pleasure Resorts Act

Although 1920 and 1921 were characterised by a return to pre-war organisational co-operation in Britain's seaside resorts, they were also years when conflict over the direction of publicity policies reached a peak. The issue which brought the inherent divisions to the surface of local resort politics was the Health and Pleasure Resorts Act, passed after some delay in 1921. A forerunner of this Bill, supported by the Federation of British Health and Holiday Resorts and the Urban District Councils' Association and enjoying the powerful support of an influential group of Members of Parliament, had only been prevented from receiving its third reading in 1914 by the outbreak of war.[33] A milestone in British resort advertising, the Act was significant in that for the first time it allowed local authorities to fund advertising from deck chair, beach tent and bathing machine revenue and from admission charges to municipal tourism attractions. Whilst it has been described as 'a modest piece of legislation' (limiting spending to the product of a penny rate and confining advertising to the press, books, leaflets, placards at railway stations and guides), it is also recognised as the 'major breakthrough in seaside promotion' during the inter-war period, for it enabled a huge expansion of municipal involvement in resort development.[34]

Although some 'select' resorts (such as Sidmouth in Devon and Frinton in south-east England[35]) preferred to rely on word of mouth, the activities of their Chambers of Commerce and voluntary sector publicity associations during the inter-war years, many more quickly took advantage of the Act.[36] Many of the larger resorts established new council departments to administer publicity and entertainments: in Torquay, for instance, a professional publicity manager was appointed in 1922. Elsewhere, as in Clacton, the Act enabled resorts to launch advertising campaigns run by professional agencies—a further example of early sophistication and subsequent continuity in promotional practice.[37] As Yates has commented, even in the more conservative resorts 'the minimum concession to the new legislation was normally the setting up of separate council committees to take on the responsibility for resort activities and promotion'.[38] The Act was extended in 1936 to allow local authorities to fund advertising through a rates levy of up to a one-and-a-third penny rate.[39] Together these two pieces of legislation facilitated an unrivalled expansion in municipal activity, both in advertising and in entertainment provision—'which few modern local authorities have the resources to imitate'.[40]

The policy of local government-subsidised advertising was not without its critics, however, and at the heart of the criticism lay the issue of social tone. Resorts (like Blackpool, Clacton and Ilfracombe) which were more economically dependent on tourism more readily embraced marketing and with it a more popular resort product.[41] Those resorts, like Torquay, which were struggling to maintain their select nature were rather more equivocal in their support. The debate was highlighted in the pages of the *Torquay Times*, and whilst the Bill was before Parliament in 1921 the paper devoted a great deal of print to the issue and to the residential opposition to the spending of ratepayers' money on publicity. One critic of the idea argued:

It is perfectly monstrous that other residents should be made to pay for a scheme which in no way benefits themselves. [The Bill will] … benefit one section of the community only, many of whom have made a good deal out of the war, and are not yet satisfied.[42]

These criticisms were ultimately unsuccessful as the benefits of subsidised marketing were increasingly recognised during the inter-war period. Local newspapers, such as the *Torquay Times,* argued that the direct advantage gained by promotion was money 'well spent … [and] the direct advantage gained by Torquay … inestimable'.[43] During the debate over the 1921 Bill, therefore, the paper was unusually vigorous in its criticism of the anti-holiday interest groupings, labelling suggestions that Torquay should be kept free of more visitors a 'selfish monopoly' on the part of 'that section of the community generally described as villa residents'. In contrast, it praised the Bill's provision to allow local authorities to use profits from entertainments to finance advertising as 'an ingenious and effective means of removing that unjustifiable and selfish opposition' of those who claimed it was 'an unjust tax on residents'.[44] Whilst the anti-development lobbies continued to oppose increases in adver-tising expenditure, others pushed for increases, arguing that their resorts 'must either go forward or go back', and if it was to be the former they must continue to advertise.[45] In Ilfracombe in the early 1920s, for instance, the *Ilfracombe Chronicle* spearheaded the calls for increased advertising and an editorial of January 1922 was typical of its campaign, proclaiming:

Wake up, Ilfracombe! What are we going to do about length-ening our summer season, both at its beginning and its end, to say nothing at all as to any movements towards booming the town as a winter resort?[46]

Consolidation and Progress in the 1920s
During the 1920s the pre-war resort marketing methods (the use of brochures, posters and press advertisements, often produced in conjunction with the railway companies) continued to prove successful. As before the war, railway companies were principal

110

partners in resort promotion schemes and they channelled considerable sums of money into resort promotion in the decade. For Devon's resorts the GWR was the most prominent, though by no means the only railway partner (for instance the Southern Railway was also highly active).[47] Early in 1922 the GWR and Torquay Council launched a £900 scheme which included £400 on press advertisements in Manchester and Birmingham—frequently target areas for Torquay publicity.[48] These joint schemes often produced large posters for nation-wide display, a good example being a scheme of 1923 which provided £1,175 over two years for 5,000 posters and £400 for 20 London buses to carry advertisements of Torquay—a policy first begun in 1920.[49]

The replacement in 1924 of the old GWR advertising department with a new publicity department under the leadership of W.H. Fraser marked the beginning of a new era in GWR publicity. Under his direction the Company's promotional activities reached their zenith. These were the 'Go Great Western' years of the mid-1920s, when more aggressive GWR publicity began to supplement the backbone of inter-war publicity—the small non-displayed advertisements which appeared in the same position each week in hundreds of local papers around the country. Between 1924 and 1928 printings of the *Holiday Haunts* guidebook doubled to 200,000 and, more importantly as far as its partner resorts were concerned, Fraser advanced an ambitious joint resort advertising programme whereby the local authorities and the GWR shared the publicity costs of campaigns including press, poster and folder schemes.[50]

The amount spent by Torquay on press advertising in the 1920s reflected its substantial ambitions which were to see it become one of the major international as well as British resorts. Confirmation of its international reputation came with successful advertising in the South of France and West Africa in 1924.[51] The following year almost £3,000 was spent on promotion: £1,150 on spring and autumn London and provincial press advertising; £400 an advertising on London buses; £200 on illuminated signs at Paddington station; and £1,125 on poster, folder and brochure expenses.[52] Other innovative promotional approaches included familiarisation trips for British and Canadian journalists to Torquay in 1923, facilitated by a wealthy resident's personal donation to the publicity fund of £3,000. This initiative was crucial in the development of Torquay as a popular holiday resort and was so successful that it was repeated in 1929 when the publicity committee hosted a dinner for 33 representatives of travel and tourist agencies and steamship companies.[53] Interestingly, such familiarisation visits and public relations activities remain very much in evidence in destination marketing today—a further confirmation of the essential continuity in such activities.[54] The second significant event of 1923 was Torquay's hosting of the International Advertising Convention, which signalled the town's intention to diversify its visitor base beyond the holiday-maker and which did much to establish Torquay as one of Britain's major conference centres.[55]

Although such individual events were significant in raising Torquay's profile, more important in the long-term development of its publicity services was the excellent organisation of the resort's promotional activities. Building on the framework established during 1906–13, partnerships and co-ordination were central to advertising success.[56] Working independently, and in concert with Torquay Council, hoteliers and trade associations did much to promote the resort and in 1927 they co-operated to provide an accommodation and information bureau at the Strand in London. As a forerunner of the modern tourism information centre networks, initiatives such as these supplemented the private advertising budgets of Torquay's hotels, estimated to be worth about £40,000 in the late-1920s—money which benefited Torquay's entire holiday industry.[57]

The fruits of this effective administration and the advances of the early 1920s were outlined in the Torquay publicity officer's 1925 annual report, which noted that during 1922–5 the numbers of visitors and the accommodation stock had increased by 40 per cent. It also reported that in 1925 Torquay had produced a folder with the GWR, continued its advertising on London buses for the fifth successive year and hosted several important conferences, including the Health and Pleasure Resorts Conference—activities which, together with a successful joint GWR autumn press campaign, had ensured a profitable winter season despite strong competition from the resorts of the English south coast. The resort was not prepared to rest on its

112

laurels, however, and the report stressed the need for continued investment, stating that a cash input in the region of £5,000 was necessary to enable Torquay to meet the challenge of its rivals.[58]

The years 1922–9 also saw consolidation in Ilfracombe's advertising activities, although these were significantly hampered by insufficient funds. Ilfracombe JAC's reliance on fund-raising events as opposed to formal subscriptions meant that the bulk of the funds came from annual fêtes and dances held at the town's Pavilion and pier—an inadequate system of funding for post-war advertising. Recognising the problem, Ilfracombe's JAC lobbied extensively for more reliable funding to support more effective advertising. For instance, at its annual meeting in 1923 it argued that since advertising in the provincial press was not as effective as advertising in national papers such as the *Daily Mail* and the *Daily Telegraph,* an improved annual press programme of £10,000 was required.[59] All these attempts to formalise the funding procedure were rejected, however, and this was to have significant consequences for Ilfracombe's ability to mount successful advertising campaigns in the years before the Second World War.[60]

After the re-organisations of 1918–24, the period 1924–9 was one of gradual expansion in the publicity activities of the leading Devon resorts. In Ilfracombe the JAC's initiatives centred on joint press advertising with the railways, both the Southern Railway and the GWR contributing £150 each out of a total of £600 in 1926–7—a substantial sum, but small in scale compared to the £3,000 publicity fund of Torquay.[61] Some 70 per cent of the press advertising for Ilfracombe was placed in London papers, and 30 per cent in the provincial press. This reflected the JAC's belief that advertisements in London publications were more effective as, in the words of one town councillor, it was 'wise to advertise in better class papers to attract better class people'.[62] Such modest advances pleased the holiday interests in both resorts but others, particularly in Torquay, where progress had been more rapid, were concerned that social exclusivity was being threatened by 'over-population'. One particular focus for such concern was the increasingly popular Sunday rail excursions—which the local paper considered 'might actually ruin the town'. Those residents and councillors who supported such views successfully prevented a GWR proposal to run Sunday trains to Torquay, forcing them to continue on to neighbouring Paignton and thus preventing influxes of excursionists from arriving at the town.[63]

Concerns over such post-war shifts in holiday patterns were expressed in many British resorts but this concern was often tempered by a recognition of the need to be proactive in promotion—as the following editorial in the *Torquay Times* illustrates:

> It behoves the Municipal Authority and those whose business it is to cater for the wants and recreation of the travelling public to broadcast the attractions of the town as widely as possible. The serious rival to well-known seaside resorts and Torquay in particular, is the Riviera whose climate and charm are so persistently advocated by posters and pamphlets.[64]

The French Riviera was regarded as one of Torquay's main rivals until the later 1950s as it competed with its resorts (especially Cannes) for the much sought-after select clientele. It was the topographical and climatic similarities between the resorts which also gave rise to the comparison, highlighted by *The Times* in 1931:

> Torquay is certainly the English equivalent of Cannes. There is no resort which, apart from a certain prime austerity in the administration of the licensing laws, comes nearer in character and amenities to the most progressive of Mediterranean Towns.[65]

The constant invoking of comparisons between Torquay and Cannes was to prove particularly significant in terms of the themes which were to dominate the former's advertising over the coming decades. These were most apparent in the cover illustrations of the official guides which signalled an early attempt by a resort to create an emotional, rather than a rational, appeal to its target audience.[66] The repetition of certain advertising designs (notably the palm tree image), evocative of the French Riviera's mild climate and sophistication, is traceable in Torquay's guidebooks from the 1920s to the 1990s. These annual publications provide valuable insights into the aspirations and the marketing of the resort, revealing its continued fascination with the Riviera analogy. The official guide of 1928 clearly alludes to this perceived similarity. The cover design, with its hillside villas and palm trees, depicts a scene very reminiscent of a star-lit Cannes, whilst the blue of the harbour—reflecting the starry sky, the lights of the parade, and the illuminated Pavilion—is intended to invoke continental summer evenings. This picture of elegance and European sophistication is completed by the figures in the foreground, the dinner-jacketed man and his companions—fashionable 'flappers' attired in furs, evening gowns and silk-stockings. The illustration is underpinned by the town's crest with its motto *'Salus et Felicitas'* (Health and Happiness) and the word 'Torquay' in bold lettering above the phrase 'The English Riviera'. The link between the French and English Rivieras is clear, as is the intended clientele: middle- and upper-class winter visitors.[67]

Resort Promotion and Political Crisis

Long a focus of Torquay's advertising, the attraction of wealthy visitors dominated the marketing activities of many more British resorts during 1931–2. These years were ones of national political and economic crisis, focusing on the creation of a coalition government under the leadership of Ramsey MacDonald in 1931. Of particular significance in tourism terms was the dramatic devaluation of the British currency in the same year—a situation which boosted the domestic holiday resorts at the expense of overseas rivals. In these years the seaside resorts of Devon intensified their winter advertising campaigns to try to attract 'patriotic' holiday-makers voluntarily exiled from the Continent. This was especially true of the more fashionable resorts such as Torquay and Sidmouth, and these provide much of the material for our discussion of this upsurge in marketing activity. Interestingly, however, it seems that publicity activities in Devon's resorts increased even before the economic crisis broke. Thus in 1929 the less select resort of Ilfracombe boasted an ambitious £930 scheme and in 1930 its publicity budget topped £860.[68] This pattern of increased advertising activity in the late 1920s and early 1930s was shared by the railway companies. During 1928–31 the GWR's *Holiday Haunts*, with its new illustrated colour cover, reached its greatest circulation, peaking at 200,000 in 1929–30 before falling to about 125,000 in 1932.[69] The period 1929–33 thus emerges as a period of intensi-

Figure 5.1: *The 1928 Torquay Guide Cover*
Images of a chic 1920s resort. The 1928 guide cover typifies Torquay's inter-war promotional literature, which conveyed impressions of an exclusive destination offering high-quality service. (Reproduced by kind permission of the Torquay Library and the Torbay Tourist Board.)

fied activity, but one in which the 1931 crisis and the subsequent 'Winter in England' campaign played contributory rather than initiating roles.

Even the conservative Sidmouth stepped up its publicity activity during these years. In 1930 a publicity scheme involving the major railways serving the resort and the town council was launched, and in the following year rate-aided publicity schemes were introduced for the first time—a major step for the resort.[70] Advertisements placed by the council and the resort's private hotels appeared frequently in *The Times* during 1931 and two of the most prestigious hotels were amongst the first to use endorsement by association strategies in their advertising, using the slogan 'where HRH the Duke of Connaught is spending the winter'.[71] Such advertising strategies were to assume even greater significance in the post-war period, especially in the 1980s and 1990s—as the early 1990s Wales Tourist Board advertising campaign based around endorsements from stars such as Sir Anthony Hopkins, Tom Jones and Dylan Thomas demonstrates.[72]

The Sidmouth hotels were capitalising on the appeal made in October 1931 by Chancellor Snowden for holiday-makers to holiday at home and improve Britain's balance of payments. This presented British resorts with a marvellous opportunity, cemented by the Duke of Connaught, 'who usually spent the winter at his villa on the Riviera' but caught the mood and 'decided to make Sidmouth ... his winter headquarters'. This was reported in detail by *The Times*, which commented 'He has thereby set an example that is hoped will be followed by many of those who usually winter abroad'.[73] The idea gained momentum and a letter from a Lieutenant-Colonel Elliott in *The Times* of 28 October provided the impetus for the establishment of the British Health Resorts' Association, a patriotic movement designed to promote Britain and a forerunner of today's British Resorts' Association.[74] In addition to this patriotic push, the devaluation of the pound also provided further incentives to stay at home as it increased foreign travel costs and made the British seaside resorts a much more economical alternative.

Torquay, like the other British resorts which had lost trade to the Continent in the 1920s, grasped this opportunity to recapture business. Advertisements proclaiming the attractions of Devon resorts appeared early in October. One in *The Times* of 9 October 1921 informed readers that Torquay had: 'health and holiday facilities equal in every respect to those of the Continental Riviera. Patriotism and National Economy demand a Winter Holiday at home ... and at Torquay.'[75] These marketing messages were echoed by other fashionable resorts and by the publicity departments of Britain's railways. As the GWR's publicity department reported:

> In view of the financial position of the country and the devaluation of the pound, with a consequent discouragement of travel to foreign resorts, special advertising has been entered into with a view to direct public attention to the merits of the English 'Riviera' ...[76]

The resultant winter advertising campaign was so successful that Torquay's hotels were heavily booked at Christmas 1931 and the local paper asked 'Are we about to Recapture our former Winter Season?'[77] The momentum of the campaign continued in 1932 and in January the nearby resort of Paignton hosted the 'Winter in Britain' conference attended by hundreds of delegates from the holiday industry and the medical profession. The conference inaugurated a series of such events all over the country to discuss ways to retain within Britain the £30 million usually spent on foreign holidays—an issue of some concern at this date, although it is usually regarded as emerging for the first time in the 1960s. The Paignton conference was one of national importance and the Home Secretary, Sir Herbert Samuel, sent 'best wishes for the success of the patriotic efforts of the British Coastal Resorts Association ... [which] will do much to increase the tendency of British people to patronise their own resorts. It may help also the excellent movement to attract foreigners to our shores.'[78] Publicity of this nature was an ideal platform for resort promotion campaigns, and the *Torquay Times* in its call for 'A wise expenditure of public funds' to attract visitors echoed the sentiments of the local press in many seaside towns at the time.[79]

The increased advertising activity in the Devon resorts was reflected in an upsurge in press advertisements placed by the town councils, the railway companies and private hotels in 1931. A content analysis of resort publicity in *The Times* from 1901 to 1971 indicates

118

the increase in publicity that year, although the evidence also points to a general increase over the decade 1921–31. Although the value of the trend data is undermined after 1951 due to changes in the format of the paper's holiday advertisements, the dramatic increase in their number between 1921 and 1931 is clearly illustrated in Table 5.1. Sidmouth outstripped Torquay in the quantity of its publicity but its advertisements were inserted by the private hotels and tended to be smaller features, whereas many of Torquay's, sponsored jointly by the town council and the GWR, were much more prominent in the newspaper.

Table 5.1: Torquay and Sidmouth Advertisements in *The Times*, 1911–1931

	1911	1921	1931
Torquay	213	204	496
Sidmouth	383	349	659

Source: *The Times*, 1911–31

Advertisements for Ilfracombe hardly figure in *The Times* during 1911–71—a reflection of its more 'popular' social tone—and whilst resorts like Sidmouth and Torquay gained from the 1931 economic crisis, Ilfracombe failed to capitalise on the 'holiday at home movement'. Unlike its more fashionable rivals, it had no winter season to build on and the local press was highly critical of the town council's and the hoteliers' failure to emulate Torquay and capitalise on the pound's devaluation. During this critical period there was a surprising lack of interest in advertising affairs and the town's JAC made several appeals for larger attendances at its meetings.[80] Although this lethargy was a serious obstacle, Ilfracombe's major problem at this time was a lack of resources and an inability to put its advertising finances on a stable and secure footing. If the resort was to create a winter season council officers considered that £10,000 was required over a five-year period—money which was simply not available.[81] This opinion confirmed an editorial which had appeared in the *Ilfracombe Chronicle* as early as 1915, commenting: 'To try to make Ilfracombe a winter resort would be putting [our] heads against a wall. Bournemouth and Torquay spent enormous sums of money; but Ilfracombe was not in a position to do so.'[82]

As Ilfracombe's hopes of creating a fashionable winter season to compete with continental resorts evaporated in the early 1930s, Torquay seized its opportunity during the 1931 crisis. It was already an established 'congress' or conference town, hosting several major annual conferences. In 1930 its sophisticated advertising campaign included: 200 council-sponsored and 170 Hoteliers' Association-sponsored posters on the London Underground; a significant early attempt at niche marketing with the production and distribution of a new Baths brochure aimed at the medical profession; and 80,000 pamphlets of Torquay produced with GWR co-operation and issued to American tourist agencies.[83]

More controversial was a move to intensify Torquay's advertising efforts through the inclusion of a clause in the 1933 Torquay Corporation Bill which would have enabled the council to expend the difference from the rates on publicity if the profits available from entertainments fell below the equivalent of a one-and-one-third penny rate. This clause became a focus of intense debate in the town in late 1933. In November its opponents urged its deletion in council but most councillors were deeply committed to the clause and the suggestion was defeated by a large majority.[84] At a public meeting convened to discuss the issue, the two key factions were 'the villa residents' and the Hoteliers' Association which led the pro-tourist group. The *Torquay Times* favoured the clause, proclaiming 'Publicity is the life-blood of Torquay'.[85] The debate was eventually resolved in favour of the clause but it later proved to be a pyrrhic victory for it was lost in the Bill's passage through the House of Lords Select Committee, forcing Torquay to continue to rely on entertainments profits to finance marketing under the 1921 Health and Pleasure Resorts Act.[86]

Advertising Advances in the Depression

Despite the successes of the early 1930s, this was a difficult decade for British resorts and the railway companies serving them, and the economic slump was reflected in the holiday advertising slogans of the time. These were the years of the 'Buy British' campaign, which found echoes in railway advertising. In 1934 it became 'Quicker by Rail'—a slogan used by all the railways in these years, in response to greater road competition. These campaigns could not prevent tumbling profits in the tourism sector of the railways' business, however, and during 1931–5 sales of the GWR's holiday brochure, *Holiday Haunts*, fell by 25 per cent.[87] Not only did railway companies increase their advertising in an effort to combat the slump—the numbers of GWR pictorial posters rising from 50,000 to 100,000 between 1932 and 1934—they also sought new markets as the numbers of traditional holiday-makers fell.[88]

These new markets, particularly those associated with camping and rambling, proved to be major growth areas for the railways, and they were encouraged by notable early 1930s advertising innovations, including the introduction of sound film: several films went on general release in Britain, including 'Dawdling in Devon' (released in 1933 and also available in the USA). Other promotional campaigns included the introduction of themed packages such as the GWR's Hikers' Specials and Mystery Trains introduced in 1932; the camping coaches and reduced fares in 1934; and, in the later 1930s, the annual booklets with directories of campsites—seven in all being issued and later re-issued in the Second World War.[89] Partnerships with resort publicity departments remained significant and indeed became increasingly sophisticated as multi-lingual versions of brochures were produced to attract overseas visitors. Towards the end of the decade Torquay was producing 80,000 folders annually in partnership with the GWR—10,000 in French and 10,000 in Dutch, an indication of the resort's international position.[90]

In addition to the familiar publicity of the railway schemes and brochure production, the Torquay publicity committee also engaged in more unorthodox enterprises in these years. These included a publicity film shown in 15,000 British and foreign cinemas and a project to attract foreign visitors in conjunction with the Travel and Industrial Development Association of Great Britain and Ireland.[91] The Torquay town council initiatives were also augmented to a considerable extent by those of the private sector, some of which (notably the town's Grand Hotel's 1935 advertising film, shown in 250 British and Irish towns) were very ambitious.[92] Perhaps the most ambitious private-sector scheme of the 1930s, however, was an advertisement for Torquay which occupied the entire front page of the *Daily Mail* on 25 May 1934 at a cost of £1,400. This was a huge success, gaining editorial coverage in the national press and generating almost 10,000 enquiries by September 1934 in direct response to the advertisement.[93]

Such public- and private-sector advertising initiatives enabled Torquay to cement its position as a premier British resort in the inter-war period. Although there was opposition to such expensive publicity, the vast majority of businesses in the resort recognised the importance of the tourism industry to Torquay's prosperity and it was not merely the hoteliers and the traders who contributed to the advertising fund in the 1930s. Clearly, advertising was not the controversial issue during 1933–9 which it had been in the 1920s and early 1930s when there was such debate over its financing. This was due to the fact that by the late 1930s Torquay's advertising seems to have been in capable hands. When war broke out in 1939 the resort had the most professional and effective publicity machine in Devon and one of the most sophisticated in Britain.

Torquay's promotional policies were in stark contrast to those of Sidmouth Council which remained low-key and conservative during 1933–9—notwithstanding the upsurge in advertising activity between 1929 and 1932. In this resort, the emphasis remained on autumn and winter advertising rather than spring and summer campaigns, and in the mid-1930s Sidmouth's annual advertising operation consisted of press advertising and the production of about 1,000 brochures and 7,000 guides—financed by the railways, the Sidmouth Hoteliers' and Caterers' Association and the town council.[94] In 1938 the railways paid half the costs and the entire contribution payable by the resort was met by hoteliers' subscriptions, the council having no financial input.[95] At the outbreak of war, Sidmouth Council operated a modest publicity machine, producing 10,000 annual brochures from a total publicity budget of £300. Compared to other British resorts such as Skegness in Lincolnshire (producing 40,000), and Exmouth and Ilfracombe in Devon (both producing about 25,000 brochures), this was a very low-key operation.[96]

Whilst Sidmouth continued its policies of exclusivity and Torquay made steady progress in resort promotion, Ilfracombe suffered more than most Devon resorts from the economic depression of the 1930s. Its problems led to confusion and disunity in the resort with some pressure groups advocating economy and others favouring expensive publicity campaigns. The resort had not reaped the benefits of the events of 1931 as had Torquay and Sidmouth and the local paper argued that 'If the experience of other resorts and big business is anything to go by, any reduction in the amount spent on advertising … will mean harder business times to come'.[97]

More problems emerged for Ilfracombe in the mid-1930s when the railways serving the resort reduced their advertising schemes by 25 per cent. This severely hit the town and this was a period of considerable internal strife over resort advertising policies. The local paper was at the forefront of this controversy, advising the council in July 1934 that:

> When a business man finds that trade is slack he re-doubles his efforts, spends more money in making his shop attractive and getting the right kind of goods, and he spends more upon advertising. That is what must be done with regard to Ilfracombe.[98]

The newspaper was convinced that the resort should be doing more to market itself and the controversy over Ilfracombe's future caused concern in all sections of the community. The president of the Hoteliers' Association, for instance, observed:

> The Council seems to be divided, there is a progressive section and a defeatist section. Our association will support whole-heartedly the progressive side of the council, and will strenuously fight the other side. Ilfracombe must go forward.[99]

In 1935 the Ilfracombe Hoteliers' Association informed the council that it viewed 'with considerable concern' the latter's 'utter disregard' of the JAC, 'believed to be the most vital link between Ilfracombe and its visitors'.[100] The Association pressed for more action as, in the words of one of their number, 'Ilfracombe is … marking time …

most of the rates come from hotels and boarding houses. We have a right to be heard in planning the future prosperity of the town.'[101] Whilst there was some innovation (such as a 1935 *Radio Times* advertisement, a magazine then with a circulation of three million, and an inclusion in a 1939 promotional film of Devon shown in 50 cinemas before the outbreak of war), the town's advertising policies remained essentially unchanged.[102] As a result, even the slight recovery in the industry towards the end of the decade could not disguise the fact that the depressed years of the 1930s had hit Ilfracombe hard.

Advertising in an Age of Austerity

The inter-war achievements provided the post-war British image creators with a solid foundation in resort advertising, although the war and its aftermath brought major challenges to resort publicity departments throughout Britain. As we have seen, the legislation of 1921 and 1936 proved the key to much of the inter-war success accomplished by seaside local authorities since it allowed them to raise a penny rate for publicity. The Second World War interrupted this progress in resort publicity and although activity did continue during the conflict it was on a much reduced scale. Some resorts, such as Sidmouth, suspended operations for the duration of the war, whilst others such as Torquay drastically curtailed their involvement, restricting their advertising to local catchment areas.[103]

At the end of the war many resorts were ill-prepared for the holiday rush and it was their differing financial resources which dictated their achievements in the years of post-war economic difficulty, although some resorts (such as Sidmouth) continued to disdain high profile advertising. Such strategies were more the exception rather than the rule, however, as the resorts' financial resources tended to be reflected in their advertising initiatives. For example, in the mid-1940s a penny rate levied in Torquay equalled £2,800, whilst in neighbouring Paignton it produced £1,356. These were both large sums, and enabled the towns to advertise extensively and employ a full-time publicity officer, as did the similarly ambitious but less well-endowed Ilfracombe.[104]

Co-operation and Co-ordination to Recapture Markets in Torquay

During the late 1940s and early 1950s British seaside resorts were presented with substantial difficulties in promotion and as a result there was a great deal of activity and experimentation in resort publicity and organisational structures during 1946–9. These were crucial years in the race to recapture inter-war trade as many foreign revivals (especially in the Vichy-controlled South of France, which had operated as a resort area throughout the War) had geared up for business as early as February 1946.[105] Many British resorts were not ready for this challenge. Although impressive schemes were proposed, post-war difficulties brought division rather than positive action even to forward-looking resorts such as Torquay. Publicity was hamstrung by a lack of resources and guide production was disrupted by paper shortages as after the First World War. Similarly, difficulties such as the national fuel crisis hampered resorts' abilities to launch effective campaigns, whilst they also had to deal with the criticisms of residents who opposed expenditure.[106] In these difficult circumstances, Torquay's fortunes were boosted by the publicity coup afforded its hosting of the Olympic Games yachting events in August 1948. The resort was already a major conference centre, hosting about 16 important events a year, but this was a significant event for the town, heightening its profile as an international resort during a problematic period.[107] The hosting of such events continues to be highly desirable at the close of the twentieth century, offering both raised profiles and increased visitor numbers—as in the case of Atlanta, whose hosting of the 1996 Olympic Games was worth $3 billion for the city's businesses and citizens.[108]

Throughout the post-war period, a considerable amount of Torquay's promotional effort was devoted to encouraging its conference market—a policy first pursued in earnest in the 1920s. During 1949–50 the Hoteliers' Association donated £550 to the new Hospitality Fund designed to attract conferences to the resort. A major success in this sphere in 1950, confirming the benefits of such publicity, was the town's hosting of the United Nations Organisation Trades and Tariffs Conference (which generated an estimated £1.4 million in hotel expenditure alone).[109] Thus the conference market attracted the financial backing of the town's hoteliers and traders throughout the 1950s and early 1960s and an increasing proportion of their donations was devoted to the town's conference rather than its advertising fund. By the early 1950s the town council was spending £5,000 a year on conference promotion and in that decade the Hoteliers' Association's contributions totalled several thousands. By the early 1960s over £11,500 was being allocated to the town's conference marketing budget each year, whilst the advertising budget totalled £14,000: a reflection of the importance Torquay attached to its conference market.[110]

These were indeed huge sums of money devoted to publicising Torquay as a holiday and conference centre during the 1950s and early 1960s—a period of rapid growth in all tourism sectors throughout Britain. These were still the pre-package holiday years and a prosperous period for British seaside resorts. Torquay had long had an excellent publicity department and from the 1950s this functioned on an even more professional footing with its publicity officer controlling an annual advertising budget of £2,000 and operating from offices which incorporated an information bureau.[111] A notable advance at Torquay in the mid-1950s was the improvement of the resort's brochure with the addition of colour pages in 1955, becoming a 144-page publication, 24 of which were in colour.[112] In contrast to the immediate post-war years, it is clear that the late 1940s and early 1950s were characterised by co-operation rather than dissension within Torquay. The marketing efforts of British resorts were also aided at this time by central government policies designed to stem the flow of sterling out of Britain, especially Chancellor R.A. Butler's move in January 1952 to cut the foreign travel allowance to £25.[113]

Uneasy Partnerships in Sidmouth

As in the first half of the twentieth century, advertising partnerships continued to be significant and resorts were assisted by the railway companies' advertising operations, which continued after nationalisation. This co-operation was, in fact, to continue until the mid-1960s when British Rail announced a nation-wide reduction in its resort advertising programme.[114] The early 1950s were thus very successful for British resorts, and even the publicity-shy Sidmouth was very active. In 1951 its town council launched an ambitious joint advertising scheme with British Rail, which committed both to press advertising, 15,000 guides and 3,000 posters for three years.[115] This scheme followed a year when Sidmouth's Entertainment and Publicity Committee spending exceeded £930, far above the original estimate. In 1951–2 the Committee increased guide production to 20,000 and targeted autumn and winter advertising at the Sunday 'quality' press.[116] In 1952, however, whilst other Devon resorts faced the post-war challenges with a degree of co-operation, Sidmouth's advertising efforts suffered from a double blow of British Rail policy changes and internal strife caused by a failure to embrace properly the partnership principle—that year the Railway Executive announced economy measures which reduced advertising by 50 per cent.[117]

The second blow to Sidmouth in 1952 was the rift between the council entertainments and publicity committee and the town's traders' and hoteliers' bodies. The council's continued refusal to allow these organisations representation on that committee had been a perennial source of friction and in 1950 they pursued independent advertising rather than join the council's winter advertising scheme.[118] In 1952 the situation reached a crisis point when the commercial sector organisations withdrew their financial support from advertising since the Council refused to co-operate in a publicity committee, warning that: 'In conveying this decision, it is strongly urged by both associations, that such co-operation, both actively and financial, is the only solution possible to our joint aim and desire to compete with those towns to whom ... much of our winter business is being lost'.[119] Sidmouth Council's refusal to grant representation for traders and hoteliers on its publicity committee reflects the low-key approach to advertising in the resort, especially as in Torquay and Ilfracombe such bodies had been closely involved from the outset. The council remained unmoved despite external pressure and the inconvenience of parallel publicity schemes, although a degree of *de facto* co-operation developed in the mid-1950s as the council's publicity agents and the Hotels' Association collaborated over press advertising to prevent duplication.[120]

Signs of Fading Fortunes at Ilfracombe

Whilst Torquay developed its advertising machine and Sidmouth grappled with its internal strife, Ilfracombe struggled to recapture its pre-war position. The years 1945–9 were ones of particular difficulty for the north Devon resort and its policy-makers were aware of the need 'to keep Ilfracombe editorially and pictorially in front of the public'.[121] Despite this, the financing of the town's advertising operations was a major problem, complicated by the attitude of the Southern Railway which argued that 'next summer our trains are going to be full whether we advertise or not…. There are millions of people taking holidays with pay, the majority of them staying in England.'[122] The railway company also considered a poster of the resort superfluous and not until 1948 was an up-to-date poster of Ilfracombe available. The resort's JAC was still short of funds as subscriptions were low and the railway companies did not enter into joint advertising until late 1948. This lack of funds forced the JAC to seek other partners and it approached Campbell's Steamer Company and the Southern National Bus Company for financial aid whilst the town council itself spent £760 on publicity, purchasing advertising space in the *New York Times Supplement*.[123]

Although many of the problems faced by Ilfracombe were a direct result of the war, some were of a more perennial nature. There were perceptual problems amongst potential holiday-makers due to the term 'north Devon' which was recognised as an advertising liability and in 1948 Ilfracombe's municipal publicity literature tried a new tack by describing the resort as on 'Devon's Atlantic Coast'.[124] Some progress was achieved despite such problems, however, and the quantity of publicity material steadily increased as Ilfracombe's JAC regained its pre-war position. In 1947 30,000 folders appeared and in 1950 35,000 guides were printed—11,000 above the pre-war maximum.[125] However, the nature of the town's advertising policies dominated local politics in Ilfracombe during 1952–4 and there were repeated calls for an information bureau to combat the slump in the resort's fortunes.[126] Ilfracombe was stagnating as a resort and its promotional activities were an obvious target for criticism. In 1953 the *Chronicle* commented, 'we must re-orientate our ideas as far as advertising is concerned. We need a microscope to see our advertising in the national press.'[127]

Ilfracombe's tourism industry was atrophying and although the numbers of tourists visiting the resort increased in the 1950s, 1960s and 1970s, with hindsight it emerges that the seeds of its decline had been sown as early as the inter-war period. Ilfracombe, like many more of Britain's small and medium-sized resorts, would struggle to respond to the challenge of package holidays, a challenge which even Sidmouth (with its clear market strategy) and Torquay (with its impressive financial resources) would find difficult to meet.

Modern Policies Reach Maturity

Whilst the period from the mid-1950s to the late 1970s witnessed continuing resort popularity, it also saw the eclipse of fashionability in many British resorts—although a small number (notably Sidmouth in Devon) managed to retain their select profile. Advertising assumed even greater significance during this period as British resorts began to respond to the threats of foreign package holiday competition. For those of Devon this was a period of mixed fortunes. Not surprisingly, Ilfracombe stagnated in this period despite sporadic campaigns to heighten the resort's profile, including the late 1950s promotion of the town as the 'Honeymooners' Paradise'.[128] The north Devon resort's malaise was too deep-seated to be alleviated by advertising campaigns alone and its remote location remained a serious difficulty. Perceptions of its northerly location remained stubbornly strong despite the official guide's reassurance that although 'the very word "North" has something cold about it ... [this] can give a false impression.... Ilfracombe is south of south Wales, south of London and south of Southend. That makes it sound almost tropical.'[129]

Despite such attempts to redress this negative image it remained strong, as in other UK resorts on eastern and northern coasts.[130] The council tried numerous slogans throughout the 1950s, 1960s and early 1970s to rid itself of the image: in the 1960s Ilfracombe was 'On Glorious Devon's Ocean Coast'; by the mid-1970s it was promoted as the 'Gateway to Devon's Golden Coast'; and in the 1980s it became 'the Centre of Attraction'.[131] Despite changes in the nature and direction of such campaigns, Ilfracombe's guide cover illustrations, in common with many other British resorts, exhibit a remarkable post-war continuity in design and photographic style, a factor which may well have contributed to (and certainly reflects) the stagnating fortune of the seaside. As we shall see, the innovative style of Torbay's mid-1980s campaign was a notable exception to this pattern and critical to its revival as a premier British resort.

Exclusivity Preserved at Sidmouth

As Ilfracombe grappled with its negative identity, there was little controversy over the direction of Sidmouth's advertising strategies in this period. The town council put its problem with British Rail and the Hoteliers' Association behind it and experimented with more 'progressive' policies, although at no time did it lose sight of the importance of maintaining a high social tone in the resort. Thus, when the council promoted the town as a conference centre in 1954 it recognised an opportunity to capitalise on 'modern' trends, but in rejecting plans for an information bureau the previous year it clung to its traditional perceptions of 'appropriate' municipal activity.[132] This conservatism was evident in Sidmouth's continued emphasis on winter rather than summer advertising: firmly associating the resort with the season of the wealthy or leisured classes rather than that of the holiday-fortnight masses.

Whilst former British winter resorts (including the still quite fashionable Torquay) accepted that the summer was now their main season, Sidmouth retained an image of an exclusive year-round resort. In the mid-1950s almost half the municipal publicity budget was allocated to autumn and winter advertising, whereas by this date most resorts saw the spring and summer season as the priority.[133] Towards the end of the decade even Sidmouth could not resist the pull of the summer season, however, and there was a further concession to changing holiday trends with the provision of municipal tourist entertainment in the shape of a repertory company.[134] It remained traditional in outlook, however, and continued to spurn attractions beyond the bowling, tennis, putting and bathing facilities which had been available since the 1920s, although the amateur band which had long provided concerts was replaced by a professional band in the early 1960s.[135] The town council continued to remain aloof from pressure to grant representation to the Hoteliers' Association and the Chamber of Commerce, informing the latter in 1960 that it was not council policy to co-opt members to the publicity committee. In the same year the council also rebuffed Exmouth's overtures to participate in a tripartite advertising scheme with Budleigh Salterton: Sidmouth was determined to remain apart from its Devon counterparts and refused to realign its image in the face of declining business in the 1960s.[136]

In fact, the resort's response to the increased foreign and domestic competition was to further emphasise its select image. In 1962 for instance, the *Western Morning News* carried a full-page advertisement and article entitled: 'Sidmouth caters for the Discriminating'. The item noted that, 'It has consistently shunned sheer popularity in order to preserve old-world graciousness ... [setting] out very positively to appeal to a particular minority of visitors and retired people'. Furthermore, it continued, 'today the town is as near united as makes no difference in deciding to remain the odd one out among Devon's larger resorts'.[137] In the 1960s, 1970s and 1980s Sidmouth continued to promote its traditional marketing messages. A small resort with a number of high-class hotels, it remained loyal to its wealthier clientele and continued to shun popular advertising methods.[138]

Throughout the post-war decades Sidmouth's official guides reflected and confirmed its image as a resort which resisted change. As in Ilfracombe (although with rather more success), the official brochure's front covers remained substantially unaltered and the message to prospective visitors focused on traditional attractions. In 1950 its compilers informed the reader that 'Sidmouth relies mainly upon its natural beauty, allied to good local government, for attracting and re-attracting its visitors'.[139] By the early 1970s the competition of foreign package holidays began to be reflected in images of sun, sand and family scenes in both the guide's text and illustrations. This was only a slight modification in Sidmouth's image, however, for the same publication emphasised that it was ideal for drives and walks in the Devon countryside and announced that its local authority and residents had retained its atmosphere of peace and quiet by

131

prohibiting 'wirelesses' in public places and enforcing the use of bathing tents. These measures were seen as maintaining the resort's character whilst ensuring that the visitor was 'not irksomely restricted'.[140]

Fashionability Eclipsed at Torquay

In contrast to this rather old-fashioned approach, the later 1950s, 1960s and 1970s witnessed much greater experimentation in Torquay's advertising initiatives as this resort sought to meet the challenges of greater competition and retain its premier status. In the later 1950s, although Torquay's activities were still hampered by national financial constraints, its resources dwarfed its Devon counterparts, as well as many other British resorts. Whilst Ilfracombe JAC's budget was limited to the product of a three penny rate (reduced to £1,250 in 1957 due to 'the general economics of the town'), during 1956–7 the Torquay publicity committee spent £4,000 on press advertising: £1,000 of this sum on out-of-season and 'prestige advertising'.[141] In 1957 the publicity committee discussed the production of a 20-minute colour travelogue of Torquay which alone cost over £3,500.[142]

In the early 1960s Torquay attempted to raise its advertising profile even further and began a concerted campaign, dispensing with the guide cover format which had served the resort throughout the 1950s: a photograph of the resort with prominent palm trees bearing the slogan 'Torquay: Queen of the English Riviera'. Instead the guide cover was a photograph of a young couple on a beach—images intended to rival the attractions of Mediterranean sun and sand destinations. This guide—quickly labelled the 'Bikini-Girl Guide'— proved highly controversial and was criticised as unsuitable for 'classy' Torquay and as unrecognisable as the resort.[143] Not all opinions were unfavourable, however, and the Hoteliers' Association approved of the cover, describing its detractors as 'a few old Grundies'.[144] This new guide heralded a vigorous campaign. In August 1960 a £15,000 advertising package was announced (a big increase on the 1959–60 budget of £10,000) and welcomed by the Association whose members spent over £40,000 on their own advertising and who virtually paid for the guide through their advertisements.[145] These

Figure 5.2: *The 1960 Torquay Guide Cover*
Torquay responds to the emergence of the package tour. This controversial guide cover marked a short-lived departure from Torquay's image of a smart palm-tree dominated resort. This photograph of a young couple under a beach umbrella, which was intended to market Torquay as a 'sand and sun' resort, met with opposition from those who considered it unsuitable for 'the Queen of the English Riviera'. (Reproduced by kind permission of the Torquay Library and the Torbay Tourist Board.)

efforts were disrupted in 1962, however, when British Rail announced that it would be the last year of joint advertising, folder production and poster display.[146] This move signalled an important though unwelcome shift in the make-up of advertising partnerships in British resorts. Resorts lost extremely valuable partners as in future they now had to provide their own posters for display at stations and pay the railway company full commercial rates.[147]

Despite such setbacks, Torquay's publicity services were those of a highly professional modern resort, boasting a huge budget—by the mid-1960s its press advertising alone cost almost £10,000.[148] Moreover, the resort's publicity operations were re-modelled in the wake of the creation of the new County Borough in 1968 and the new Torbay County Borough Council operated a resort services department in which the functions and resources of the previously separate resort publicity departments of Torquay, Paignton and Brixham were merged. This new department was responsible to a committee chaired by a former chairman of the Torquay publicity committee and prominent member of the Torquay Hoteliers' Association—a reflection of Torquay's dominance in Torbay and of the continuing influence of the holiday-interest in policy-making.[149]

This administrative change brought with it problems of both images and nomenclature. In 1968 the 'new' resort of Torbay produced a single guide but each of its three constituent 'old' resorts of Torquay, Paignton and Brixham had differing images, markets and needs.[150] Furthermore, the Torbay publicity committee was concerned that if the County Borough was marketed as Torbay—as it had been in a Sunday national press advertising scheme in 1966— it would have a weak image. The resort publicity officer advised that the old names were more effective, as the modern image-makers have proved.[151] Indeed, these are problems which have continued to dog resort marketing activities throughout the later twentieth century and local government reorganisation has often led to authorities being more concerned to market their municipal names rather than their resort products.[152]

The new Torbay Borough enjoyed a publicity budget of almost £20,000, making its resort services department the richest and most effective single agent of tourism promotion in Devon, notwith-

Figure 5.3: *The 1968 Torbay Guide Cover*
A colourful depiction of Torquay's harbour, pavilion and seafront gardens, this painting introduced the 1968 Torbay guide, the first produced by the publicity committee of the new Torbay County Borough. Incorporating the new 'Torbay' term together with the familiar palm tree in the foreground, the illustration conveys the resort's aspirations to rival the French Riviera and confirms the dominance of Torquay within the new Borough. (Reproduced by kind permission of the Torquay Library and the Torbay Tourist Board.)

standing the creation of the West Country Tourist Board under the 1969 Development of Tourism Act. Together with the efforts of its numerous large hotels, this department endowed Torbay with an impressive financial and technical resource base. In 1970 Budleigh, Ilfracombe, Sidmouth, Teignmouth and Torbay of the Devon resorts boasted municipal information bureaux, but the numbers of guides distributed by these resorts vastly differed, reflecting both the scale of their tourism industries and their ambitions: Torquay produced almost 70,000, whilst Ilfracombe produced 45,000 and Sidmouth only 16,000.[153]

New Markets—New Strategies?

As we saw in Chapter 3, British seaside resorts have experienced fluctuating fortunes in the 1980s and 1990s (as has the British tourist industry as a whole) and the slight recovery which has occurred has largely been due to improved standards of service, customer care and advertising. British tourist resorts did much to re-align their marketing strategies in the later 1980s and early to mid-1990s, and in Devon the marketing strategies of Ilfracombe, Sidmouth and Torbay offer contrasting approaches. The promotional literature of Ilfracombe has clearly been updated, but at the beginning of the 1990s the resort was still marketed in a very traditional fashion, its brochures being similar to the guides of the 1950s, 1960s and 1970s. This was also the case in the publications produced by Sidmouth, but here, however, the guides consciously seek to exploit popular images of nostalgia and a more traditional style of holiday resort, whereas in Ilfracombe it was (and is) more the result of stagnation and a lack of dynamism.

In contrast, Torbay attempted to reposition its image in the 1980s and achieve a 'popular fashionability' in response to a downward slide in its resort fortunes and tone. A 1982 report by the English Tourist Board signalled the beginning of a new Torbay Tourist Board (TTB) advertising initiative which was spearheaded by eye-catching guide covers and poster designs.[154] Printed on high-quality paper, these guides were of a new, larger format and incorporated a controversial new palm logo and the TTB's corporate colours of blue, jade, yellow and white. All the brochure designs market Torbay as a highly stylised image not as a location—very different from those of resorts such as Ilfracombe and Sidmouth which feature photographs of the resort (often the same photograph year after year). By producing a different cover each year, Torbay ensured that its guide stood out from other such publications. Moreover, by embracing a highly branded identity, Torbay was attempting to sell a concept rather than a product—an emotional rather than a resort attribute.[155]

Produced within the resort, these brochures of the 1980s and 1990s have achieved a considerable impact and their designs have won national acclaim—that of 1988 scooping the Creative Circle Honours Award for the best travel advertisement. Costing £100,000, the design was launched at the World Travel Market in winter 1987 and appeared on 200,000 English Riviera brochures. Although its depiction of seaside huts was criticised in Torbay itself as too old-fashioned (the hoteliers commenting that it conjured up images of a quaint and antiquated seaside which the resort sought to escape), the poster was highly successful according to TTB research and certainly capitalised on burgeoning trends in the holiday market such as the nostalgia trend.[156]

The 1985 Torbay design is a good example of the resort's new image. The brochure cover depicts a waiter serving drinks to a young woman in a swimming pool. White-jacketed and bearing aloft his tray of cold drinks at the pool-side, the waiter indicates a high standard of service. His dress means style, evocative of popular conceptions of inter-war elegance, an image reinforced by the art-deco style of the title's lettering of 'The English Riviera'. Yet at the same time the design also incorporates images associated with a very contemporary holiday since the swimming pool and the deeply suntanned, bikini-clad woman convey images of sunshine more reminiscent of Mediterranean holiday-making. Thus this design—typical of contemporary Torbay publicity material—cleverly mixes traditional and modern images, creating an impression of a very modern resort capable of providing old-fashioned service and elegance, a sophisticated and successful blend.

This appeal to nostalgia in the 1980s and 1990s was not peculiar to Torbay and Sidmouth. In the early 1980s a Brighton poster campaign depicting a 1920s couple in a Brighton-bound car

Figure 5.4: *The 1988 Torbay Guide Cover*
Traditional British seaside architecture in a modern marketing message. The Torbay guide design of a palm tree shadow falling across a row of beach huts won national acclaim as the best travel advertisement of 1988. Heavily criticised in the resort for presenting an old-fashioned image, it clearly appealed to the revival of the nostalgia dimension in the British tourist market. (Reproduced by kind permission of the Torbay Tourist Board.)

Figure 5.5: *The 1985 Torbay Guide Cover*
Repositioning the Torbay tourism product. The 1985 guide cover indicates the branding and packaging of the resort of Torbay initiated in the marketing strategy of the early 1980s. (Reproduced by kind permission of the Torquay Library and the Torbay Tourist Board.)

proclaimed 'We've cleaned up the dirty weekend', and at the end of the 1990s pier refurbishments in the resorts of Eastbourne and Clacton echo Edwardian themes.[157] Some time ago Yates concluded, 'the elements of the new resort publicity of the 1970s and 1980s recreated in a new guise many of the themes of the 1920s and 1930s: the claim of good value or greater investment, the images of glamour or modernity—sometimes even the appeal to nostalgia'.[158] In the 1990s this seems even more applicable and the nostalgia angle has been successfully pursued in Torbay since the beginning of the decade when the TTB promoted Torbay via its 'Mystery on the English Riviera' campaign—an international festival of mystery and suspense marking the centenary of Agatha Christie's birth in Torquay. This marketing promotion was so successful that it became established as an annual event and won the overall prize at the 1989 British Tourism Authority UK Tourism Marketing Awards. The triumph of Torbay's marketing strategies has been widely acclaimed by the industry and in 1990 an Association of British Travel Agents spokesperson commented that whilst 'many resorts are still stuck with a kiss-me-quick image … the English Riviera is a good example of what solid investment and skilful marketing can do'.[159]

Whatever the future for its advertising operations, Torbay has successfully implemented a new promotional strategy by clearly defining its audience, its message and the channels of communication. Having developed its marketing position or 'branding', the resort promotes its message in all communications, and the palm logo has become an integral part of the resort package, appearing on all literature and incorporated in the designs of the new Fleet Walk retail and leisure complex—which we will discuss in Chapter 6.

Despite the changes in resort promotion since 1900, the most striking conclusion which emerges from the analysis of this chapter must surely be the essential continuity in this area. At the end of the twentieth century it is difficult to identify any major areas of advertising activity or techniques which were not in use at its beginning. Technical innovation has obviously facilitated development: for instance, the World Wide Web has become a powerful new advertising medium and resorts (including Torbay) are becoming an increasingly significant presence on the Internet.[160] The basic organisation of British resorts' marketing departments remains largely unchanged, however, and they still concentrate the bulk of their efforts on brochure production, press and poster advertising and public relations activities. Moreover, the fundamental attractions of the domestic holiday remain constant: the lure of sun and sea are still powerful in the British context despite the impact of continental travel and therefore the underlying message of the publicity material is not dissimilar to that of the 1920s, 1930s and 1950s.

Clearly, the resorts of Torquay, Ilfracombe and Sidmouth have all pursued quite different objectives whilst operating within the same broad marketing framework. Sidmouth emerges as a resort which deliberately remained traditional in outlook, and was largely successful in retaining an exclusive social tone, whilst Ilfracombe and Torquay sought to project a more popular image to potential holiday-makers. The resorts all experimented in advertising policies, but continuity, conservatism and tradition were the watch-words of many of Devon's advertising policy-makers. Within this traditional approach, however, Torquay's publicity became very sophisticated and the recent Torbay programmes demonstrate how far the promotion of Torquay has developed since the establishment of its JAC in 1906. Over the years the promotion of Torquay has evolved from an amateur and piecemeal approach into an impressive organisation administered by professional council officers utilising modern advertising methods. Much of this transformation occurred at a relatively early stage, however, for although the publicity changed in scale and in form, its continuity is clearly discernible. This is even more applicable to Sidmouth, described in its 1988 guide as 'a quiet, dignified town which has retained much of its old-fashioned charm'—a description which would certainly have pleased those responsible for its publicity direction in earlier years.[161] As we will see in the provision of tourism facilities in Chapter 6, such continuity is not unique to resort promotion and indeed is observable in many spheres of resort policies.

6

Planning Resort Entertainment

Hitherto, … Torquay has been one of the finest resorts in the country—without Sunday games. Today we have to make up our minds if we are to continue as a snobbish seaside resort which I and many other people prefer. If Blackpool sells tripe there is no reason why we should. We have been a select resort for years; I hope members see we remain so, and will keep our Sunday respectable.

Councillor Ely, Torquay Alderman, 1949[1]

In Chapter 5 we demonstrated how the evolution of resort advertising and the promotional policies of seaside resorts have articulated social tone throughout this century. By focusing on case studies drawn from Devon, it provided an insight into the processes by which resorts targeted their markets, and revealed internal disputes over the social tone to which they aspired. Equally crucial in the development of Britain's seaside resorts in the twentieth century was the public-sector provision of entertainments and facilities to attract tourists. This subject, like advertising, is equally intertwined with social tone, since certain types of entertainments and sports were seen to attract certain tourists, either high spending, up-market visitors or less affluent down-market tourists whose patronage would lower resort social tone. As such, resort amusements and the provision of public-sector sports and entertainment facilities also demonstrate the different policies adopted by resorts and throw light on the divisions which characterised seaside communities. As Huggins has said of organised sports at the seaside, such topics provide 'another focus for conflict between classes and lifestyles, since wealthy and status-conscious visitors and residents often wanted very different sorts of sport than did plebeian locals and excursionists'.[2]

Throughout the twentieth century, and especially since the inter-war period, British resorts have implemented a range of policies in their provision of tourism facilities and entertainments. Some resorts, such as Blackpool, Barry Island, Clacton, Rhyl (and to a lesser extent Ilfracombe in Devon), elected to attract the popular mass market, whilst others—notably Torquay, Brighton and Bournemouth, attempted to secure a kind of popular fashionability. Still others chose to pursue exclusivity—the Devon resorts of Sidmouth and Budleigh Salterton being prominent examples. This chapter discusses the internal mechanisms which underpinned the implementation of entertainment policies in these different types of resorts. It examines the development of the local authority entertainment committees which dictated these policies and prevented those amusements deemed as 'undesirable' and explores the debates surrounding the nature of the attractions which were so influential in the maintenance of resort social tone. In doing so, it highlights the critical involvement of local authorities in resort infrastructural development in a century largely characterised by central government disinterest in tourism.

As we outlined in Chapter 3, before the 1960s the public-sector attitude towards tourism was characterised in Britain by a *laissez-faire* approach in which policies 'focused on specific markets or sites'.[3] Prior to the 1969 Development of Tourism Act central government showed little interest in the sector and grants for tourism projects were excluded from regional development policy during 1934–65. There was, as we have seen, however, a much greater involvement at the local level, although resort development was initially motivated by the commercial self-interest of entrepreneurs. Municipal activity increased substantially after the reform of local government between 1884 and 1894 and councils began to assume responsibility for infra-structural improvements, attractions and promotion.[4] In the twentieth century seaside resort development in Britain has been a partnership between the public and private sectors. The former invested in the creation and enhancement of the public tourism infra-structure (building promenades, piers, gardens and concert halls), whilst the private sector developed areas such as accommodation and entertainment which augmented the income of the resorts and in turn increased property tax receipts for the local authority.[5]

This public-sector development of the tourism infrastructure was by no means universally welcomed in the resorts and this chapter illustrates how the provision of facilities designed for resort entertainment more often than not provoked intense conflict in seaside communities. As we have already established, most seaside resorts have long had significant retired populations on fixed incomes which often opposed rate-subsidised tourism development. Ranged against this interest group were those in the holiday industry whose livelihoods depended on the attraction of tourists. As well as demanding effective marketing and resort promotion, this trade lobby also argued that visitor numbers depended upon the provision of piers, spacious promenades, elaborate gardens and entertainment halls—facilities which were usually beyond the means of the private sector. The high cost of providing an extensive range of facilities and entertainments was clearly a drain on local authority resources and the fact that many seaside councils expended huge sums on such attractions demonstrates their commitment to the tourist industry. Yet such commitment was rarely automatic and the expenditure was often approved after considerable deliberation in resort communities.

Focusing principally on Torquay and Ilfracombe, this chapter will therefore examine, not the total development of public- and private-sector resort facilities in this century, but the building, promotion and management of local authority facilities. In taking this approach it demonstrates that certain resorts were advantaged in the provision of essential tourism facilities by their size and relative wealth. Other smaller resorts which drew their clientele from less prosperous markets were disadvantaged, despite often spending a higher proportion of their income on tourist attractions, and experienced significant degradations in their resort environments quite early in the twentieth century.

Resort Entertainment Policies

In the twentieth century the overwhelming majority of Devon's

144

public- and private-sector entertainment facilities have been concentrated in its resort areas where local authorities were more likely to build and operate winter gardens, theatres, swimming pools and dance halls, many of these amenities being heavily subsidised as tourist attractions.[6] All the seaside local authorities recognised the potential of their role in this area of resort development, but some adopted a highly pro-active approach, providing entertainments and facilities, whilst others declined to become involved in such direct provision, intervening only to control 'undesirable' amusements which would lower resort social tone. Although the type of their entertainments varied, the active councils included Torquay, Ilfracombe, Exmouth and Paignton—resorts which targeted a cross-section of tourists and drew many from the 'popular' market. Those Devon resorts which largely declined to organise municipal entertainments included Budleigh Salterton, Lynton and Lynmouth and, above all, Sidmouth—all resorts which were committed to maintaining an exclusive and 'quiet' resort atmosphere.

The Organisation of Entertainment

The achievements of those British resorts which sought to attract a popular market in the first half of the century were largely attributable to a solid organisational framework founded upon the work of entertainments committees and, in some cases, professional entertainments officers. In Devon, Torquay, Ilfracombe and Exmouth all employed professional staff to promote entertainments. The importance attached to the provision of public-sector entertainment by the different resorts was also reflected in the organisation of their committees and the contrast between those of Torquay, Ilfracombe and Sidmouth epitomises the different policies adopted by the three councils. As early as 1911 Torquay Council created a new standing entertainment committee 'to organise and manage all entertainments promoted by the Council'. The new committee resolved that:

> the working, letting, management, and maintenance of the Pavilion, Princess Gardens, Pier and Concert Hall, as well as the engagement of bands, musicians, and vocalists, and all other

matters appertaining thereto as shall, in the committee's opinion, be the means of popularising and encouraging the use of Pavilion, Pier, and Gardens be vested in this committee.[7]

In contrast, the provision of entertainment played a minimal part in the business of Sidmouth Council, and its entertainments committee (in much the same way as its advertising equivalent) had a much lower profile, meeting much less frequently than its counterparts in Torquay and Ilfracombe. Not until 1947 was it given responsibility 'To co-ordinate programmes throughout the year' and provide tourist attractions on a small budget.[8] In this post-war decade Sidmouth did invest more resources in its entertainments, and throughout the mid- and late 1940s a musical band in the town's main pleasure grounds was heavily subsidised.[9] In the 1950s the resort adopted even more 'progressive' policies, although it was careful to maintain the quality of the attractions. During the 1950s the entertainments committee provided autumn and winter 'high class concerts' and towards the end of that decade a highly successful repertory company was engaged for the town's Manor Pavilion, itself re-modelled at a cost of £4,375 in 1957.[10] At all times, however, Sidmouth Council was conscious of the need to maintain a high degree of exclusivity in the nature of the entertainments it provided.

Entertainments and Social Tone

As we saw in Chapter 5, it was after the First World War that the resorts of Devon cemented their images, both popular and fashionable. Just as critical to the development of resort social tone as advertising, however, were the entertainment policies adopted by resorts during the inter-war period. Indeed, by the end of the Second World War Devon's resorts had become much more individual in character and tone so that the primary markets of each were clearly discernible—a process clearly illustrated by the development of Torquay and Ilfracombe. Prior to the First World War both resorts were fashionable and offered similar numbers and types of entertainment. In the depression of the 1920s and 1930s, however, the north coast resort lost ground to its southern rival. This is apparent in the numbers of private- and public-sector entertainment facilities in each town, for whilst those of Torquay almost trebled during 1919–39, the number of attractions available to Ilfracombe's visitors narrowed after the war and stagnated in the following two decades (Table 6.1).

Table 6.1: Entertainment Facilities in Torquay and Ilfracombe, 1910–1939

	1910	1919	1930	1939
Torquay	5	8	10	13
Ilfracombe	5	3	3	4

Source: Kelly's Directories of Devonshire, 1910–39.

The entertainments available in the resorts of Devon did not merely differ in number, more crucially, they also differed in kind. Before the war, for instance, Exmouth, one of the more popular resorts, offered attractions including roundabouts, a bowling green and tennis courts. In the 1920s and 1930s, however, its entertainments (many of them provided by Exmouth Council) expanded in both quantity and range to include a seasonal musical band, bathing pools, bowling greens, tennis courts, mini-golf and indoor entertainments at the town's pavilion. On the foreshore the local authority also provided many beach entertainments and in the early 1920s it expanded its operations, purchasing £2,000 of beach equipment.[11] This enabled it to let sites for amusements including refreshment tents, deck chairs, mini-golf, ice-cream vendors, donkey and pony rides, sand artists, photographers, Punch and Judy entertainers, roundabouts and fishponds.[12]

These entertainments—designed to appeal to working-class day-trippers—proved very successful for Exmouth and during the mid-1930s annual crowds of 20,000 flocked to its municipal orchestra and concert party performances, which proved highly lucrative for the authority. In 1936 the council's foreshore and pleasure grounds committee announced that: 'As an indication of the growth of the Council's activities the Committee desire to report that their receipts from these sources constitute a record'.[13] Exmouth's policy in this area was similar to that of Weston-super-Mare—one of the most 'popular' resorts in the South West of Britain—where entertainments in the 1920s included donkey rides, beach stalls, pier entertainments, concerts, dancing at the Assembly Rooms and steamer trips on the Bristol Channel.[14] Entertainments of this type were frowned upon at most Devon resorts, particularly those attempting to attract middle- rather than working-class tourists. Thus, whilst Exmouth allowed palm-readers on its seafront in the mid-1930s, Ilfracombe repeatedly refused requests from operators wishing to provide such entertain- ment throughout the inter-war years.[15]

This is not to suggest that Ilfracombe pursued a staid or unimag- inative entertainments policy, indeed it was the most active resort local authority in Devon in the inter-war years. 'The Municipality ... [did] everything in its power to organise entertainments and to encourage others to organise them privately.'[16] It provided a pavilion, concerts, bands, theatres, tennis, bowling and putting greens, swimming pools, operated two bathing beaches and let numerous sites for a variety of seafront amusements. The town's most ambitious inter-war project, the laying-out of the Victoria Pleasure Grounds and the building of a new concert hall during 1922–8, was also a council initiative.[17] Such investment underlined Ilfracombe's commit- ment to foster a lucrative tourist trade, as one commentator wrote: 'Ilfracombe is quite clearly out to get the type of tourist which Sidmouth and Torquay desire to keep at arm's length. It aims at being a popular tourist resort and wishes to draw the maximum possible numbers.'[18] This was an approach which earned Ilfracombe the disap- proval of its more 'select' rivals and a survey of the county's tourism industry in the mid-1940s noted that 'It is generally supposed in Devon that Ilfracombe has "debased itself"'.[19]

In complete contrast, Sidmouth, together with resorts such as Lynton and Lynmouth and Budleigh Salterton, disdained such direct municipal provision and preferred to rely on natural attractions. Budleigh Salterton Council refused to organise any entertainments and in 1921 *The Times* wrote of Lynton and Lynmouth: 'Although [they] ... cannot boast the musical attractions of the neighbouring town of Ilfracombe, ... the "twin villages" have charms peculiarly their own'.[20] It is Sidmouth, however, which was the classic Devon example of a resort which provided few organised amusements and tightly controlled private operators to ensure the maintenance of a high social tone. In 1945 the Nuffield tourism survey commented: 'The facts about Sidmouth are amazing. It is deliberately the mecca of the "right people".'[21] From the 1920s to the 1950s it offered only bowls, tennis, croquet, and putting greens, and depended 'mainly upon its natural beauty ... for attracting and re-attracting its visitors'.[22] This proved to be a remarkably successful policy, for by discouraging day-trippers and weekend visitors the resort attracted 75,000 annual domestic residential visitors in the mid-1950s, virtually all of them from the luxury end of the market.[23]

In the inter-war years and in the decades immediately after the Second World War Torquay adopted a *via media* between the approaches typified by Sidmouth and Ilfracombe, although Sidmouth considered that this abandonment of a thoroughly select policy reduced Torquay to the status of a 'fallen sister'.[24] As the Nuffield survey compiler concluded: 'Torquay cannot really be said to have a distinct type of clientele, but it is not a "popular resort"'. In fact, whilst it 'is in many ways similar to Sidmouth', Torquay 'aims at exclusivity but is more active in its policy ... it has a pier and pavilion with concert parties, straight theatre and amenities'.[25] In the late 1940s its facilities, which included an art gallery, museum, theatres, cinemas, concert parties, ballrooms, open-air concerts, a Marine Spa and a municipal orchestra, made Torquay the most impressive of all Devon's resorts, and one of the leading ones in Britain.[26]

The Policing of Suitable Entertainment

British resort authorities were not only the providers of entertainment, they were also effective at policing it, intervening to restrict, license or prohibit those activities, such as mixed-sex bathing (in the earlier decades of the century) or street trading and entertainment, deemed 'undesirable'. As in the nineteenth century, twentieth-century resort social tone continued to be maintained by the enforcement of by-laws which dictated the conduct of traders and hawkers, prevented hoteliers, boarding house keepers and charabanc organisers from touting for business, and controlled tourists' behaviour in public places, especially on the promenades, pleasure grounds and beaches.[27] The extent and nature of such municipal regulation and control frequently signalled the depth of a resort's commitment to maintaining the integrity of its social tone. For instance, Laura Chase has shown how in the 'select' resort of Frinton (on the south-east coast of England) the local council discouraged activities and services such as picnicking, public entertainment, beach vendors, coach parties and pubs. By a process of economic and social sanction such resort authorities were able to enhance exclusive images. As Chase comments, such sanction 'was not a matter of explicit legal prohibition, but a more complicated set of economic, social and licensing constraints'.[28]

The control of public bathing before the Second World War provides a valuable illustration of the policing of leisure and entertainment in Britain's seaside resorts. Before the First World War it was strictly regulated with the sexes segregated by both spatial and temporal zoning. In Torquay, for instance, there were five beaches for men and four for women; and bathing machine proprietors such as those in Exmouth were fined for breaches of the segregation by-laws.[29] Such controls were being increasingly challenged by bathing practices on the continent, however, and in 1896 Paignton became the first resort in the South West to permit 'continental' or mixed bathing,[30] a move which Torquay quickly followed in 1900. Such was the shift in resort attitudes that in 1912 the *Torquay Times* commented:

> It is clear that mixed bathing with all its delights will be more popular than ever, and whilst there have been one or two instances in which public authorities have endeavoured to put a stop to sea front promenading in bathing costumes, it seems that there is a tendency to follow the freedom which prevails at the American and continental resorts.[31]

Despite this apparent relaxation in opinions, bathing continued to be strictly controlled in many resorts. Regulation Oxford dress swimming costumes were still obligatory bathing attire before the First World War in Torquay and in the 1920s mixed bathing was regulated at the town's Torre Abbey Sands; bathing tents and machines were in use at Teignmouth, Sidmouth and Exmouth; and family bathing was only allowed up to 8 o'clock in the morning in some resorts.[32] These by-laws were enforced at the larger Devon resorts by council staff, such as the bathing and boating inspectors employed by Exmouth from the mid-1920s. These employees policed the beach and seafront, prevented Sunday bathing, and collected charges for the use of private tents and the rent of municipal beach tents. Undressing on the beach remained an offence at many resorts in the inter-war years and although bathing machines were still in use at some in the mid-1920s, most resorts used council-rented tents— a lucrative source of income.[33] In this sense, the enforcement of social tone served a dual purpose of regulating public behaviour whilst providing the revenue to finance the provision of tourist facilities. Indeed, in the later 1930s many British resorts complained that the increasing practice of changing on the beaches behind towels was depriving resort authorities of much-needed income.[34]

In Sidmouth, changing on the beach was prohibited altogether and the use of bathing tents and huts was obligatory until after the Second World War. This, together with the control of the beach traders, ensured the high tone of the resort. As the *Western Morning News* commented in 1956: 'That elusive quality, "tone", is given to the seaward side of the town, by the absence of ice-cream salesmen, photographers, and whelkstands on the front'.[35] This regulation of traders was common to all resorts, and, of course, remains an important role of local government today in Britain. In the 1920s and 1930s even the 'popular' Exmouth limited stalls and carts to the south-western side of the promenade and the eastern part of the Esplanade and fined offenders.[36] Similar by-laws operated in Ilfracombe and Torquay and were vigorously enforced by special constables until after the Second World War.[37] It was Sidmouth's *total* prohibition of such traders until well into the 1960s which was rather unusual and typical of its attempt to maintain an exclusive resort atmosphere.

Social tone was not only achieved by the policing of leisure behaviour and private-sector traders, it was also secured through the regulation of public-sector entertainment. Many resorts prohibited musical concerts and games on Sundays, an issue which remained

151

contentious in some Devon resorts until as late as the 1950s and early 1960s, a fact which is quite remarkable given that these decades witnessed massive cultural changes in the values and norms which characterised social behaviour. Although some resorts had unsuccessfully attempted to introduce Sunday concerts before the First World War—as in Ilfracombe in 1914—it was during the early interwar years that they became popular.[38] In the summer of 1919 Ilfracombe introduced controversial Sunday concerts on the pier, the council's band committee defying organised local clerical opposition to provide 'vocal and instrumental concerts on Sundays on the pier or such other place as they may from time to time decide, such concerts to be arranged so as not to commence in the evening before 8.15 and in the afternoon before 3.15 p.m.'.[39]

These concerts proved tremendously popular, as did the Torquay Corporation Sunday afternoon Pavilion concerts which regularly attracted crowds of over 1,000 that same autumn. Similarly, whilst Church opposition prevented afternoon concerts at Paignton, the resort's hour-long Sunday evening performances proved very successful.[40] Even in these relatively progressive resorts, however, many activities remained prohibited on the Sabbath and during the early 1920s there was concern that those domestic resorts, especially on the south coast, which 'sternly discountenanced' Sunday entertainment were contributing to the threat foreign competition increasingly posed to the British resort product. Indeed, *The Times* advised in 1923 that holiday-makers might be drawn to resorts in Europe which offered more attractions all weekend, saying: 'The more cheerful continental Sunday is such a very little way away that many visitors may ... alter their plans on this account'.[41]

Despite this, many British resorts were slow to change their policies: for instance, Exmouth did not consider offering Sunday concerts until 1926.[42] Indeed, during the 1920s and 1930s the debate over Sunday entertainments intensified and centred around the prohibition of Sunday games and sports on municipal pleasure grounds. Whilst concerts were largely acceptable, more active pursuits, especially those which attracted large working-class crowds, were discouraged. During the late 1920s and early 1930s Exmouth, for instance, prohibited Sunday entertainments at the resort's pier.[43]

152

Some resorts, like Paignton, allowed games including bowls and tennis on their seafronts and in their parks, but many more prohibited activity in certain places and at certain times. Others enforced blanket-bans on even these 'middle-class', relatively sedate, games which could pose no conceivable threat to public order or to a select atmosphere.

Torquay Council prohibited Sunday games at all the facilities it owned or operated throughout the inter-war years. Despite severe criticism of the policy by the railway companies, the local Hoteliers' Association and the Chamber of Commerce, six separate attempts to open the municipal tennis courts and bowling and putting greens on Sundays were defeated during 1927–39.[44] The issue aroused strong feelings within the town and when the *Torquay Times* attacked the inconsistency of a policy which allowed tourists to hire deck chairs but prevented them from playing on a putting green or bowling rink, supporters of the policy dismissed such comments as moves to 'Blackpoolise Torquay'. On the council itself the issue became a class debate, and one defender of the *status quo* argued that: 'The Blackpool game of rowdyism is not popular here with our visitors. They come here for a quiet peaceful holiday…. It would be better to keep that class of visitor who would sustain the tone of Torquay.'[45]

It was the social and cultural upheaval caused by the Second World War which provided a breakthrough for Sunday entertainments in Devon's resorts. Entertainments had been introduced on Sundays in many resorts to relieve the tedium of the war for both soldiers and civilians, and in peacetime this policy proved difficult to reverse.[46] A poll of residents revealed a two to one majority in favour of the continuance of Sunday cinema and entertainments at Exmouth in 1946, and in the following year Teignmouth Council (which already allowed the Sunday use of its tennis courts and putting greens) extended this concession to the bowling greens.[47] Ilfracombe Council, supported by a majority of the ratepayers, continued the wartime Sunday cinemas and in 1948 controversially decided by four votes to allow Sunday games—a policy successfully defended the following year.[48] In many resorts the initiative to introduce such policies came from Chambers of Commerce which were worried about the loss of tourism trade. In Dawlish, for instance, the Chamber lobbied the council to allow Sunday putting, tennis, bowls and cricket in the early 1950s.[49]

In Torquay, however, despite the efforts of its Chamber of Commerce and other tourism pressure groups, the advance towards Sunday games was much more protracted. In 1947 the council terminated the wartime Sunday opening of the bowling and putting greens and rejected its reintroduction by 17 votes to 15 in 1948. This refusal to 'slavishly emulate other resorts' was heavily criticised by the hoteliers, particularly those from smaller establishments—a point which reveals that Torquay's entertainments policy differentially restricted and constrained the behaviour of tourists. Up-market, affluent visitors to the larger, more luxurious hotels had access to various entertainments, including dances and hotel amenities, denied to those less advantaged visitors. For the latter, virtually the only attractions which were available on a Sunday were the resort's beaches and musical concerts at the town's Pavilion.[50] Despite the fact that this issue achieved a high profile in the late 1940s, becoming a local election issue in May 1949, the council remained resolute in its opposition to any relaxation in its approach, rejecting four attempts to overturn the policy between November 1948 and July 1949.[51]

The issue was finally resolved in the mid-1950s and the pressures which eventually led to its resolution provide an interesting commentary on the power relations which underpinned the regulation of leisure behaviour. In 1955 Torquay's Trades Council and other groups pressed the council to open all forms of Sunday games after 2 p.m. On this occasion, Church opposition and a petition of (largely retired) ratepayers combined with council hard-liners to defeat the proposal by 18 votes to 11, but in 1957 this alliance was finally defeated.[52] The policy change was precipitated by the council's purchase of private members' tennis facilities—their subsequent closure on Sundays once in council ownership caused an outcry amongst members of a relatively privileged group who now found their recreational behaviour curtailed. This development provided a significant boost to those campaigning for change and subsequently a private referendum was commissioned which revealed overwhelming support for the lifting of Sunday restrictions.[53] The authority ended the ban on Sunday afternoon games in Torquay in

154

1957, although the controversy over Sunday entertainment was only finally buried in 1967 when the new Torbay County Borough brought Brixham (whose previous council had not allowed Sunday games even at this late date) into line with Torquay and Paignton.[54]

The Provision of Municipal Tourism Facilities

It is clear from the above discussions that the restriction of certain entertainments have long been seen as an effective tool in the creation of 'desirable' atmospheres in those resorts seeking to attract the more up-market tourist. Yet all resorts, whatever their market, endeavoured to improve the physical tourism environment by creating open spaces, pleasure grounds, promenades and piers, whilst many also provided ambitious beach facilities, pavilions, bandstands and theatres. As Chapter 3 outlined, resorts around Britain were highly active in acquiring and laying out large areas of parkland and pleasure gardens throughout the twentieth century, particularly during the inter-war period. The tourism boom which followed the First World War prompted many resorts to improve their amenities and purchase lands and parts of beach foreshores in order to provide 'for organised sports or games suitable to a first-class residential seaside town or for such other purpose as may conduce to the amenities of [their] district'.[55] Such policies were almost universally adopted and even 'select' and conservative resorts such as Sidmouth followed similar policies in the creation of open spaces, since this was in line with their perceived social tone.[56]

In many resorts councils purchased foreshores with the intention of increasing revenue through the renting of deck chairs, tents and pitches for traders and the provision of beach entertainment.[57] Before the Second World War such policies were successful as beach under-takings were generally profitable and many councils ran the facilities directly from their own departments. In the post-war decades, however, although beach undertakings remained a focus for municipal seaside investment, they became an increasing drain on resources. Between 1961 and 1963, for instance, Torquay alone invested almost £110,000 in upgrading its beaches.[58] Many beach facilities continued to be run directly by the local authorities, although some were leased to private operators. By the early 1970s, however, whilst beach huts and cafés were still profitable, deck chairs and the ageing piers became increasing liabilities. Overall, beach operating costs escalated so that many resorts found the expense crippling. Thus, of the major Devon resorts, only Dawlish, Exmouth, Teignmouth and Torquay were actually making a profit on their beach operations in the early 1970s.[59]

The differential operating costs of tourist facilities were exacerbated by the different resources available to resorts. In 1970 Torquay was capable of raising rates of 264 shillings per head of population compared with 181 in Ilfracombe, whilst the operating profits of tourism facilities were also often greater in the south of the county. Thus, whilst the running costs of Ilfracombe Harbour were £10,419, resulting in a loss of over £1,000, in Torquay costs were similar (£9,540) but profits were significantly greater (£5,365). Similarly, just as in its advertising activities, Ilfracombe was spending a higher proportion of its resources on its tourism facilities than Torquay in the late 1960s. It could never, however, match the economic power of its southern rival.[60] The financial resources and the relative sizes of the resorts' tourism industries meant that whereas Torquay and Ilfracombe had the same number of entertainment facilities at the beginning of the twentieth century, by the early 1970s the latter had been eclipsed. By this date the vast majority of Devon's amusement facilities (amusement arcades, bowling alleys, night clubs, and cinemas) were located in the resorts and centres of the south coast, particularly in the Plymouth and Torbay areas.[61] The resorts of Devon, in much the same way as others across Britain, were thus undergoing a process of concentration with facility investment in some and facility downsizing and closure in others: bigger and more prosperous resorts were on the whole better placed to meet the late-twentieth-century challenges of product improvement and facility enhancement.

Even in the larger resorts the cost of providing and maintaining these amenities was high and during the 1960s and 1970s the quality of both public- and private-sector resort facilities generally declined in Britain. As we saw in Chapter 3, whilst in the early 1970s there was considerable investment in amusements in the larger resorts (especially in the public sector in conjunction with local government reorganisation), in the smaller ones units were not large enough to cover the capital costs.[62] Indeed, the rising capital costs of tourism facilities forced both the private and public sectors to maximise their returns throughout Britain, although many municipal amenities continued to be heavily subsidised to provide attractions for tourists, especially in the 1970s when the seaside theatres' traditional summer shows declined in the face of falling audiences and rising overheads.[63]

Piers—Sites of Entertainment and Conflict

Although the cost of tourism facilities became increasingly burdensome in the 1970s, 1980s, and 1990s, local authorities were involved in heavy municipal investment throughout the century and, as we have seen, this often provided the focus of fierce debates in seaside resort communities. Proposals to build and enhance piers provide an interesting case in point. Popular particularly during 1860–1900, by the turn of the century piers had become characteristic of the British seaside and a prominent feature of most resort seafronts, although after 1939 many increasingly acquired an air of neglect.[64] Piers provided focal points for visitors and were frequently the sites of resorts' amusements. Yet, just as they provided sites for entertainment, so too (as expensive and prestigious amenities) they provided the focus for much struggle and conflict in resort communities—as the struggle over Torquay's Princess Pier illustrates.

Whilst Torquay's pier and surrounding gardens provided an ideal site for a theatre, its proposed development provoked heated controversy. The struggle centred around whether the pier was primarily intended for entertainment purposes or simply to shelter the harbour. In many ways the debate surrounding the purpose and proposed utilisation of piers foreshadowed the debates which were to emerge towards the end of the century over marina developments. These were often mooted to boost ailing resort infrastructures—a subject we shall return to later in this chapter. After much debate, the entertainment ethos triumphed in Torquay and by the late 1890s the pier was hosting open-air concerts and a canvas awning was erected for summer concerts. Despite the success of this venture, the resources available for such entertainment continued to be hotly disputed and when existing facilities became inadequate at the turn of the century the council's proposals for a purpose-built concert hall were fiercely debated. After the rejection of a £15,000 pier head bandstand plan by a ratepayers poll, the council was forced to construct a more modest £1,500 structure in 1901.[65]

As well as providing the focus for division, when they were of crucial significance to the local prosperity of a resort, piers could conversely be the focus of unified action. Thus, the attempts to reconstruct Ilfracombe pier in the aftermath of the Second World War demonstrated how resorts could unite behind the tourism lobby. By the mid-1940s this pier urgently needed reconstruction since financial constraints had prevented a major renovation in the late 1930s and the outbreak of war had precluded anything more than cosmetic repairs. By 1945 years of neglect (compounded by partial dismantling as an anti-invasion precaution during 1939–40) meant that the structure required immediate attention if passenger steamers were to continue landing there.[66] Between 1946 and 1948 the Ilfracombe Council pursued every avenue of enquiry, in the face of much resistance from the Ministry of Transport, to gain sanction to borrow £45,000 from the Public Works Loan Board for repairs. This proposed loan became increasingly critical as the resort recognised that: 'The visitors which these steamers bring with them are an important item in the prosperity of the town and unless adequate and safe berthing can be provided for these vessels, the traffic will deteriorate'.[67] Despite the urgency of the situation, the Ministry of Transport remained unmoved and recommended a 'policy of mend and make do'.[68] Negotiations continued during 1948, however, and in December the Ministry approved a £41,000 repair project, the pier eventually being re-opened in 1952.[69]

Pavilions—Building and Management Disputes

Whilst the investment in Ilfracombe's pier illustrates how a resort community could be united in the promotion of its tourist industry, when we examine the building and subsequent management of Torquay's Pavilion, we are presented with 'a classical example of the acute and permanent division of the opinion between the mass of the residents on the one hand and the traders and hotel and boarding house keepers on the other'.[70] Throughout its history the Torquay Pavilion, as the most prestigious municipal entertainment facility in the town, was often the focus for debates over the resort's tourism industry and the town council's policies that shaped its development. These debates also trace and echo the resort's fortunes over the decades: in times of economic depression the pressures from some quarters to cut-back on tourism spending intensified, whilst in times of economic resurgence such expenditure was less controversial.

In the 1890s a pavilion proposal emerged as a practical scheme for the first time but this planned development was rejected by a ratepayers poll.[71] In 1903 the pressure for action from the business community increased with the newly formed Torquay Chamber of Commerce playing a lead role (just as it did in the advertising of the town at this date). That February the Chamber convened a public meeting on the pavilion issue and in July it advised that 'such a building connected with the Princess Gardens, where adequate visual and other attractions might be provided, would enhance the winter attractions of Torquay to residents and visitors, and would prove of indirect benefit to the trade of the town'.[72] Whilst the business community regarded the provision of such entertainments as essential if Torquay was to advance as a resort, residential interests continually opposed investment in tourism. After much internal wrangling, however, the tourism lobby triumphed with the Pavilion project eventually being given the go-ahead by the local authority in March 1910.[73] Built at a cost of £17,500, the 'White Palace', as the Pavilion became known locally, had a carnival opening in August 1912 attended by local and national press representatives.[74]

Intended as the town's showpiece, money was lavished on the Pavilion's façade. The brickwork was faced with imitation marble soapy surface stone, whilst the portions facing the gardens and harbour, which were to be used as an open-air promenade and a sea-facing tea room, had an asphalt covering. Perhaps the most imposing feature of the building was its £750 domed copper roof surmounted by a figure of Britannia and circled by four octagonal summer pavilions for promenaders. The interior of the building, furnished at a cost of £3,000, was equally impressive. The main hall was 140 feet by 60 feet with a small stage, as the Pavilion was originally built as a concert hall and not a theatre. A balcony encircled three sides of the Pavilion hall and the intricate roof decorations incorporated the town crest and motto.[75]

The completion of the Pavilion did not remove it from the centre of controversy, however, as the operation of the facility continued to provide a forum for political debates, especially during the 1920s. Indeed, arguably, these debates encapsulated many of the issues which animated Torquay's political scene at that time. Initial concerns centred around whether the Pavilion should be operated directly as a public facility or let for commercial operation. Having investigated the management arrangements in similar concerns in other resorts, the council chose the former option[76] and the enterprise operated very successfully on this basis in the inter-war period when the Pavilion blossomed into Torquay's most famous asset. Much of its reputation was linked to the Torquay Municipal Orchestra, which the Pavilion hosted from its creation in 1912 until its disbandment in 1953. It was an excellent attraction, raising the resort's profile through the orchestra's BBC radio appearances and epitomising Torquay's fashionability during the 1930s.[77]

Despite this obvious success, the Chamber of Commerce and the Hoteliers' Association were concerned over the rather 'select' or staid nature of the Pavilion entertainments, considering that more popular music or a variety group should be included to broaden the resort's appeal. This suggestion was eventually incorporated into the enter-tainment programme in the winter of 1919 when the Pavilion orchestra played classical concerts on two evenings in the week and more popular entertainments during the remainder. This programme was highly successful and during 1918–19 the Pavilion was Torquay's most profitable municipal enterprise.[78] The spectacular successes of these immediate post-war seasons were short-lived, however, and although the inter-war years witnessed the halcyon days of Torquay's musical entertainments, they soon became a persistent drain on the council coffers.

Indeed, the management of the Pavilion, with its café and orchestra, became highly contentious, and experienced frequent and often acrimonious shifts of direction, especially during 1923–8. The

Pavilion lost money throughout 1921–3 and in 1924 the council reduced staff and cut back on winter refreshments as pressure increased to let the Pavilion café to private operators. Although this was rejected, the advocates of economy succeeded in deferring £3,000 of improvements.[79] The issue remained unsettled, however, and in the economically difficult year of 1926 (that of the General Strike) debate raged over the facility, with heated exchanges in the council elections and in the council chamber, and animated letters to the local press. The local newspaper strongly disapproved of the suggestion to privatise the facility, contending that the Pavilion was intended, not as a paying proposition, but as an attraction for the town, an argument familiar to other resort councils across Britain then, as now.[80]

Such was the division on council that in April 1926 there was a vote of no confidence in the entertainments committee over its handling of the issue.[81] Although it survived, the council debates reveal that, like the town, it was divided between those who advocated subsidising the holiday industry, and those who believed that all facilities should be self-financing. Many Torquay councillors considered that municipal control was vital to ensure the continuance of 'quality' concerts, winter entertainments, and to prevent the conversion of the town's Pavilion into a more popular but far less prestigious cinema—although a substantial minority regarded it as a failure and an economic liability.[82]

Although the Pavilion survived this scrutiny and remained extremely popular with tourists, it continued to be a drain on Torquay's municipal resources throughout the inter-war years, and the post-war period was an even more difficult time for the facility. The town lost its winter season after the 1940s—a major blow to its pretensions to be a select resort—and the Pavilion building was used for less fashionable purposes, becoming the venue not only for plays and concerts, but for bingo and roller skating, seriously undermining the resort's social tone.[83] During 1947–53 the future of the Pavilion and the municipal orchestra was hotly debated as the resort faced the challenges of post-war austerity. From 1948 to 1952 overall takings at the Pavilion Theatre fluctuated but the municipal orchestra itself made consistent losses, the deficit between 1948 and 1951 being in

the region of £15,000.[84] Despite the value of the orchestra in enter-
taining thousands of visitors, such losses became increasingly difficult
to justify and there were calls for an inquiry into the operation of the
Pavilion and the orchestra. Throughout 1951–2 the town council
managed to side-step such demands, but although the losses on the
orchestra were reduced, its supporters could not fight the inevitable
and the orchestra was disbanded in 1953.[85] A chapter in the history
of Torquay's entertainments was closed and one of the foundations
of Torquay's reputation as a fashionable resort was destroyed.
Torquay, in fact, was entering a very difficult period in its fortunes.

Throughout the 1950s the Pavilion continued as Torquay's premier
municipal entertainments venue but by the end of the decade both
its theatre and its restaurant were sustaining heavy losses. There were
two separate moves to demolish it and redevelop the land between
1965 and 1973. Suggested schemes ranged from the complete demolition of the Pavilion and the landscaping of the area, to proposals
that the structure be re-developed as a retail and entertainment
complex. The latter proposal incorporated plans for a 1,500 capacity
theatre, two ballrooms, shops, a restaurant and an information centre,
but the retailing element aroused fears that the tone of the seafront
would be lowered and councillors stressed the need for a more
'dignified' development.[86]

By the late 1960s, echoing Torquay's failing resort fortunes, the
Pavilion provided only summer entertainments and functioned in
winter as a bingo venue. Yet it was very popular as a summer amenity
and its summer shows and concerts attracted over 90,000 patrons
annually in the early 1970s. Despite such popularity, the facility was
very much a liability and in 1969 Torquay's finance committee
chairman commented that it was 'foolish … to sink yet more money
into extending the life of these worn-out buildings which occupy what
are probably the two best and most valuable sites in the West of
England'.[87] This reflected the majority opinion on council and the
Pavilion was scheduled for demolition, being saved rather ironically
by a local pressure group, 'The Friends of the Pavilion', whose
campaign secured grade II listed building status for the theatre in
1973.[88]

This decision required any future re-development to harmonise

162

with the splendid Edwardian architecture of the seafront building, and this was achieved in a substantial restoration programme in the mid-1980s when the Pavilion formed the centrepiece in the rejuvenation of Torquay as a fashionable and up-market resort. In 1987 it re-opened as a shopping complex housing high-quality retailing units. Its elegant exterior was renovated whilst the interior design blended the original decor with the modern corporate logo of the Torbay palm tree. The second floor was refurbished as a café, restaurant and bar, with its live music echoing the style of the Pavilion's inter-war heyday.[89] The success of this project encapsulated Torquay's revitalised resort fortunes in the 1980s and 1990s in much the same way as the problems of the Pavilion had characterised its decline in the preceding decades.

The disputes that raged over the building and management of the Torquay Pavilion were not unusual and when we examine the re-modelling of the Ilfracombe Victoria Pavilion and Pleasure Ground during 1921–5 we find these debates mirrored. In the 1920s Ilfracombe Council pursued an ambitious policy of resort development against a backcloth of depression and slump, investing almost £80,000 in tourism-related ventures.[90] Initially planned in the 1919–21 boom, by 1922–5 these seafront improvement schemes had assumed a counter-cyclical dimension, intended both to improve the resort's attractions and to relieve unemployment.[91] The second phase of this development—a 750-seat theatre—stimulated particularly heated debate on the council and in the wider community and again demonstrates the inherent divisions in resorts which tourism spending often brought to the surface.[92]

As in Torquay in 1903–12, this scheme polarised opinion in Ilfracombe and widened the rift between its holiday interest and the town's residential group. The scheme was overwhelmingly condemned by two separate ratepayers' meetings in October 1923 and 1924.[93] More seriously, it also split the unity of the council (at this time heavily dominated by councillors with interests in the tourism industry) and at the public inquiry on 23 October 1923 the project's opponents included prominent councillors.[94] Opposing the development both on economic grounds and because they felt it would prove aesthetically detrimental to the seafront (since it involved the partial

Figure 6.1: *Ilfracombe Pavilion and Pleasure Grounds, c. 1922*
During the inter-war years the seaside resorts of Britain benefited from heavy investment in numerous seafront improvement schemes. At Ilfracombe the first phase of a seafront enhancement project was completed in 1922 with the laying out of new walled greens costing over £6,000. (Reproduced by kind permission of the Ilfracombe Museum.)

Figure 6.2: *Ilfracombe Pavilion Theatre, c. 1925*
The seafront at Ilfracombe c. 1925. Dominated by the new Pavilion Theatre, walled gardens and the bandstand, this area was usually thronged with visitors throughout the summer months. The exclusive Ilfracombe Hotel, located on a prime site, was demolished in 1976, having become a massive drain on municipal resources. (Reproduced by kind permission of the Ilfracombe Museum.)

demolition of the glass Victoria Pavilion), a group of councillors continued to fight the plan even after the Ministry of Health sanctioned the loan to finance it in 1924.[95] The question continued to dominate the town's politics even after work had begun, right up until the controversial hall opened on 18 May 1925 at a total cost of £9,402.[96] Located on the Parade at the hub of Ilfracombe's seafront attractions, it remained a major element of the resort's amenities until its eventual demolition in 1997, being replaced by a national lottery-funded theatre and winter gardens in 1998—itself a highly controversial scheme.

Band Enclosure Schemes and the Success of Residential Opposition

The pavilions at Torquay and Ilfracombe are examples of some of the most prestigious municipal seaside entertainment facilities built in spite of public controversy in Devon in the first half of the twentieth century. Similarly controversial were proposals for a new band enclosure in Torquay. Unlike the eventually successful pavilion schemes, this one illustrates how indecision by the local authority and opposition from certain sections of the community thwarted the ambitions of a resort's holiday interests. These band enclosure schemes were recognised by resorts as significant wet weather facilities, particularly as the seaside band—playing in bandstands, concert halls and pavilions or on pleasure grounds and promenades—was an integral component of the entertainment 'package' at any British resort before the 1960s. Many resorts heavily subsidised municipal bands and, as in Ilfracombe in the 1920s, most attempts to lengthen their summer seasons were invariably linked to longer band engagements. In the inter-war years Paignton was typical of Devon resorts in providing bands virtually all year round—summer and winter. At neighbouring Torquay the town boasted a municipal orchestra throughout 1921–53, an entertainment which drew large crowds to the Pavilion, but in the 1920s and 1930s the resort's summer bands made heavy losses and there were suggestions that a new purpose-built all-weather venue for the band was required.[97]

Crucial to these proposals in Torquay were plans to utilise a reclaimed seafront site for an entertainments complex—a scheme

Figure 6.3: *Victorian Pavilion Interior, c. 1900*
The interior of the Ilfracombe Pavilion, known locally as the 'cucumber frame'. It was used principally as a concert hall until it was remodelled in the mid-1920s. (Reproduced by kind permission of the Ilfracombe Museum.)

167

which formed the basis of three unsuccessful band enclosure projects during 1927–9.[98] These schemes, which ranged from costs of £25,000 to £50,000, were welcomed by those who depended upon Torquay's holiday industry and drew particularly fervent support from the town's Hoteliers' Association, its Motor Hirers' Association and its Chamber of Commerce. However, there was on council, as the *Torquay Times* pointed out, 'a body of men ... strongly opposed to these proposals'.[99] These included a section of the town council which advocated economy and a group of councillors who were concerned that any reclamation project would reduce harbour space at a time when the resort was attempting to promote itself as a yachting centre. Thus, financial stringency combined with concerns over their suitability to obstruct re-development plans for the seafront Princess Gardens site in the late 1920s.

Nonetheless, the need to improve Torquay's wet weather entertainment facilities remained apparent, and the height of the indecision over the project came in the early 1930s. Between September 1929 and November 1931 several council committees were preoccupied with proposals to develop the Princess Gardens at costs ranging from £55,000 to £114,000, schemes being constantly approved and then deferred. These vacillations were caused not only by the internal rifts and personality clashes on council but also by the fact that the so-called 'progressive', tourism-oriented party, which supported the principle of a band enclosure development, was itself divided over which of the various options it should champion.[100]

The procrastination of the local authority frustrated both the members of its entertainments committee (many of whom were in favour of building a band enclosure) and the holiday traders. But whilst the council was aware of 'the urgent need of a permanent band enclosure ... for visitors during the autumn and winter months', and recognised that inadequate facilities hindered tourism development, it continued to be hamstrung by indecision.[101] Between 1932 and 1936 further council deliberations over three separate re-development schemes, all of which incorporated plans for a band enclosure and one of which was estimated at a cost of £250,000, yielded no tangible results. This lack of activity provoked criticism from those who were urging the immediate improvement of Torquay's attractions and the

Torquay Times remarked that, as plans for an enclosure had been discussed for over 15 years, the very mention of the proposal had become 'unpalatable'.[102] In October 1936, however, the council discussed an impressive £70,000 seafront scheme which incorpo-rated an underground car park, a £15,000 band enclosure and a £40,000 swimming pool on land reclaimed from the harbour. A ballot of the ratepayers over the Torquay Corporation Bill (which included enabling legislation for the scheme) revealed almost a 17,000 majority in favour of the Bill and, encouraged by this mandate, Torquay Council forged ahead with the project which was supported by many in the town, and not merely by the holiday interests.[103]

These ambitious local authority plans were disrupted by the inter-national crisis and by the outbreak of war in the summer of 1939, and early in 1940 the Borough was forced to defer the project indefi-nitely.[104] After the war the Princess Gardens frontage improvements emerged as a priority within Torquay's strategic plan for resort devel-opment, but the financial restrictions of the post-war years curtailed progress in this area. It was not until 1958 that work began on the £350,000 Princess Gardens Development Scheme which incorpo-rated pleasure gardens, an elliptical two-tier promenade and the £180,000 Princess Theatre which won a prestigious award for tourism enterprise in 1961.[105]

Although the Princess Gardens band enclosure was never completed in the form originally conceived in the late 1930s, this does not detract from the fact that before the Second World War, Torquay Council had been prepared to invest £250,000 in schemes to improve the resort's attractions. The band enclosure was merely the most prominent and expensive project; others included a £19,000 seafront road scheme, a £60,000 promenade enhancement, a £20,245 Pavilion refurbishment, and a new concert hall costing £8,164.[106] Together these constituted by far the largest proposed spending programmes in the resort since the £77,284 developments of 1912 which had included the Pavilion and Princess Gardens. This impressive financial outlay in the late 1930s had been intended to keep Torquay in the front-rank of British resorts, for these years witnessed massive invest-ment in the plant of the tourist trade throughout Britain. For example, in 1938 the resorts of the south coast, including Bournemouth,

Brighton and Hastings, spent £2 million on recreational facilities such as tennis courts, golf courses, swimming pools and bowling greens. Brighton alone spent £500,000 pounds on capital works during the decade, whilst both Paignton in Devon and Scarborough in Yorkshire were engaged in improvements in 1938, the latter building a £26,000 municipal bathing pool.[107]

Baths, Spas and Leisure Pools

Although piers, pavilions and band enclosures were important resort facilities, perhaps the most vital attractions for any traditional British seaside resort were its beaches and swimming baths. Throughout this century local authorities in seaside resorts across Britain have invested heavily in improving these amenities, both to maintain their towns' attractions and to increase municipal profits. The construction of artificial bathing facilities such as swimming pools, spas and leisure pools are capital intensive operations, demanding considerable commitment from the public sector. With the exception of theatres, they were the largest and most expensive facilities most resorts built in this century, yet many resorts regarded such amenities as vital and schemes of this nature abounded.

As with many types of facilities, it was again the inter-war years which witnessed particularly heavy investment in these projects (although the early 1970s was also a significant period in the provision of local authority leisure complexes). In Exmouth, for instance, a new seafront baths was built during 1931–2 at a cost of over £5,000, whilst at the same time the South Wales resorts of Porthcawl and Barry also built sea-water pools on their fronts.[108] There were also numerous swimming pool schemes mooted in Ilfracombe and Torquay throughout the inter-war period. The issue of bathing facilities was particularly contentious in the north coast resort, and the failure to construct a major amenity of this kind was regarded as a notable failure in the resort at the outbreak of the Second World War. In Torquay the building of a new pool was discussed as early as February 1919 but no major facility was built and the issue re-appeared in the mid-1930s. During 1932–4 the council considered a new bathing pool 'in order to meet a very much-needed want, and also to keep abreast of other seaside resorts in this direction as well as providing work for the unemployed'. Although it was supported by the press, the hoteliers' lobby on council, and the council's own harbour and baths committee, the council decided that the development would be prohibitively expensive.[109]

One reason why Torquay failed to build a major new swimming pool between 1919 and 1939 was the existence of the Marine Spa complex on the Beacon Quay overlooking the town. A baths complex has stood on the Quay since the Bath Salons were built there in 1817. These were replaced in 1853 by the Medical Baths which (later re-named the Marine Spa) stood on the site until 1971–2 when construction began on the Beacon Leisure Complex, which itself later became the Coral Island Leisure Complex. The re-modelling and subsidisation of these often unprofitable bathing facilities illustrates the extent of a local authority's commitment to encourage (and capacity to fund) tourism development in the twentieth century.

The first major refurbishment of the Bath Salons in the twentieth century came during 1913–16. Incorporating six ladies' and five men's baths at a cost of £15,000, when the new baths opened in 1916 they were soon in service treating shell-shocked and wounded troops, a use which attracted central government subsidies.[110] From the first the Baths incurred a deficit, however, and by the early 1920s the amenity that many had welcomed as a potential asset had become a major liability.[111] In August 1921 a subcommittee appointed to investigate the Baths' operations confirmed that their sale would not recoup the capital outlay and that no private firm could make the facility profitable. It concluded:

> The sub-committee do not think that the Medical Baths can ever be expected entirely to pay their own way even under the most favourable circumstances, but they regard the undertaking as undoubtedly a great asset to the town, and they view with apprehension any suggestion that the Medical Baths should be abolished, and this view is shared by proprietors of hotels and large boarding houses.[112]

As a result, the Baths were reprieved, for, although a notable group in Torquay argued for their closure and warned of large losses, the facility was backed by a more powerful lobby which included the press and the tourism industry and which argued that the amenity was understaffed and underfunded.[113] The *Torquay Times* argued that closure of the Baths would be 'suicidal' if the town was to remain a first-class resort.[114] Swayed by such arguments, the council rejected proposals to lease the Baths, approved a major renovation and gave the facility a vote of confidence by appointing a general medical and swimming baths manager in January 1922.[115] Despite the inter-war fashionability of the Baths, described as Torquay's 'chief rendezvous for dancing' in the summers of the early 1920s,[116] it faced constant difficulties in the financially constrained inter-war years. That the council continued to subsidise the facility heavily in spite of such losses confirms the Borough's commitment to its tourism industry, although the Baths' annual admissions figures did increase considerably in these years, rising from 30,000 in 1922 to almost 157,000 in 1930.[117]

In the later 1920s and 1930s the Baths consolidated its position as a major feature of Torquay's attractions and was recognised as integral to the resort's reputation as a health spa. Despite extensive refurbishment in the mid-1930s which meant that the baths (now renamed Torquay Marine Spa[118]) were still relatively modern when war ended in 1945, the post-war period proved a difficult time. Immediately after the war it soon became apparent that the facility's high overheads were increasingly difficult to justify. Between 1948 and 1957 the continuing losses provoked several concerted attempts to close the Spa's medical baths section and its stay of execution was only due to the support it drew from the local press and from a powerful group on the town council. Like all of Torquay's attractions, it required upgrading, but it did remain the main bathing facility in the town and, as such, was an important aspect in the marketing of the resort. As late as 1956 the official guide boasted that 'for the invalid requiring expert treatment to recover health, Torquay is the ideal choice', and even in 1961 the guide highlighted the Turkish, Vichy and sea-water tonic baths available at the facility.[119] The calls for closure persisted, however, and it was clear that the medical treatment centre was obsolete: since the mid-1950s visitor admissions had rarely topped 700 per annum.[120]

In the later 1950s the council remained divided over the future of the Marine Spa complex. During 1955–8 the area was reviewed as part of a major improvement scheme and only financial constraints prevented the implementation of a plan to re-develop the entire area and demolish the medical section at the close of the decade.[121] From 1962 until its eventual demolition in 1971, the Marine Spa remained a focus of discussion and a drain on resources. Its closure was only a matter of time as the Spa incurred substantial maintenance costs in the 1960s[122] but it was not until September 1971 that work finally began on the demolition of the Spa and the construction of the new £1.5 million Beacon Leisure and Entertainment Centre. This complex was in turn succeeded in 1977 by the Coral Island development which, like its forerunners, inherited some of the problems of the rather remote site and closed in September 1988 for 'economic reasons'.[123] It is interesting that the use of the site may come full circle, for in 1991 the Torbay Council approved an £8 million redevelopment of Coral Island into a sea-water health treatment centre with restaurant and hotel facilities.[124] However, this development, reflecting the renewed interest in health tourism at the end of the twentieth century,[125] remains on the drawing board.

Marinas and Shopping Malls

In the late 1990s the public sector remains vitally involved in the provision of many tourist facilities at the British seaside, but, whereas previously the local authorities were active initiators and entrepreneurs, now they increasingly play an enabler role in partnership schemes with the private sector. Since the 1970s the UK's national tourist boards have encouraged the development of indoor recreation centres and swimming pools to provide wet weather tourist facilities and in this 'The role of local authorities in the resorts is felt to be crucial in giving a lead to the many individual operators whose activities in total determine the economic wealth of the resort towns'.[126]

Two types of leisure-orientated schemes which have proved very successful in revitalising British resorts are marina developments for yachts and small sailing craft, and high-quality indoor retailing complexes or shopping malls. Indeed, it would not be an exaggeration to contend that marinas have been perceived to be the saviours of many failing resorts and hence proposals sprang up all over Britain, especially in the 1980s. Both developments have appeared in Devon's seaside resorts in recent decades and, like other tourism facilities before them, have been hotly debated. To examine marina developments first, the creation of these facilities has been a highly contentious issue in many British resorts in the 1970s, 1980s, and 1990s, and in none more so than in those of Torbay, Teignmouth and Exmouth. Until interest rates soared in the recession of the early 1990s, restricting consumer spending, property-led marina development was an attractive investment and by 1990 there were nearly 4,000 marina berths and moorings on the south coast of Devon.[127]

This maritime leisure boost created a rash of marina proposals of varying degrees of feasibility in the late 1980s around the British coastline, from Aberystwyth and Newport in Wales to Ilfracombe in Devon. In the latter, a working party appointed by the council to investigate the feasibility of the creation of a 220-berth marina reported in 1987 that whilst the harbour remained 'the town's principal tourism asset providing a focus in terms of visitor amenity and visual appeal', the area was characterised by shabby shop frontages and an air of neglect.[128] The need to revitalise Ilfracombe and the success of other marina projects in the Bristol Channel, including the re-development of the former merchants' area of Bristol docks, the marina and barrage at Swansea[129] and the Cardiff Bay Development Corporation's designs for a marine lake (now nearing completion), strengthened arguments for such a project. The case was also lent credibility by the fact that Ilfracombe is the most important harbour of refuge at the entrance to the Bristol Channel. However, a marina's operational success is vitally dependent upon the nature of an area's micro-economy, and the feasibility study concluded that:

> In the case of Ilfracombe, the topography of the harbour precludes sufficient developments surrounding it and, therefore finance must be generated from productive developments in other parts of the town of Ilfracombe to assist with the funding of the marina in the harbour.[130]

Although the resort was targeted by the West Country Tourist Board as a focus for investment in retail and leisure businesses and in the harbour area, with no specific European Community grants available, financing these projects proved an insurmountable problem in the 1980s.[131] Developments in Ilfracombe in the 1990s— as in so many other British resorts—have been largely restricted to public-sector partnerships since investment monies from the private sector have proved to be very difficult to attract, as the experiences of Barry Island and Rhyl underline.[132] The public-sector investments, financed by government agencies and local authorities, have tended to focus on townscape enhancement projects, including the pedestrianisation of major streets, the planting of urban greenery and the improvement of seafronts. Further proposals for the redevelopment of Ilfracombe's harbour zone as a residential and leisure area with a new breakwater and sheltered squares and piazzas constructed around a botanical garden were defeated by a lack of financial resources in the late 1980s, although, as we have seen, a new theatre and winter gardens have been developed on the seafront in 1998.[133]

Although proposals failed in the north Devon resort, marina developments have proceeded apace on the south Devon coast, frequently provoking controversy reminiscent of those surrounding tourism schemes at the beginning of the century. At Brixham, for instance, after 12 months of debate, a proposal was launched in early 1988 to build a £16 million harbourside scheme with 600 berths. Local groups opposed the plans on the basis that the marina would destroy the £8 million fishing industry which had made Brixham the fourth most important British fishing port, arguing that it 'would turn Brixham harbour from a fish and commercial port into a port dominated by recreational interest. In particular it would be dominated by one group—those people of sufficient means to own and operate a yacht from a marina.'[134] Such comments illustrate the conflicts over space so frequently highlighted in the tourism industry, in this case between resort industrial interests and tourists. Here the local authority promoted the interests of affluent tourists above those of its own less lucrative—and therefore less powerful—fishing industry. At a public inquiry in 1988 the evidence presented by Brixham's fishing interest that the marina would be detrimental to its industry failed to defeat

175

the proposals as the inquiry concluded that there would be no conflict with the recreational use of the harbour.[135]

In addition to the marina at Brixham, there have also been marina developments at the south Devon resorts of Dartmouth and Kingswear, and their success, together with the boom in water sports, with an estimated 1.5–2 million people participating in these activities whilst on holiday in Britain in the early 1990s, provoked further proposals in Devon.[136] One plan concerned Exmouth's once thriving docks: after the docks were declared unsafe, they were closed on 1 January 1990 and, despite the efforts of 4,000 objectors, a proposal for a £69 million marina development was accepted, although planning wrangles subsequently held up its development.[137]

During the 1980s Torbay also capitalised upon the boom in the maritime leisure industry and Torquay's 500-berth marina has proved a significant income-generator for the resort. Equally significant in the revitalisation of the town, however, has been the heavy investment in shopping malls. These leisure-related retail developments have already proved successful in attracting visitors and revitalising those resorts able to sustain such developments throughout Britain. In many ways, their success indicates and capitalises on the increasing leisurization of shopping and its significance as a tourism activity in the late twentieth century.[138] Clearly, since Torbay's £12.5 million retail turnover was the third highest in Devon in the early 1980s, the resort's tourism-planners anticipated that leisure-retailing had the potential to bring further prosperity to Torbay in the 1990s.[139] A significant phase in the 1980s and early 1990s re-positioning of Torquay was the £35 million Fleet Walk retailing scheme. This incorporates a covered mall, car parking provision and a large Winter Gardens rotunda with a glass elevator at its heart. This impressive complex of arcades and pedestrianised streets is themed throughout with the resort's palm tree logo and is linked to the Torquay Pavilion by a raised walkway. Whilst such developments are proving to be very significant in the remaking and reimaging of Britain's larger resorts, the obvious inability of smaller to medium-sized resorts to sustain such investment does not auger well for their fortunes in the coming years, given that tourists' expectations are likely to become increasingly demanding.

Partnerships in Provision

As this chapter has illustrated, resort local authorities in the twentieth century have been intimately concerned with the need to entertain and provide facilities for visitors. The increasing requirement at the end of the twentieth century for high-quality wet weather facilities is merely one example of the essential continuity in resort provision. Similarly, given the investment patterns in resorts throughout the twentieth century, it is possible to argue that the pattern of many resorts' fortunes was set at relatively early stages of their development. From the start, the larger, more prosperous resorts have been able to dominate the seaside product because of their abilities to raise substantial revenues, thereby funding large-scale facility development, enabling them to maintain their appeal to existing and new markets.

It would be a mistake, therefore, to suggest that British resort authorities were not prepared to invest in their products and therein lay the seeds of their ultimate decline. The experience of the twentieth century reveals that many resorts were prepared to invest substantial sums of money, particularly when the municipal authorities involved were relatively dynamic and pro-tourism development in outlook. In many resorts, such authorities created the infrastructural product which the private sector then capitalised on by investing in amusements and entertainment facilities. However, the increasing local authority shift since the 1980s away from direct provision towards facilitating and enabling private-sector investment has severely constrained the ability of resorts to reinvent themselves continually and respond to rising consumer expectations. As local authority involvement in entertainment provision has declined, so too have investment levels across resorts since the private sector has not invested in the seaside resort product to any great extent in recent decades, apart from certain exceptions such as the grand hotels.

There is no doubt that the decline of the dynamic local authority leisure provider and operator has much to do with the overall decline of many British resorts. The future success of resorts would now appear to rest on the ability of joint public–private sector projects such as that which has proved to be so successful in Torquay.

However, arguably its experience and its ability to attract private-sector investment is unlikely to be replicated in many of the small- to medium-sized resorts across Britain. Evidence from resorts in Wales which have benefited from public funding partnerships designed to act as catalysts for private investment suggests that whilst the former have made significant contributions to the environment of resorts, they have not been matched by reciprocal investments from the latter.[140] This is no doubt due in large part to the small-scale and fragmented nature of the resort-based private sector and it has also been exacerbated by the failure of resorts to compete adequately with other tourism sites and products for that investment capital which is available.

7

Power and Politics at the Seaside

> ... an English holiday often means one spent in some decaying
> mausoleum of mid-Victorian standards of enjoyment combined
> with ... [high] prices. It is a legitimate incentive to the improve-
> ment of the drearier English watering places to leave them for
> more attractive quarters elsewhere.
>
> *The Times*, 28 July 1926

This book has demonstrated the crucial role played by British seaside
local authorities in fostering resort development ambitions. In particular it has focused on the two key areas of municipal promotional
activities and the public-sector provision of tourism facilities.
Throughout this century these activities have been surrounded by
controversy, and the debates concerning their implementation reflect
the inherent divisions within resort communities. We have also
examined the micro-politics of resort communities and revealed the
rifts between those who depended on the tourism industry for their
livelihoods (often led by the local hoteliers' associations and chambers
of commerce) and the resorts' residential groups. The latter were
frequently dominated by those who wanted to see resorts maintain a
high social tone and those retired inhabitants (frequently incomers)
who wanted low rates and were resistant to tourism development
which 'threatened' their quality of life. Indeed, the struggle between
these factions emerged as a key theme in Chapters 5 and 6 where we
discussed resort advertising campaigns and tourism facilities.

Such struggles at the local, political level in Britain's seaside communities confirm the contention that tourism—like all forms of

leisure—articulates the power and politics of everyday life. This, perhaps, is the essence of our book. It has, of course, also tried to provide an overview of the development of the British seaside industry in the twentieth century and to trace the evolution of Devon's resorts in the same period. In doing so, however, its underlying aim has been to illustrate that in the twentieth century the development of the seaside has been shaped by conflicts between those seeking to control leisure space and time and those seeking to utilise them. In suggesting this, we are arguing that the notion of 'social tone'—long familiar to historians of nineteenth-century resorts—remains as durable today as it was at the turn of the last century. In 1900 all of Devon's resorts were 'select' and 'respectable', largely because distance and inaccessibility had protected their social tone for a somewhat longer period than was the case for other British resort areas. As a result, Devon's physical remoteness from the main centres of population in England ensured that its resorts entered the 'mass' holiday market later than the resorts of, for example, the South East and the North West.

Over the century some resorts, such as Ilfracombe and Exmouth, developed as 'popular' resorts. Only one, Torquay, which dominated the county's holiday industry as its largest resort, was able to sustain a fashionable image whilst supporting a more 'popular' dimension. A handful of others (including Budleigh Salterton, Lynmouth and Seaton) strove to retain a genteel atmosphere. Remaining relatively 'select' well beyond the Second World War, we have seen how the resort of Sidmouth was able successfully to pursue policies designed to discourage influxes of working-class tourists and day-trippers throughout the twentieth century. Moreover, we have also seen that the concept of social tone remains important to both residents and tourists at the end of the 1990s. It is at the heart of many current tourism development policies: in reality, references to 'market segmentation', 'resort specialisation' or 'target audiences defined by lifestyle' are often merely refinements of social tone divisions, defined by socio-economic class.

Patterns of Power

In Chapters 1 and 2 it was contended that leisure relationships are underpinned by the power relationships inherent in society. As leisure both reflects and realises social divisions, there is no doubting Walton's contention that 'The seaside … *expressed* class and cultural differences…'¹ as local groups sought to control the extent and the nature of access to their resorts. Moreover, as we have seen, the 1930s and 1960s emerge as key decades of conflict in British resorts, coinciding with continuing rising levels of real income amongst the working class that facilitated consumer revolutions—themselves part of the general shift from a production to a consumption culture. These were the decades when remoter holiday regions like Devon experienced considerable pressure from the increasing influx of holiday-makers. Resort communities across Britain faced decisions over whether to encourage and facilitate or attempt to resist the changes in popular holidaymaking patterns. The different paths chosen by the communities dictated the subsequent development of their resorts and determined their degree of success in the reshaped British tourism industry. Throughout the twentieth century the seaside resorts of Devon have had a much more 'middle-class flavour' than those of most other areas of Britain. This emphasis on the 'quality' segment of the holiday market would appear to have placed many resorts in Devon in a relatively favourable position to meet the challenges of the next century.

The Policies of Exclusion

The development of Devon's seaside resorts clearly exemplifies of the operation of leisure power relations on a micro-scale. Even in the later decades of the twentieth century, the distance of the county's resorts from the major urban catchment areas of England enabled the resorts' controlling groups to manipulate holiday-makers' access to and use of leisure space. Indeed, residential opposition effectively defeated several moves to open up areas of Devon to the lower middle and working classes. Not only was access constrained by the economic barrier of distance, but the local authorities of some of the more 'select' resorts (notably Sidmouth and Budleigh Salterton) actively discouraged transport improvements which would alleviate such access issues. Furthermore, almost all of Devon's resorts (including Ilfracombe) disdained the most 'popular' entertainments which attracted working-class visitors to resorts such as Blackpool.

Perhaps some of the most striking examples of the attempts to control 'undesirable' tourism developments in Devon were the opposition during the inter-war period to Sunday concerts, steamers, charabancs and Sunday sports, and the opposition to the holiday camp scheme near Sidmouth. In opposing the holiday camp, the local ratepayers' groups and the accommodation operators articulated fears, not simply of the threat of competition in the marketplace, but also of the camps' perceived impact on the social tone of the resorts of south-east Devon. The concern over the influx of charabancs— similar to the views of other resorts in Britain—are an even louder echo of the conflicts inherent in leisure relationships. The resorts' concerns over drunkenness, rowdiness and litter associated with the popularisation of these cheaper holiday trips were reflected in by-laws and bans imposed by a number of British resort authorities, and in Devon this inter-war working-class influx into its resorts and the county's hitherto 'inaccessible' interior aroused considerable hostility amongst the county's ruling elites.[2]

The impact of such policies, or to phrase it differently the continuing relevance of social tone, is apparent in the differing experiences of Devon's resorts. It emerges that, of these, Torquay has been one of the more successful in adapting to the changing tourism patterns of the twentieth century. As a large resort it has been able to sustain more than one character and image and has been able to attract more than one market: as early as the late 1930s (although more clearly from the mid-1950s) it achieved a 'popular fashionability'. Most of the other Devon resorts have been uncertain of their desired image or tone or tried to cultivate more than one and failed (see Table 4.1). This highlights the importance of a successful policy of resort specialisation or effective target marketing. Certainly, Lewes, writing in the 1960s, considered that 'the most successful resorts' in Devon 'seem to be those which have set out, intentionally or perhaps accidentally, and succeeded in appealing to a particular section of the market'.[3]

Teignmouth in south Devon, for instance, has long targeted family holiday-makers. In the late 1950s over 80 per cent of its visitors were in family groups—a trend the Teignbridge District Council attempted to sustain in the late 1980s through policies designed to 'maintain the character of the area as one suitable for family holiday enjoyment'.[4] Further down the south Devon coast, Salcombe (a resort isolated by land and unsuitable for industrial development, but with a good sheltered harbour) has concentrated on sailing and other forms of pleasure boating. Here (and at Dartmouth, another Devon yachting centre), appeal to a particular part of the market or market segmentation has led to an economically sustainable resort. In east Devon, Budleigh Salterton has opted to develop its function as a limited, quiet resort. Providing essentially for a resident retired population, it has always prevented the development of caravan or chalet sites and does not have large purpose-built hotels. 'The result seems to be a social organisation based on retired leisure, which older people find satisfying.' Economically the town has prospered from this strategy, although its growth has been limited by the need to preserve the secluded atmosphere.[5]

Sidmouth, with its very sheltered position and Georgian townscape, provides perhaps the best example of resort specialisation in twentieth-century Devon. Throughout the century, the town has catered for a specific market by cultivating a 'select' atmosphere. As we have seen, the cornerstones of this policy have been the pursuit of a low-key and selective advertising strategy; a refusal to provide either 'popular' municipal entertainment or build large, rate-subsidised facilities; the discouragement of improved transport access to the resort; and opposition to caravan or campsite developments. Today, Sidmouth has a very large number of high-quality hotels for a modest-sized resort, and the market which it continues to target is visitors who enjoy a quiet, expensive holiday. In the late 1980s almost 65 per cent of Sidmouth's tourists were drawn from the highest socio-economic groups (a substantial number being aged 55 or over)—groups with high living standards, significant disposable incomes and a large leisure budget.[6] Sidmouth's success in capturing and retaining this market seems to promise a reasonable future for the resort, since the tourist industry's recent emphasis on high standards of service is unlikely to wane.

Patterns of Success: Torquay and Ilfracombe

Torquay has proved the most adaptable of Devon's seaside resorts. It has successfully repositioned itself in the changing tourism market of the second half of the twentieth century by pursuing a *via media* between the selectivity of Sidmouth and the popularity of resorts such as Paignton, Exmouth and Ilfracombe. Its adept responses to the changes in holiday-making patterns have enabled it to maintain its role as Devon's premier resort and one of the foremost resorts in Britain (Table 7.1). Its ability to adapt to these changing holiday-making patterns is not simply explained by its geographical location, its good communications networks and the strength of its financial resources, although clearly these were critical to its success. The investment policies of its local authority and its willingness to work in partnership with the local tourism industry also proved vital ingredients in the success story.

Table 7.1: Resorts Forming the Core of the British Seaside Resort Industry in the 1990s

Scarborough	Torbay
Great Yarmouth	Newquay
Brighton	Blackpool
Eastbourne	Tenby
Isle of Wight	Llandudno
Bournemouth	Rhyl

Source: Middleton V.T.C. (1989) 'Seaside Resorts', *Insights*, English Tourist Board, 5–9.

The inter-war period which provided the platform for Torquay's development as a 'modern' resort proved to be critical. Although the resort was often riven by disputes in the face of economic difficulties (particularly in the later 1930s), the tourism lobby usually won the arguments over the desirability of generating more tourism business. Despite these various internal rifts, the resort community as a whole displayed a high level of commitment to the promotion of its tourism industry, and throughout the century Torquay proved a successful and eclectic adopter and adapter of tourism development schemes. This is most evident in the town's advertising strategies, which throughout the second half of the century sought to attract a more 'popular' market without undermining the resort's 'smart' image.

By the 1960s and early 1970s, however, Torquay's market—like that of the British tourism industry as a whole—was shifting in the face of continental competition. In these years the resort suffered something of a crisis, losing direction as its more exclusive hotels experienced a loss of trade and down-market amusements and retail outlets flourished in the town's harbour area. By the end of the 1970s, Torquay was facing a serious decline in business. Despite its ability to ride out periodic depressions and adapt to market changes, Torbay could not remain immune from the collapse of the domestic tourism market at the beginning of the 1980s. Yet, at the same time, Torbay was anticipating a revival on the back of assistance received under the English Tourist Board's Tourism Development Action Programme. In 1988 its multi-million pound retailing and leisure developments outlined in Chapter 6 won it the British Resorts 2000 competition and national acclaim as the resort that best exemplified successful private and public sector partnership schemes.[7]

By comparison, Ilfracombe has failed to adapt to the changing holiday-making patterns of this century. In contrast to the geographical advantages of Torquay in the south, much of Ilfracombe's difficulties stem from its rather physically isolated location on the exposed north Devon coast—a remoteness exacerbated by poor communications links. Throughout the twentieth century the resort's local authority sought unsuccessfully to counteract this drawback. As early as the 1920s the Ilfracombe Council was pre-occupied with the town's inadequate rail service and, from the later 1940s, with its inferior road network, complaining that the rail companies and Devon County Council neglected its needs and demands in favour of the south Devon coast. Yet, despite the activities of its local authority—perhaps the most energetic and interventionist of all Devon's resorts—Ilfracombe's problems of geographical location have seemed insurmountable. Ilfracombe was simply too remote from the major British centres where the population enjoyed high disposable incomes to become a successful day-trip or short-break destination.

Ilfracombe's main problem was that it increasingly positioned itself as a more 'popular' resort from the inter-war period, yet failed to capture this market. In a sense, it is an example of failed resort specialisation. In 1931 one of the town's prominent councillors voiced his view of the problem:

> the policy pursued by the Council is catering for the masses rather than the classes.... That is a matter about which there will always be varied opinions. There are many in the town—especially after the experiences of the war years—who lament that the town was not developed along the lines of catering for the classes. However, the opposite policy has been in favour for so long that it would appear hopeless to attempt to change it now. For good or ill, Ilfracombe must remain a 'popular' seaside resort, and I think everyone must acknowledge that the Council are doing their best to make it so within the limits imposed by financial considerations.[8]

As this comment highlights, together with its unfavourable location, one of the major obstacles in Ilfracombe's attempt to establish itself as a prosperous 'popular' resort was its limited financial resources. Time and again, the local authority's enthusiasm for tourism development projects, so essential to upgrade its infrastructure, was undermined by its impecuniousness. Ilfracombe has long lacked a diverse economy, and relying almost exclusively on the seasonal holiday industry, it has been unable to adapt to the changed domestic holiday scene since the late 1960s. It remains the case that, suffering from relative remoteness, poor communications and a poor image, Ilfracombe does not have an easily 'packaged' modern tourism product. Despite recent major environmental schemes and the construction in 1998 of a new national lottery-funded theatre and winter gardens, the resort needs still further investment in its resort infrastructure (particularly from the private sector) and more aggressive and dynamic marketing if it is to prosper as a significant medium-sized resort.

186

Prospects: Local Authorities and Resort Development Beyond 2000

If Ilfracombe and other British resorts like it are to participate in a revival of the domestic seaside, the role of local government would seem to be vitally important. The previous chapters, particularly those on resort marketing and facility development, have demonstrated that local authorities, more than any other agents, played a vital role in resort development over the twentieth century. Many of these municipal achievements were often accomplished in the face of considerable opposition from central government in periods of financial retrenchment. In the absence of any direction from central government until the late 1960s, municipal bodies played the leading role in the formulation of tourism policies, although there was little attempt at strategic planning. Not only did central government give little lead to the British tourism industry, but in contrast to the activities of district and borough councils there was also little support from the second tier of local government, the more 'remote' county councils. Many of these had minimal interest in tourism until the later 1960s, even in areas heavily reliant on the tourism industry. In Devon, for instance, the agriculturally dominated county council had no official forum for the discussion of tourism issues until the 1970s and there was little concern with formulating a coherent county-wide tourism strategy.[9] Only the controversy over the 1969 Development of Tourism Act lifted the county council out of its apathy to establish that year an industry and tourism sub-committee and allocate a tourism budget for the first time—initiatives followed up in 1973 with the appointment of a county tourism officer.[10]

Justified on social, economic and political grounds, borough and district government intervention in British resort development in the twentieth century has operated in key areas including planning, resource provision, supervision and regulation, direct ownership of certain key components and tourism promotion. Since the 1980s, however, this involvement has become much more of an enabler role: local government proving an infrastructural and strategic framework within which the public and private sector components of the industry co-ordinate their investment and marketing plans.[11] The vital role

187

local and (to a lesser extent) central government can have in assisting the traditional resorts was emphasised in the late 1980s by the chairman of the British Resorts' Association Working Party appointed to report on the problems of seaside resorts. He urged government to establish 'resort development programmes with a system of targeted funding' and called for increased partnership initiatives and a more cohesive promotion, marketing and representation approach in a fragmented industry. In his conclusion that, 'To be successful, resorts must adapt to change and seize market opportunities in a more direct way and with the same purpose being displayed by some of the new inland tourist attractions ... resorts must make themselves more appealing, improve their image and improve standards of service', he was, in fact, identifying many of the initiatives pursued by Torbay since the early 1980s.[12]

British resorts must strive to offer a quality experience, to improve standards of beach hygiene, traffic and visitor management, and so effectively market the coastal product. For some parts of Britain (particularly Wales and some parts of Devon and Cornwall) the seaside is pre-eminent in their tourism product and whilst there has been some diversification, particularly into countryside and activity-oriented holidays—the vast majority of tourism trips are still taken on the coast. Thus the need to produce the right seaside product is critical not just to their seaside industries but also to their tourism industries as a whole.[13] The experience of Welsh, and many English, resorts suggests that this task will not be an easy one. One of the most important continuing problems is an apparent inability to attract private-sector investment. Regeneration schemes in Wales which have attempted to secure public–private partnerships have failed in this respect. Whilst the public-sector agencies have improved resorts' environmental and infrastructural qualities, this has not been matched by a similar response from the private sector.[14] The failure of the private sector to initiate complementary schemes must raise some worrying questions over the ability of the industry to meet the challenges of the next century. Moreover, at a strategic level, the success of these regeneration schemes—assessed in terms of other long-term impacts on the continued health and development of the industry—needs to be tempered with a consideration of the overall imperatives which frame the public support of tourism.

Despite its tradition as a leisure site and some recent economic successes, the future of Britain's seaside remains uncertain. Whilst the leisure market will continue to develop, it is very likely that the leisure experience will continue to be constructed around inequality of leisure opportunity, and therefore concepts such as market segmentation and resort specialisation will continue to be important. Clearly the British resort product faces a difficult market in the future. That market will be shaped by higher consumer expectations, greater global competition, health and environmental concerns, and (given demographic changes in Britain) dominated by fewer young adults, more childless couples and family-formers and more older consumers. The domestic tourism industry will not only need increased private-sector investment but, moreover, both the private and the public sectors will need to cultivate an imaginative consumer-oriented approach focusing on management, design, and marketing to target these more discerning consumers of the future.

This is vital as evidence indicates that the first decade of the third millennium will witness an increasing diversification of lifestyles which will entail a concomitant diversity of leisure experiences.[15] The numbers in less affluent groups (such as single parents and the elderly) will increase, as will those of the relatively affluent young professionals or recently retired, and income inequality is predicted to widen as the labour market becomes even more polarised. This will create a well-rewarded core and a poorly rewarded periphery or so-called second market, comprising the unemployed, those on welfare benefits and the low paid and low skilled—now accounting for 30 per cent of British households.[16] The implications of these forecasts for the seaside resorts of Britain are as yet unclear. The domestic tourism industry is slowly becoming aware of the potential of 'social tourism'—the previously untapped market of more than 10 million people in Britain unable to take holidays. Denied tourism opportunities, these people include those on low incomes and benefits, single parents, the elderly and over 6 million people with disabilities.

Despite social tourism-oriented campaigns, such as *Tourism for All* launched in the later 1980s, it seems clear that it will be the well-rewarded core groups, especially the childless, full-time employed workers and the affluent middle-aged, who will enjoy a more fulfilled leisure experience in the future. These groups will continue to provide the target markets for those seaside resorts investing in the supplementary holiday, short-break and conference markets. In contrast, the peripheral or 'second market', who are less likely to be able to afford foreign holidays, might offer a potentially lucrative market opportunity for the more popular or day-trip resorts. Such a view of the future of tourism predicts the continuance of seaside resort 'social tone' debates in the twenty-first century, although in a re-shaped form as these communities continue to display concerns over holiday-makers' use of leisure time and leisure space. Social zoning at the seaside (as at other tourism sites) has not ended and, indeed, resorts continue to be socially differentiated, from the Indian Ocean to the Mediterranean. Indeed, with the growth in needs for 'secure' tourism (such as all-inclusive Caribbean resorts and Centre Parcs in Europe) as a result of the fear of crime and the need to holiday with others who are 'like oneself', social tone is likely to remain a prime shaper of tourism development for the foreseeable future.[17]

Notes

Abbreviations used in the notes:

BTA	British Tourism Authority
DCC	Devon County Council
ETB	English Tourist Board
EUDC	Exmouth Urban District Council
IC	*Ilfracombe Chronicle*
IUDC	Ilfracombe Urban District Council
JAC	Joint Advertising Committee
NDDC	North Devon District Council
SUDC	Sidmouth Urban District Council
SWEPC	South West Economic Planning Council
TMBC	Torquay/Torbay Municipal Borough Council
TT	*Torquay Times*
WCTB	West Country Tourist Board
WMN	*Western Morning News*
WT	*Western Times*
WTB	Wales Tourist Board

CHAPTER 1

1   Durant H. (1938) *The Problem of Leisure*, G. Routledge & Sons, London: 22.
2   Lewis R. (1980) 'Seaside holiday resorts in the United States and Britain: a review', *Urban History Yearbook*, 44–52; Towner J. (1996) *An Historical Geography of Recreation and Tourism in the Western World 1540–1940*, John Wiley & Sons, Chichester; Walton J.K. (1997) 'The seaside resorts of Western Europe 1750–1939', 24–38 in Fisher H.E.S. (ed.) *Recreation and the Sea*, University of Exeter Press, Exeter.
3   Walton J.K. (1997) 'Seaside resorts and maritime history', *International Journal of Maritime History* 19 (1) 125–47: 127.
4   For instance, see Goodall B. (1992) 'Coastal resorts: development and redevelopment', *Built Environment* 18 (1) 5–11; Cooper C. (1992) 'The life cycle

191

concept and strategic planning for coastal resorts', *Built Environment* 18 (1) 57–66; and Evans M., McDonagh P. and Moutinho L. (1992) 'The coastal hotel sector: performance and perception analysis', *Built Environment* 18 (1) 67–78.

5   Shaw G. and Williams A. (eds) (1997) *The Rise and Fall of the British Coastal Resort. Cultural and Economic Perspectives*, Cassell, London.

6   Walton, 'Seaside resorts and maritime history': 128.

7   Walton J.K. (1983) *The English Seaside Resort. A Social Hisory 1750–1914*, Leicester University Press, Leicester.

8   Durie A. (1994) 'The development of the Scottish coastal resorts in the central Lowlands, c. 1770–1880', *Local Historian* 24, 206–16; Durie A. (1997) 'The Scottish seaside resort in peace and war, c. 1880–1960', *International Journal of Maritime History* 9 (1) 171–86; and Davies K.M. (1993) 'For health and pleasure in the British fashion: Bray, Co. Wicklow, as a tourist resort, 1750–1914', and Heuston J. (1993) 'Kilkee: the origins and development of a west coast resort', both in O'Connor B. and Cronin M. (eds) *Tourism in Ireland: A Critical Analysis*, University of Cork, Cork.

9   Morgan N.J. and Pritchard A. (1996) 'Welsh seaside resort strategies', paper presented to the third Urban History Conference, Budapest; and Morgan N.J. (1998) 'Welsh seaside resort strategies. Changing times, changing needs at the end of the twentieth century', 193–216 in Starkey D. and Jamieson A.G. (eds) *Exploiting the Sea. Aspects of Britain's Maritime Economy Since 1870*, University of Exeter Press, Exeter.

10   P.A. Cambridge Economic Consultants (1992) *Prospects for Coastal Resorts*, Wales Tourist Board, Cardiff.

11   Enloe C. (1989) *Bananas, Beaches and Bases. Making Feminist Sense of International Politics*, Pandora, London: 40.

12   O'Grady, R. (ed.) (1980) *Third World Tourism*. Singapore, Christian Conference Asia: 3, quoted in Crick M. (1989) 'Representations of international tourism in the social sciences: sun, sex, sights and servility', *Annual Review of Anthropology* 18, 307–44: 320.

13   Young R.C. (1977) 'The structural context of the Caribbean tourist industry. A comparative study', *Economic Development and Cultural Change* 25, 657–71.

14   Pritchard A., Morgan N.J., Sedgley D. and Jenkins A. (1998) 'Reaching out to the gay tourist: opportunities and threats in an emerging market segment', *Tourism Management* 19 (3).

15   Morgan N.J. and Pritchard A. (1998) *Tourism Promotion and Power: Creating Images, Creating Identities*, John Wiley & Sons, Chichester.

16   Shields R. (1991) *Places on the Margin. Alternative Geographies Of Modernity*, Routledge, London: 260.

17   Shields, *Places on the Margin*: 6.

18   Shields, *Places on the Margin*: 3.

19   Shields, *Places on the Margin*: 3.

20   Shields, *Places on the Margin*: 4.

CHAPTER 2

1   Hoggart R. (1969) *The Uses of Literacy*, Penguin, Harmondsworth: 147.
2   For a detailed discussion of this developing theory see Morgan N.J. and Pritchard A. (1998) *Tourism Promotion and Power: Creating Images, Creating Identities*, John Wiley & Sons, Chichester: chapter 1.
3   Said E. (1991) *Orientalism. Western Concepts of the Orient*, Penguin, London: 5.
4   Urry J. (1990) *The Tourist Gaze. Travel and Leisure in Contemporary Societies*, Sage, London; Cohen E. (1972) 'Towards a sociology of international tourism', *Social Research* 39, 164–82; and MacCannell D. (1976 and 1989) *The Tourist. A New Theory of the Leisure Class*, 2nd edn, Schocken Books, New York.
5   Enloe C. (1989) *Bananas, Beaches and Bases. Making Feminist Sense of International Politics*, Pandora, London: 28.
6   See, for instance, Yeo E. and Yeo S. (eds) (1981) *Popular Culture and Class Conflict 1590–1914: Explorations in the History of Labour and Leisure*, The Harvester Press Ltd, Brighton; and Clarke J. and Critcher C. (1985) *The Devil Makes Work: Leisure in Capitalist Britain*, University of Illinois Press, Champaign.
7   Eisenschitz A. (1988) 'The politicisation of leisure', paper presented at the Leisure Studies Association International Conference, Brighton: 1
8   Enloe, *Bananas, Beaches and Bases*; and Selwyn T. (ed.) (1996) *The Tourist Image: Myths and Myth Making in Tourism*, Wiley & Sons, Chichester.
9   Dann G. (1996) *The Language of Tourism: A Sociolinguistic Perspective*, CAB International, Oxford.
10 Morgan and Pritchard, *Tourism Promotion and Power*.
11 O'Grady R. (ed.) (1980) *Third World Tourism*, Singapore, Christian Conference Asia: 3, quoted in Crick M. (1989) 'Representations of international tourism in the social sciences: sun, sex, sights and servility', *Annual Review of Anthropology* 18, 307–44: 320.
12 Kinnaird V. and Hall D. (1994) 'Introduction', in Kinnaird V. and Hall D. (eds) *Tourism: A Gender Analysis*, John Wiley & Sons, Chichester: 6.
13 Urry J. (1991) 'The sociology of tourism', 48–57 in Cooper C. (ed.) *Progress in Tourism, Recreation and Hospitality Management*, vol. III, Belhaven Press, London.
14 Aitchison C. (1997) book review of Apostolopoulos Y. *et al.* (eds) (1996) *The Sociology of Tourism: Theoretical and Empirical Investigations*, Routledge, in *Leisure Studies* 16, 53–4: 53.
15 Foucault M. (1980) *Power/Knowledge: Selected Interviews and Other Writings 1972–1977*, ed. Gordon C., Random House, New York: 187.
16 Wilson J. (1988) *Politics and Leisure*, Unwin Hyman, London: 12.
17 Rojek C. (1985) *Leisure and Capitalist Theory*, Tavistock, New York: 146–7.
18 Wilson, *Politics*, 11; and Rojek, *Leisure*, 16.
19 Wilson, *Politics*, 11–12. See also Shields R. (1991) *Places on the Margin. Alternative Geographies of Modernity*, Routledge, London: 96.
20 Rojek, *Leisure*: 13.

193

21 Parker S. (1981) 'Change, flexibility, spontaneity, and self-determination in leisure', *Social Forces* 60 (2) 323–31.

22 Rojek presents a convincing critique of Parker's model in chapter 4 of Rojek, *Leisure*, especially 99–101.

23 Duncan N. (1996) 'Sexuality in public and private spaces', 127–45 in Duncan N. (ed.) *Bodyspace: Destabilizing Geographies of Gender and Sexuality*, Routledge, London: 135.

24 See, for instance, Rojek *Leisure*, and Duncan, *Bodyspace*.

25 Clegg S.R. (1989) *Frameworks of Power*, Sage, London: 182–3.

26 Morgan and Pritchard, *Tourism Promotion and Power*.

27 Clarke and Critcher, *The Devil Makes Work*: 174.

28 Kinnaird and Hall, 'Introduction': 5.

29 Rojek, *Leisure*; Clarke and Critcher, *The Devil Makes Work*; Wilson, *Politics*; and Hargreaves J. (1986) *Sport, Power and Culture*, Polity Press, Cambridge.

30 Hargreaves, *Sport, Power and Culture*: 41.

31 The phrase 'compensatory function' is Rojek's, *Leisure*: 51.

32 Hargreaves, *Sport, Power and Culture*: 41.

33 See, for instance, Joyce P. (1991) *Visions of the People. Industrial England and the Question of Class, 1848–1914*, Cambridge University Press, Cambridge, especially his 'Introduction: beyond class?'

34 Williams G. (1985) 'Community, class and rugby in South Wales 1880–1914', *Society for the Study of Labour History* 50, 10–11.

35 Stedman Jones G. (1977) 'Class expression versus social control? A critique of recent trends in the social history of leisure', *History Workshop* 4, 162–70.

36 Jones S. (1986) *Workers at Play: A Social and Economic History Of Leisure, 1918–1939*, Routledge & Kegan Paul, London: 6–7.

37 Joyce P. (1991) *Visions of the People*: 3.

38 Stedman Jones, 'Class expression': 168 and 163.

39 Clegg, *Frameworks of Power*: 149.

40 Hall S. (1997) 'The work of representation', 13–74 in Hall S. (ed.) *Representation: Cultural Representations and Signifying Practices*, Sage and the Open University, London: 98.

41 Foucault M. (1977) *Discipline and Punishment*, Tavistock, London: 27.

42 Foucault, M. (1980) *Power/Knowledge*, Harvester, Brighton: 119.

43 Cross G. (1993) *Time and Money. The Making of Consumer Culture*, Routledge, London: 1. See also Durant H. (1938) *The Problem of Leisure*, London, one of the first works to highlight the inequalities of leisure access.

44 See, for instance, Walvin J. (1975) *The People's Game: A Social History of Football*, Allen Lane, London; Vamplew W. (1976) *The Turf: A Social and Economic History of Horse Racing*, Allen Lane, London; Vincent D. (1983), 'Reading in the working-class home', 207–2 in Walton J.K. and Walvin J. (eds.), *Leisure in Britain 1780–1914*, Manchester University Press, Manchester; Walton J.K. (1983), *The English Seaside Resort: A Social History 1750–1914*, Leicester University Press,

Leicester; and Cross, *Time and Money*

45 For example, Yeo and Yeo (eds) (1981) *Popular Culture and Class Conflict*; Bailey P. (1987) *Leisure and Class in Victorian England: Rational Recreation and the Contest for Control 1830–1885*, Methuen, London; and Rojek C. (1989) 'Leisure time and leisure space', 191–204 in Rojek C. (ed.), *Leisure for Leisure*, Sage, London.

46 Stedman Jones, 'Class expression'.

47 Stedman Jones, 'Class expression': 170, our emphasis.

48 Marx K. and Engels F. (1957) *Verke*, Berlin, vol. III: 539, quoted in Williams R. (1985) 'Culture', 15–55 in McLellan D. (ed.), *Marx: The First 100 Years*, Oxford University Press, Oxford: 22.

49 Williams, 'Culture': 23.

50 Yeo E. and Yeo S. (1981) 'Ways of seeing. Social control and leisure versus class and struggle', 128–54 in Yeo and Yeo (eds) *Popular Culture and Class Conflict*: 150, original emphasis.

51 Yeo E. and Yeo S., 'Ways of seeing': 150.

52 Reid D. (1976) 'The decline of Saint Monday 1776–1876', *Past and Present*, 71, 76–101; and Howkins A. (1981), 'The taming of Whitsun. The changing face of a nineteenth century rural holiday', 187–208 in Yeo and Yeo (eds) *Popular Culture and Class Conflict*.

53 Wrightson K. (1981) 'Alehouses, order and reformation in rural England 1590–1660', 1–27 in Yeo and Yeo (eds) *Popular Culture and Class Conflict*; and Williams R. (1966) *Communications*, Penguin, Harmondsworth.

54 Bailey, *Leisure and Class*: 2.

55 Stedman Jones G. (1983) *Languages of Class*, London: 86–7, quoted in Cross *Time and Money*: 5.

56 Joyce, *Visions of the People*: 3.

57 Joyce, *Visions of the People*: 2.

58 Bailey, *Leisure and Class*: 170.

59 Harrison B. (1967) 'Religion and recreation in nineteenth century England', *Past and Present*, 38, 98–125. See also Walvin, *Leisure and Society*: 9–10.

60 Ashplant T.G. (1981), 'London working men's clubs, 1875–1914', 241–70 in Yeo and Yeo (eds) *Popular Culture and Class Conflict*.

61 Jones, *Workers at Play*: 6–7.

62 Cunningham H. (1980) *Leisure in the Industrial Revolution 1780–1880*, Croom Helm, London: 10.

63 Bailey *Leisure and Class*: 2. See also Briggs A. (1960) *Mass Entertainment: The Origins of a Modern Industry*, Griffin Press, Adelaide.

64 Jones, *Workers at Play*. See also Thompson F.M.L. (1990) *The Cambridge Social History of Britain 1750–1950, Vol. 2, People and their Environment*, Cambridge University Press, Cambridge.

65 Cross, *Time and Money*.

66 Walvin J. (1978) *Beside the Seaside: A Social History of the Popular Seaside Holiday*,

195

Allen Lane, London; and Walton, *English Seaside Resort.*

67 Pimlott J.A.R. (1947) *The Englishman's Holiday: A Social History*, Faber and Faber, London.

68 Hern A. (1967) *The Seaside Holiday: The History of the English Seaside Resort*, Cresset, London, see especially 28–9 and 151.

69 Walton *The English Seaside Resort.*

70 Durie A. (1997) 'The Scottish seaside resort in peace and war, c. 1880–1960', *International Journal of Maritime History*, 9 (1) 171–86; Chase L. (1997) 'Modern images and social tone in Clacton and Frinton in the interwar years', *International Journal of Maritime History*, 9 (1) 149–69; Demetriadi J. (1995) 'English and Welsh Seaside Resorts—with special reference to Blackpool and Margate', University of Lancaster unpublished PhD; and Agarwal S. (1994) 'The life cycle approach and south coast resorts', 194–208 in Cooper C. and Lockwood A. (eds) *Progress in Tourism Recreation and Hospitality Management*, vol. 5, Wiley, Chichester.

71 Perkin H.J. (1976) 'The social tone of Victorian seaside resorts in the North West', *Northern History* 11, 187–94. See also Cannadine D. (ed.) (1982) *Patricians, Power and Politics*, University of Leicester, Leicester.

72 Huggins M. (1984) 'Social tone and resort development in North East England: Victorian seaside resorts around the mouth of the Tees', *Northern History* 20, 187–206.

73 Walton, *English Seaside Resort*: 5.

74 Lowerson J. and Myerscough J. (1977) *Time to Spare in Victorian England*, Harvester Press, Hassocks.

75 Walton J.K. (1983) 'Municipal government and the holiday industry in Blackpool 1876–1914', 159–85 in Walton and Walvin (eds.) *Leisure in Britain*; and Walton J.K. (1994) 'The re-making of a popular resort: Blackpool Tower and the boom of the 1890s', *Local Historian* 24, 194–205: 199–200.

76 Roberts R. (1983) 'The corporation as impresario: the municipal provision of entertainment in Victorian and Edwardian Bournemouth', 137–58 in Walton and Walvin (eds.) *Leisure in Britain.*

77 Chase, 'Social tone in Clacton and Frinton': 150.

78 Joyce, *Visions of the People*: 1.

79 Joyce, *Visions of the People*: 1.

80 Walton J.K. (1974) 'The social development of Blackpool 1788–1914', unpublished University of Lancaster PhD: 125 and 137. See also Perkin, 'Social tone of Victorian seaside resorts': 181.

81 Walton, 'Social development of Blackpool': 125 and 137. See also Perkin, 'Social tone of Victorian seaside resorts': 181.

82 Morgan N.J. (1992) 'Perceptions, patterns and policies of tourism. The development of the Devon seaside resorts in the twentieth century with special reference to Torquay and Ilfracombe', unpublished University of Exeter PhD; and Chase, 'Social tone in Clacton and Frinton'.

83 Walton, *English Seaside Resort*: 225, original emphasis.

84 Hoggart, *The Uses of Literacy*: 147.
85 Walton, *English Seaside Resort*: 3.
86 Walton, *English Seaside Resort*: 3.
87 Walton, *English Seaside Resort*; Parry K. (1983) *The Resorts of the Lancashire Coast*, David and Charles, Newton Abbot; and Whyman J. (198) 'Water communi-cations and their direct effect on the growth and character of Margate c.1750–1840', 138–51 in Sigsworth E.M. (ed.) *Ports and Resorts in the Regions*, Proceedings of the Conference of Regional History Tutors, Hull College of Higher Education, Hull.

CHAPTER 3

1   Williams A. and Shaw G. (1997) 'Riding the big dipper: the rise and decline of the British seaside resort in the twentieth century', 1–20 in Shaw G. and Williams A. (eds) *The Rise and Fall of British Coastal Resorts. Cultural and Economic Perspectives*, Cassell, London: 13.
2   Cross G. (1993) *Time and Money: The Making of Consumer Culture*, Routledge, London: 178.
3   Yates N. (1989) 'Selling the seaside', *History Today* 38, 2–27.
4   Morgan N.J. (1992) 'Perceptions, patterns and policies of tourism. the devel-opment of the seaside resorts of Devon in the twentieth century with special reference to Torquay and Ilfracombe', unpublished University of Exeter PhD: 50–85. See also Henley Centre for Leisure Forecasting (1989) 'The discerning consumer', *Leisure Management* 9 (5) 34–6.
5   Yates, 'Selling the seaside': 21.
6   Yates, 'Selling the seaside': 21–4.
7   Durie A. (1997) 'The scottish seaside resort in peace and war, c. 1880–1960', *International Journal of Maritime History* 9 (1) 171–86.
8   Walvin J. (1978) *Beside the Seaside: A Social History of the Popular Seaside Holiday*, Allen Lane, London: 120; and Yates, 'Selling the seaside': 20–2.
9   Lewes F.M.M. *et al.* (1969) 'The holiday industry', 244–58 in Barlow F. (ed.) *Exeter and its Region*, University of Exeter Press, Exeter: 245.
10 Parry K. (1983) *The Resorts of the Lancashire Coast*, David and Charles, Newton Abbot: 92.
11 Walton J.K. (1974) 'The social development of Blackpool 1788–1914', unpub-lished University of Lancaster PhD: 224.
12 Walvin, *Beside the Seaside*: 107; and Beveridge W. (1944) *Full Employment in a Free Society*: 63, quoted in Jones S. (1986) *Workers at Play: A Social and Economic History of Leisure 1918–1939*, Routledge & Kegan Paul, London: 43.
13 Walton J.K. (1983), *The English Seaside Resort: A Social History 1750–1914*, Leicester University Press, Leicester: 221.
14 The authors are grateful to Tim Gale of University of Wales Institute, Cardiff for this information, taken from his PhD in progress on Rhyl.

15 Walvin, *Beside the Seaside*: 117.

16 Chase L. (1997) 'Modern images and social tone in Clacton and Frinton in the interwar years', *International Journal of Maritime History* 9 (1) 149–69.

17 Graves R. and Hodge A. (1940) *The Long Weekend: A Social History of Great Britain 1918–1939*, Faber and Faber, London: especially 36–49.

18 Delisle Burns C. (1932) *Leisure In The Modern World*, Allen and Unwin, London : 7.

19 Walton J.K. (1997) 'The seaside resorts of England and Wales, 1900–1950: growth, diffusion and the emergence of new forms of coastal tourism', 21–48 in Shaw and Williams (eds) *The Rise and Fall of British Coastal Resorts*: 41.

20 See Yates, 'Selling the seaside': 21–4 and Morgan, 'Perceptions, patterns and policies': chapter 6.

21 Brunner E. (1945) *Holiday Making and the Holiday Trades*, Nuffield College, Oxford: 9 and 13; Pimlott J.A.R. (1947) *The Englishman's Holiday: a Social History*, Faber and Faber, London: 219–22; Martin G.E. (1968) 'Some aspects of the provision of annual holidays for the working classes down to 1947', unpublished University of Leicester MA thesis: 86–88; and Jones, *Workers at Play*: 19–20.

22 Walton J.K. and O'Neill C. (1993) 'Numbering the holidaymakers: the problems and possibilities of the June census of 1921 for historians of resorts', *Local Historian* 23 (4) 205–16: 205.

23 Walton, 'The seaside resorts of England and Wales': 37.

24 Morgan, Perceptions, patterns and politics: 120–1.

25 IUDC Minutes 3 Oct. 1939.

26 IUDC Minutes 5 Mar. 1940 and 4 Mar. 1941; *IC* 1 Mar., 21 June and 26 July 1940; 14, 21 and 28 Feb. and 4 April and 2 May 1941. See *IC* 30 May, 27 June and 22 Aug. 1941 for reports of tension between evacuees and residents.

27 IUDC Minutes 4 Nov. 1952 and 17 Aug. and 7 Sept. 1954.

28 IUDC Minutes 2 Oct. and 10 Nov. 1945; *IC* 2 Nov. 1945; IUDC Minutes 2 April, 21 May and 2 July 1946, and 7 Jan. 1947; and *IC* 22 Mar. 1946.

29 *IC* 23 April 1948 and IUDC Minutes 1 June 1948.

30 *IC* 29 Mar., 21 June and 12 July 1940 and IUDC Minutes 1 Oct. 1940 and 2 May 1944.

31 Lickorish L.J. and Kershaw A.G. (1958) *The Travel Trade*, Practical Press Ltd, London: 116.

32 Marquand D. (1986) 'Sir Stafford Cripps', 155–77 in Sissons M. and French P. (eds) *Age of Austerity 1945–51*, Oxford University Press, Oxford: 158–9.

33 *IC* 11 June 1948.

34 *IC* 30 May 1947.

35 *TT* 10 Aug. 1945 and 19 Aug. 1947.

36 *The Times* 7 April and 8 Nov. 1951.

37 *TT* 16 Mar. 1945, 9 Jan. 1948 and 2 June 1950; and *WMN* 18 Oct. 1946.

38 IUDC Minutes 1945–53.

39   *IC* 14 May 1948, IUDC Minutes 4 Oct. 1949 and *WT* 4 Feb. 1949.
40   Lickorish and Kershaw, *The Travel Trade*: 116.
41   *The Times* 13 and 28 April 1950; and 29 Sept. 1961.
42   *The Times* 6 Aug. 1951, and 13 April and 29 Sept. 1961.
43   BTA (1967) *South Western Counties Tourist Study: Interim Report*, BTA, London: vii; and SWEPC (1967) *Region with a Future*, SWEPC, London: 146 and 76.
44   SWEPC, *Region with a Future*: 53–4 and 146; SWEPC (1976) *Economic Survey of the Tourist Industry in the South West*, SWEPC, London: 20 and 45; and Lewes F.M.M. *et al.* (1970) *The Holiday Industry of Devon and Cornwall*, HMSO, London: 70, 54–5 and 217.
45   ETB (1983) *Tourism and Leisure: A Statement of Development Intent*, ETB, London: 3–5.
46   Countryside Commission (1980) *Trends in Tourism and Recreation 1968–78*, Countryside Commission, Cheltenham: 1.
47   *The Times* 13 April 1961; and Barker T. (1985) 'The international history of motor transport', *Journal of Contemporary History* 20, 3–19: 6–7.
48   Good A. (1980) 'The coastal resort', 87–95 in DCC, *Coastlines of Devon*, DCC, Exeter: 91; Lickorish and Kershaw, *The Travel Trade*: 179; Barker, 'The international history of motor transport': 6–7; Burton T.L. (1965) 'Holiday movements in Britain', *Town and Country Planning* 33, 118–23: 118; and Countryside Commission, *Trends in Tourism and Recreation*: 1.
49   Walton, 'The seaside resorts of England and Wales': 46.
50   Walton, 'The seaside resorts of England and Wales': 46.
51   SWEPC, *Economic Survey of the Tourist Industry*: 30.
52   Waterman D. (1984) 'Seaside resorts to a theme for a dream', *Town and Country Planning* 53, 104–6: 104.
53   Farley R. (1967) 'The British seaside resort—can it survive? Part one: the facts', *Hotel and Catering Review*, July, 12–15: 14. For further evidence of the flight of the affluent abroad, see *The Times* 5 Aug. 1961.
54   Demetriadi J. (1997), 'The golden years: English seaside resorts 1950–74', 49–78 in Shaw and Williams (eds) *The Rise and Fall of British Coastal Resorts*: 58.
55   BTA, *South West Counties Tourist Study*: 217; and SWEPC, *Region with a Future*: 108.
56   Demetriadi, 'The golden years': 59.
57   East Devon Action Project (1987) *Tourism in East Devon: A Report of a Set of Surveys Conducted in East Devon, June 1986–June 1987*, Totnes: 12; DCC (1981, 1983 and 1987 edns) *Devon Tourism Review*, DCC, Exeter; and ETB, *Tourism and Leisure*: 18.
58   Morgan, 'Perceptions, patterns and policies: chapter 5. The authors are grateful to Tim Gale of the University of Wales Institute, Cardiff for the details of Rhyl.
59   Williams and Shaw, 'Riding the big dipper'.
60   *Teignmouth Post* 28 Mar. 1980; ETB (1981) *Tourism Fact Sheets: West Country*, ETB, London: 6; and DCC (1981) *Devon Tourism Review*, DCC, Exeter: 5.

61 ETB, *Tourism Fact Sheets: West Country*: 6; and ETB, *Tourism and Leisure*: 18.

62 ETB, *Tourism Fact Sheets: West Country*: 6; and ETB, *Tourism and Leisure*: 18.

63 East Devon Action Project, *Tourism in East Devon*: 12.

64 The English Tourist Board, the Northern Ireland Tourist Board, the Scottish Tourist Board and the Wales Tourist Board (1994) *The UK Tourist* (Scotland): 18–19.

65 Williams and Shaw, 'Riding the big dipper': 5.

66 Walton, 'The seaside resorts of England and Wales': 24.

67 Quoted in Pimlott, *The Englishman's Holiday*: 237.

68 Hargreaves J. (1982) 'Sport, culture and ideology', 30–61 in Hargreaves J. (ed.) *Sport, Culture and Ideology*, Routledge & Kegan Paul, London: 36.

69 Pimlott, *The Englishman' s Holiday*: 215; and Urry J. (1990) *The Tourist Gaze: Leisure and Travel in Contemporary Societies*, Sage, London: 6, quoting Cabinet Office (Enterprise Unit) (1983) *Pleasure, Leisure and Jobs: The Business of Tourism*, HMSO, London.

70 Walvin, *Beside the Seaside*, 100.

71 Pember Reeves M. (1913) *Round About a Pound a Week*, Penguin, Harmondsworth. See also Spring Rice M. (1939) *Working Class Wives. Their Health and Conditions*, Penguin, Harmondsworth.

72 Beales H.L. and Lambert R.S. (1934) *Memoirs of the Unemployed*: 237.

73 Walvin, *Beside the Seaside*, 109.

74 Pimlott, *The Englishman's Holiday*: 232; and Martin, 'Some aspects of the provision of annual holidays': 58.

75 Smith M., Parker S. and Smith C. (eds) (1973), *Leisure and Society in Britain*, Allen Lane, London: 236, citing BTA figures.

76 Williams and Shaw 'Riding the big dipper': 8.

77 WTB (1997) *All Wales Visitor Surveys 1996*, WTB, Cardiff.

78 Hudson R. and Williams A.M. (1995) *Divided Britain*, 2nd. edn, John Wiley & Sons, Chichester: 124.

79 Morgan N.J. and Pritchard A. (1998) *Tourism Promotion and Power: Creating Images, Creating Identities*, John Wiley & Sons, Chichester: chapter 5.

80 Mintel International Group Ltd (1995) *Targeting the Rich and Poor*: executive summary.

81 Mintel International Group Ltd, *Targeting the Rich and Poor*: executive summary.

82 Walvin, *Beside the Seaside*: 100; The Pilgrim Trust (1938) *Men Without Work*, Cambridge University Press, Cambridge: 102–3; and Humphries S. (1981) 'Steal to survive: the social crime of working class children 1890–1940', *Oral History* 9 (6) 24–33.

83 Walvin, *Beside the Seaside*: 133.

84 Walvin, *Beside the Seaside*: 136 and 27.

85 Walvin, *Beside the Seaside*: 136 and 27.

86 WTB (1994) unpublished qualitative findings for the Quality Assurance Schemes Report (1994), WTB, Cardiff.

87 Walvin, *Beside the Seaside*: 133.

88 A.H. Halsey quoted in Walvin, *Beside the Seaside*: 148.

89 Walton, 'The social development of Blackpool': 224.

90 Walton, 'The seaside resorts of England and Wales': 39.

91 Williams A. and Shaw G. (1988) 'Tourism: candy floss industry or job generator', *Town Planning Review* 59, 81–104.

92 Williams and Shaw, 'Riding the big dipper': 12.

93 Morgan N.J. and Pritchard A. (1996) 'Welsh seaside resort strategies', paper presented to the third Urban History Conference, Budapest.

94 Agarwal S. (1997) 'The public sector: planning for renewal?' 137–58 in Shaw and Williams (eds) *The Rise and Fall of British Coastal Resort*: 139.

95 Walton, 'The seaside resorts of England and Wales': 42.

96 Buck N. *et al.* (1989) 'The Isle of Thanet: restructuring and municipal conservatism', 166–97 in Cooke P. (ed.) *Localities*, Unwin Hyman, London: 175.

97 Walton, 'The seaside resorts of England and Wales': 42. See also Walton J.K. and Walvin J. (eds) (1983) *Leisure in Britain 1780–1939*, Manchester University Press, Manchester.

98 Walton, 'The seaside resorts of England and Wales': 43.

99 Ward S.V. (1988) *The Geography of Inter-war Britain: The State and Uneven Development*, Routledge, London; and Morgan, 'Perceptions, patterns and policies': chapters 4 and 5.

100 Walton, 'The seaside resorts of England and Wales': 44.

101 Denman R. (1994) *A Record of Achievement*, WTB, Cardiff.

102 Selby M. and Morgan N.J. (1996) 'Reconstruing place image. A case study of its role in destination market research', *Tourism Management* 17 (4) 287–94.

103 Agarwal, 'The public sector: planning for renewal?': 156–7.

104 Shaw G. and Williams A. (1997) 'The private sector: tourism entrepreneurship—a constraint or resource?, 117–36 in Shaw and Williams (eds) *The Rise and Fall of British Coastal Resort*: 118.

105 Morgan N.J. (1998) 'Welsh seaside resort strategies: changing times, changing needs', 206–16 in Starkey D. and Jamieson A.G. (eds) *Exploiting the Sea. Aspects of Britain's Maritime Economy Since 1870*, University of Exeter Press, Exeter.

106 Greenwood J., Williams A.M. and Shaw G. (1990) 'Policy implementation and tourism in the UK: implications from recent research in Cornwall', *Tourism Management* 11 (1) 53–62.

107 Shaw and Williams, 'The private sector: tourism entrepreneurship': 130.

108 Shaw and Williams, 'The private sector: tourism entrepreneurship': 130.

109 Morgan, 'Perceptions, patterns and policies': chapter 4.

110 Walton, 'The seaside resorts of England and Wales': 44.

111 Turner B. and Palmer S. (1976) *The Blackpool Story*, Blackpool Corporation, Cleveleys, and Stafford F. and Yates N. (1985) *The Later Kentish Seaside*, Alan Sutton, Gloucester, both quoted in Walton, 'The seaside resorts of England and Wales'.

112 Walton, 'The seaside resorts of England and Wales': 44.

113 Morgan, 'Perceptions, patterns and politics': 78.

114 Morgan, M. (1991) 'Majorca: dressing up to survive', *Tourism Management* 12 (1) March.

115 Lewes *et al. The Holiday Industry of Devon and Cornwall*: 91–2, 95, 101 and 107.

116 Shaw and Williams, 'The private sector: tourism entrepreneurship': 120.

117 ETB (1991) *The Future for England's Smaller Resorts*, ETB, London.

118 Ventures Consultancy (1989) *Seaside Resorts in England Market Profile*, ETB, London: 127.

119 Morgan and Pritchard, 'Welsh seaside resort strategies'.

120 Agarwal, 'The public sector: planning for renewal?'

121 Gale T., Botterill D., Morgan N.J. and Shaw G. (1995) 'Cultural change and the British seaside resort—implications for the quality and integrity of resort environments', 129–34 in Healy M.G. and Doody J.P. (eds) *Directions in European Coastal Management*, Samara Publishing, Cardigan.

122 Urry J. (1997) 'Cultural change and the seaside resort', 102–116 in Shaw and Williams (eds) *The Rise and Fall of British Coastal Resorts*: 107.

123 Urry, 'Cultural change and the seaside resort': 108.

124 Urry, 'Cultural change and the seaside resort': 109.

125 Hall D. (1998) 'Reconstruction, modernization and sustainability: prospects for the role of tourism in Albania', 321–30 in Nahrstedt W. and Kombol T.P. (eds) *Leisure Culture and Tourism in Europe*, Institut fur Freizeitwissenschaft und Kulturarbeit, Bielefeld.

126 Urry, 'Cultural change and the seaside resort': 112.

127 Williams and Shaw, 'Riding the big dipper': 16.

128 Walton J.K. (1997) 'Seaside resorts and maritime history', *International Journal of Maritime History* 9 (1) 125–47: 129; and Shields R. (1991) *Places on the Margin: Alternative Geographies of Modernity*, Routledge, London: chapter 2.

129 Shields, *Places on the Margin*: 73–4.

130 Shields, *Places on the Margin*: 74.

131 Shields, *Places on the Margin*: 75.

132 Walton, 'Seaside resorts and maritime history': 137. See also Joyce P. (1991) *Visions of the People: Industrial England and the Question of Class, 1848–1914*, Cambridge University Press, Cambridge.

133 Walton, 'Seaside resorts and maritime history': 135.

134 Walton, 'Seaside resorts and maritime history': 138.

135 Walton, 'Seaside resorts and maritime history': 133.

136 Moser C.A. and Scott W. (1961) *British Towns*, Oxford University Press, London: 31, quoted in Walton, 'The seaside resorts of England and Wales'.

137 Walton, 'The seaside resorts of England and Wales': 45.

CHAPTER 4

1   DCC (1981) *Devon County Structure Plan*, DCC, Exeter: 144–5.

2   TMBC (1932) *Torquay Official Guide*.

3   Pritchard A., Morgan N.J., Sedgley D. and Jenkins, A. (1998) 'Reaching out to
    the gay tourist: opportunities and threats in an emerging market segment',
    Tourism Management 19 (3).

4   Stanes R. (1978) *A History of Devon*, Harvester Press, Sussex: 11.

5   Morgan N.J. (1992) 'Perceptions, patterns and policies of tourism: the devel-
    opment of the Devon seaside resorts during the twentieth century with special
    reference to Torquay and Ilfracombe', unpublished University of Exeter PhD:
    chapter 3.

6   Gardiner V. *et al.* (1977) 'Scenic qualities of the south east Devon coast',
    Transactions of the Devonshire Association 109, 171–8.

7   DCC, *Structure Plan*: 124.

8   Gregory K.J. (1976) 'The face of the South West is its fortune', *Geographical
    Magazine* 48. 539–47, quoted in Gardiner, 'Scenic qualities'.

9   SWEPC (1967) *A Region with a Future*, SWEPC, London: 48; Stanes, *A History
    of Devon*: 107–8; and Starkey D. (1994) 'The ports, seaborne trade and shipping
    industry of south Devon, 1786–1914', 32–47 in Duffy M. *et al.* (eds) *The New
    Maritime History of Devon*, vol. II, Conway Maritime Press and University of
    Exeter Press, London/Exeter.

10 Hoskins W.G. (1959) *Devon and its People*, University of Exeter, Exeter: 159.

11 SWEPC, *Region with a Future*: 20 and DCC (1987) Devon Tourism Review,
    DCC, Exeter: 7.

12 DCC, *Structure Plan*: 107; DCC (1987) *Devon Tourism Review*: 15; and WCTB
    (1989) *Towards a Strategy for the 1990s and Beyond: A Review and Key Issue Report*,
    consultative document, WCTB, Exeter: 49.

13 Lewes F.M.M. *et al.* (1969) 'The holiday industry', 244–58 in Barlow F. (ed.)
    Exeter and its Region, University of Exeter Press, Exeter: 244; Good A. (1980)
    'The coastal resort', 87–95 in DCC *Coastlines of Devon*, DCC, Exeter: 87;
    Hoskins, *Devon and its People*: 120; and Nuffield College Social Reconstruction
    Survey (1944) *The Devon Tourist Trade*: 2.

14 Lewes, 'The holiday industry': 244.

15 Lewes F.M.M. *et al.* (1970) *The Holiday Industry of Devon and Cornwall*, HMSO,
    London: 4 and Lewes *et al.* , 'The holiday industry': 244–55.

16 Hoskins, *Devon and its People*: 117–18; Lewes *et al.*, *The Holiday Industry of Devon
    and Cornwall*: 4; and Lewes *et al.*, 'The holiday industry': 244–6.

17 Travis J.F. (1988) 'The rise of holidaymaking on the Devon coast with special
    reference to health and entertainment', unpublished University of Exeter PhD:
    14 and 189–91.

18 British Rail (1949) *Western Region Holiday Guide*: 212.

19 Nuffield College Social Reconstruction Survey (1944) *The Devon Tourist Trade*:

8; Papers of the Rev. Dr J. McIntyre, compiler of Nuffield College Social Reconstruction Surveys on Devon Industries and Tourism, 1941–3; and EUDC Foreshore and Pleasure Grounds Committee Minutes, 1919–38.

20 Walton J.K. and O'Neill C. (1993) 'Numbering the holidaymakers: the problems and possibilities of the June census of 1921 for historians of resorts', *Local Historian* 23 (4) 205–16: 215

21 Census Report, 1921.

22 Walton and O'Neill 'Numbering the holidaymakers': 205

23 Traffic at GWR stations, PRO Rail 266/45. See Morgan, 'Perceptions, patterns and policies': 62.

24 Lewes *et al.* 'The holiday industry': 244.

25 *The Times* 2 Aug. 1929.

26 *IC* 24 July and 18 Sept. 1920.

27 *IC* 24 July and 18 Sept. 1920.

28 *The Times* 2 Aug. 1929.

29 Nuffield College Social Reconstruction Survey (May 1941) *Devon Industries* (with special reference to South Devon): 4.

30 BTA (1967) *South West Counties Tourist Study: Interim Report*, BTA, Exeter: vii; and SWEPC, *Region with a Future*: 146 and 76.

31 SWEPC, *Region with a Future*: 53–4 and 146; SWEPC (1976) *Economic Survey of the Tourist Industry in the South West*, SWEPC, London: 20 and 45; and Lewes *et al.*, *The Holiday Industry of Devon and Cornwall*: 70, 54–5 and 217.

32 BTA, *South Western Counties Tourist Study*: viii; SWEPC, *Region with a Future*: 146; SWEPC, *Economic Survey*: 3, 33 and 37–8; Lewes *et al.*, *The Holiday Industry of Devon and Cornwall*: 69; WMN 31 July 1970; and DCC, *Structure Plan*: 108.

33 *WMN* 9 Oct. 1968; and DCC (1971) *Background. An Information Summary of Devon County Council* Oct./Nov./Dec., Exeter: 2.

34 SWEPC, *Region with a Future*: 55; EUDC Minutes 24 July 1956; *The Times* 13 April 1961.

35 SWEPC, *Economic Survey*: 21 and SWEPC, *Region with a Future*: 55. See IUDC files on reduced fares for resorts, 1956, and the closure of the Barnstaple–Ilfracombe railway line, 1966–8. Opposition to the Beeching report can be traced in the local press: see for instance *WMN* 28 Mar., 1 May and 12 June 1963.

36 SWEPC, *Region with a Future*: 30, 19 and 35; and DCC (1958) *Teignmouth: A Survey of Holidaymakers* 1957, DCC, Exeter.

37 Census report, 1971.

38 Lewes *et al.*, *The Holiday Industry of Devon and Cornwall*: 131; and DCC (1977) *Devon in Figures*, DCC, Exeter: 159.

39 *WMN* 19 Oct. 1968

40 BTA, *South West Counties Tourist Study*: x and viii; and SWEPC, *Economic Survey*: 36.

41 BTA, *South West Counties Tourist Study*: vi.

42 Lewes *et al.*, *The Holiday Industry of Devon and Cornwall*: 139.
43 *Independent* 26 Aug. 1989.
44 DCC (1987) *Devon Tourist Review*: 17; and DCC (1983) *A Discussion Paper on Tourism: The First Alteration of the Devon County Council Plan*, DCC, Exeter: 3.
45 DCC (1987) *Devon Tourist Review*: 17; and DCC, *A Discussion Paper on Tourism*: 3.
46 DCC, *Structure Plan*: 123–4.
47 DCC (1987) *Devon Tourism Review* 15–6.
48 DCC *Devon Tourism Review* 1981, 1983 and 1987.
49 DCC (1981) *Tourism and Recreation Topic Report*: 3; and DCC (1984) *Tourism and Recreation Topic Report*: 3; and East Devon Action Project, *Tourism in East Devon*: 14–15.
50 Lewes *et al.*, *The Holiday Industry of Devon and Cornwall*: 15; DCC (1984) *Devon Tourism Review*: 5 and DCC (1987) *Devon Tourism Review*: 14; and DCC (1981) *Tourism and Recreation Topic Report*: 3.
51 Census Report 1981 and Office of Population, Censuses and Surveys (1984) *Key Statistics for Local Authorities*, HMSO, London.
52 Grafton D.J. and Bolton N. (1986) 'Planning policy and economic development in Devon and Cornwall 1945–1984', in Gripaios P. (ed.) *The Economy of Devon and Cornwall*, Occasional Papers Series, No. 9, South West Papers in Geography, Plymouth Polytechnic, Plymouth.
53 Walton J.K. (1997) 'The seaside resorts of England and Wales, 1900–1950: growth, diffusion and the emergence of new forms of coastal tourism', 21–48 in Shaw G. and Williams A. (eds) *The Rise and Fall of British Coastal Resorts. Cultural and Economic Perspectives*, Cassell, London: 40.
54 Walton, 'The seaside resorts of England and Wales': 40.
55 Stanes, *A History of Devon*: 111.
56 Census Reports 1911–51.
57 Census Reports 1911–51; and *Express and Echo*, 24 June 1958.
58 Census Reports 1921–81.
59 DCC, *Structure Plan*: 30; SWEPC, *Region with a Future*: 14; and Lewes *et al.*, *The Holiday Industry of Devon and Cornwall*: 28.
60 Lewes *et al.*, *The Holiday Industry of Devon and Cornwall*: 32; and DCC (1977) *Devon in Figures*: 116.
61 DCC, *Devon in Figures*: 135.
62 DCC, *Devon in Figures*: 135.
63 DCC, *Structure Plan*: 23–5.
64 Lewes *et al.*, *The Holiday Industry of Devon and Cornwall*: 32; and DCC, *Devon in Figures*: 116.
65 Central Statistical Office (1985) *Regional Trends*, HMSO, London; and Census Report 1981.
66 May F.B. (1978) 'The Development of Ilfracombe as a seaside resort in the nineteenth century', unpublished University of Wales MA.

67 Councillor Houlford, quoted in *IC* 16 Sept. 1924.
68 Morgan, 'Perceptions, patterns and policies': chapter 5.
69 Councillor Woodward, quoted in *IC* 19 Sept. 1925.
70 Reports of ratepayers meetings, *IC* 7 and 11 Nov. 1930.
71 Mayoral address, reported in the *TT* 13 Nov. 1931.
72 *TT* 15 Jan. 1926.
73 Mr Knill, quoted in *IC* 29 Nov. 1946.
74 Middleton V.T.C. (1989) 'Seaside resorts', *Insights*, B5–13, ETB.
75 *TT* 13 Mar. 1970.
76 *TT* 13 Mar. 1970.
77 IUDC General Purposes Committee 18 April 1972.
78 *WMN* 13 April 1966 and *Herald Express* 25 Nov. 1988.
79 Morgan, 'Perceptions, patterns and policies': 133.
80 Devon Alliance of Amenity Societies (1978) *Report of a Survey on the Effects of Tourism in Devon*, Exeter.
81 *Herald Express* 5 Nov. 1976.
82 DCC, *Structure Plan*: 107; and NDCC (1979) *Ilfracombe District Plan*, NDCC, Barnstaple: 153–4.
83 Travis J.F., 'Lynton in the nineteenth century: an isolated and exclusive resort', 152–67 in Sigsworth E.M. (ed.) (1980) *Ports and Resorts in the Regions*, Proceedings of the Conference of Regional History Tutors, held at Hull College of Higher Education, Hull; Travis, 'The rise of holidaymaking on the Devon coast'; and Travis J.F. (1993) *The Rise of the Devon Seaside Resorts 1750–1900*, University of Exeter Press, Exeter.
84 May F.B. (1978) 'The growth of Ilfracombe'; May F.B. (1980) 'The rise of Ilfracombe as a seaside resort in the nineteenth century', 137–59 in Fisher H.E.S. (ed.) *West Country Maritime and Social History*: Exeter Papers in Economic History 13, University of Exeter, Exeter; and May F.B. (1983) 'Victorian and Edwardian Ilfracombe', 186–205 in Walton J.K. and Walvin J. (eds) *Leisure in Britain 1780–1939*, Manchester University Press, Manchester.
85 Travis, 'The rise of holidaymaking': 638–9.
86 Walton, 'The seaside resorts of England and Wales': 40.
87 Walton, 'The seaside resorts of England and Wales': 39.
88 See Huggins M.J. (1997) 'Sport and the English seaside resort, 1800–1914', *International Journal of Maritime History* 9 (1) 213–32.
89 Good, 'The coastal resort': 89; Stanes, *A History of Devon*: 114–15; Travis, 'The rise of holidaymaking': 148 and 158–60.
90 Brown B.J.H. (1971) 'A survey of the development of the leisure industries of the Bristol region, with special reference to the history of the seaside resorts', unpublished University of Bath PhD: appendix 5.
91 Travis, 'The rise of holidaymaking': 639.
92 *IC* 8, 15 and 22 June 1934.
93 May, 'The development of Ilfracombe': 12, 431.

94 Morgan, 'Perceptions, patterns and policies': chapter five.

95 *IC* 26 Nov. 1910.

96 Major Peto, MP, *IC* 21 and 28 April 1938.

97 Nuffield College (1944) *Devon Tourist Trade*: 7; and Papers of the Rev. Dr J. McIntyre, detailing his interview of Mr R. Pickard, clerk of the SUDC.

98 SUDC Pleasure Grounds Committee Minutes, 1923–35.

99 SUDC Publicity Committee Minutes, 1928–57, and Entertainments and Publicity Committee, 1957–62; and Nuffield College, *Devon Tourist Trade*: 6–7.

100 Morgan, 'Perceptions, patterns and policies': 97–8.

101 Letter to the *TT* 18 Mar. 1910.

102 Mr Levi Powell, a prominent Torquay resident, quoted in the *TT* 18 Mar. 1910.

103 *WT* 17 May 1920.

104 *TT* 6 July, 1923.

105 *TT* 21 April 1922, original emphasis.

106 *TT* editorial 9 Aug. 1929.

107 Lewes *et al.*, *The Holiday Industry of Devon and Cornwall*: 92.

108 Walvin J. (1978) *Beside the Seaside: A Social History of the Popular Seaside Holiday*, Allen Lane, London: 117; Pike J., unpublished material on Torquay held in Torquay Central Library. See also Morgan, 'Perceptions, patterns and policies', chapter 4.

109 Letter to the editor, *TT* 16 Aug. 1935.

110 *TT* 22 Aug. 1947.

111 ETB (1982) *Torbay Tourism Study*, ETB, London: 18.

112 *Independent* 26 Aug. 1989.

CHAPTER 5

1 Councillor Bennetto, IUDC, quoted in *IC* 23 Dec. 1948.

2 Chase L. (1997) 'Modern images and social tone in Clacton and Frinton in the interwar years', *International Journal of Maritime History* 9 (1) 149–69: 150.

3 See Morgan N.J. (1997) 'Seaside resort strategies: the case of inter-war Torquay', 84–100 in Fisher S. (ed.) *Recreation and the Sea*, University of Exeter Press, Exeter.

4 For instance, Goodall B. and Ashworth G.J. (1988) *Marketing Tourism Places—The Promotion of Destination Regions*, Croom-Helm, London; Ashworth G.J. and Goodall B. (1990) *Marketing Tourism Places*, Routledge, London; and Gold J.R. and Ward S.V. (eds) (1994) *Place Promotion: The Use of Publicity and Marketing to Sell Towns and Regions*, John Wiley & Sons, Chichester.

5 Yates N. (1988) 'Selling the seaside', *History Today*, 38, 20–7: 21.

6 Yates, 'Selling the seaside', and Walton J.K. (1974) 'The social development of Blackpool 1788–1914', unpublished University of Lancaster PhD: 343–50, 354 and 367.

7 Yates, 'Selling the seaside': 22.

8 Yates, 'Selling the seaside': 20.

9 Chase, 'Social tone in Clacton and Frinton': 165.

10 Pimlott J.A.R. (1947) *The Englishman's Holiday: A Social History*, Faber and Faber, London: 245–6.

11 SUDC Publicity Committee Minutes, 1928–39.

12 May F.B. (1978), 'The development of Ilfracombe as a resort in the nineteenth century', unpublished University of Wales MA: 348–52; Lamplugh L. (1984) *A History of Ilfracombe*, Harvester Sussex: 95; and IUDC Minutes 1 June 1909.

13 Torquay Chamber of Commerce Annual Reports, 1903–6.

14 Torquay Chamber of Commerce Annual Report, 1906.

15 IUDC Minutes 7 Nov. 1911. 9 Jan. 1911 and 5 Mar. 1912; and *IC* 25 Mar. 1911 and 15 April 1911.

16 IUDC JAC 21 Jan. 1913 and 2 Dec. 1913; and IUDC Minutes 2 Dec. 1913.

17 IUDC JAC 1 Dec. 1913; *IC* 10 Jan. 1914 and 7 Feb. 1914.

18 Middleton V.T.C. (1994) *Marketing in Travel and Tourism*, 2nd edn, Butterworth Heinemann, Oxford: parts one and five.

19 TMBC JAC 26 April 1911, 13 June 1911 and 6 Dec. 1911; 8 May 1912 and 5 Feb. 1913.

20 *TT* 9 Feb. 1912.

21 TMBC JAC 30 Oct. and 6 Nov. 1911; and 12 Jan. 1912.

22 *TT* 19 Sept. 1913.

23 May, 'The devlopment of Ilfracombe': 353; Burdett Wilson R. (1970) *Go Great Western: A History of GWR Publicity*, David and Charles, Newton Abbot: 24; Simmons J. (1982) 'The railway in Cornwall 1835–1914', *Journal of the Royal Institution of Cornwall*: 11–29; and Simmons J. (1984) 'Railways, hotels and tourism in Britain, 1839–1914', *Journal of Contemporary History* 19 (2) 201–22.

24 Simmons, 'The railway in Cornwall': 21–22; and Burdett Wilson, *Go Great Western*: 25, 27 and 80.

25 Pike, J. Studies in local history, unpublished and undated material held in Torquay Library, briefly mentions the launching of the guide in 1913.

26 Yates, 'Selling the seaside': 21–4 and Walvin J. (1978) *Beside the Seaside: A Social History of the Popular Seaside Holiday*, Allen Lane, London.

27 TMBC Baths Committee 11 Mar. 1918.

28 *TT* 23 May 1919.

29 *IC* 5 Oct. 1918; and *TT* 3 and 24 Jan. 1919.

30 *TT* 22 Feb. 1920.

31 *IC* 14 May 1921; *TT* 11 Mar. 1921, 25 Feb. 1921; 8 April 1921 and 28 Oct. 1921; TMBC Entertainments Committee 13 April 1921 and Baths Committee 14 June 1921 and 8 July 1921.

32 TMBC Baths Committee 12 April 1920; Entertainments Committee 17 Nov. 1920 and 15 Dec. 1920; and Baths Committee 13 Dec. 1920, and 10 Jan. 1921; and *IC* 14 May 1921.

33 Federation of British Health and Holiday Resorts (1915) *Annual Report*: 6–7;

and *TT* 8 May 1914 and 27 Aug. 1920.

34 Yates, 'Selling the seaside': 23. See also Pimlott, *The Englishman's Holiday*: 244–6.
35 Chase, 'Social tone in Clacton and Frinton': 165.
36 Yates, 'Selling the seaside': 23.
37 Chase, 'Social tone in Clacton and Frinton': 166–7.
38 Yates, 'Selling the seaside': 23.
39 Pimlott, *The Englishman's Holiday*: 244–6.
40 Yates, 'Selling the seaside': 23.
41 Chase, 'Social tone in Clacton and Frinton', and Morgan N.J. (1992) 'Perceptions, patterns and policies of tourism. The development of the Devon seaside resorts during the twentieth century with special reference to Torquay and Ilfracombe', unpublished University of Exeter PhD: chapters 3 and 5.
42 *TT* 25 Mar. 1921.
43 *TT* 27 Aug. 1920.
44 *TT* editorial 18 Mar. 1921.
45 *TT* editorial 10 Mar. 1922.
46 *IC* 24 Sept. 1921 and editorial 21 Jan. 1922.
47 TMBC JAC 25 Feb. 1924 and Baths and Publicity Committee 11 June 1925.
48 TMBC Baths and Beaches Committee: 13 Feb. 1922.
49 TMBC JAC 16 Oct. 1923.
50 Burdett Wilson, *Go Great Western*: 43 and 30.
51 TMBC JAC 15 Jan. 1924.
52 *TT* 10 April 1925.
53 Pike, unpublished material on Torbay: 13; and *TT* 26 July 1929.
54 Snelling A. (1997) 'Letter from America: marketing Wales in the USA', *Leisure Monitor,* 3.
55 *TT* 16 Feb. 1923; Pike, Torbay: 13; and Russell P. (1960) *A History of Torquay and the Famous Anchorage of Torbay*, Torquay: 14.
56 *TT* 18 May 1923.
57 *TT* 28 Oct. and 8 July 1927.
58 *TT* 24 Dec. 1925.
59 *IC* 31 Mar. 1923; IUDC Minutes 10 April 1923 and 1 May 1923.
60 IUDC Minutes 4 Mar. 1924.
61 *IC* 17 Oct. 1925 and 27 Jan. and 6 Feb. 1926, *TT* 2 April 1926.
62 *IC* 27 Feb. 1926.
63 Morgan, 'Perceptions, patterns and policies': chapter 4.
64 *TT* editorial 19 Oct. 1928.
65 *The Times* 21 Dec. 1931.
66 Pritchard A. and Morgan N.J. (1998) '"Mood marketing". The new destination branding strategy. A case study of "Wales" the brand', *Journal of Vacation Marketing* 3 (4): 215–29.
67 TMBC (1928) *Official Torquay Guide*, Torquay.
68 *IC* 17 Jan. 1930.

69 Burdett Wilson, *Go Great Western*: 115–18.

70 SUDC Publicity Committee: 25 April 1930.

71 *The Times* 11 Dec. 1931.

72 Morgan N.J. and Pritchard A. (1998) *Tourism Promotion and Power: Creating Images, Creating Identities*, John Wiley & Sons, Chichester: chapter 4.

73 *The Times* 24 Oct. and 21 Dec. 1931.

74 *TT* 7 Oct. and 4 Aug. 1932.

75 *The Times* 9 Oct. 1931.

76 Quoted in Burdett Wilson, *Go Great Western*: 45.

77 *TT* 1 Jan. 1932.

78 *TT* 2 Jan. 1932.

79 *TT* 16 Sept. 1932.

80 *IC* 9 Oct. 1931.

81 *IC* 25 Dec. 1931.

82 *IC* 20 Nov. 1915.

83 *TT* 27 June 1930; and TMBC Publicity Committee 10 April, 13 Feb. and 25 Nov. 1930; and Baths Committee 25 Nov. 1930.

84 *TT* 20 Oct. 1933 and 24 Nov. 1933.

85 *TT* 27 Feb. 1934.

86 *TT* 22 Dec. 1933, 11 May 1934 and editorial 25 May 1934.

87 Burdett Wilson, *Go Great Western*: 27–31 and 34.

88 Burdett Wilson, *Go Great Western*: 76.

89 Burdett Wilson, *Go Great Western*: 128 and 101.

90 TMBC Publicity Committee 24 Nov. 1936 and 14 Oct. 1937.

91 *TT* 12 May and 16 June 1937, 30 June 1933 and 7 Sept. 1934 and TMBC Publicity Committee 21 Aug. 1934.

92 *TT* 22 Mar. 1935.

93 *TT* 30 Mar. 1934; TMBC Publicity Committee 12 April 1934 and 13 April 1934 and *TT* 28 Sept. 1934.

94 SUDC Publicity Committee 11 Oct. 1935 and 25 Sept. 1936.

95 SUDC Publicity Committee 12 April 1938.

96 SUDC Publicity Committee 7 Mar. 1939 and IUDC Minutes 1940.

97 *IC* 9 Sept. 1932.

98 *IC* 27 July 1934.

99 *IC* 14 Dec. 1934.

100 IUDC Minutes 1 Jan. 1935 and *IC* 4 Jan. 1935.

101 *IC* 15 Feb. 1935, quoting Mr W. Joslin.

102 *IC* 8 Feb. 1935 and 20 Jan. and 24 Nov. 1939.

103 *IC* 24 Nov. 1939, and 20 Dec. 1946; TMBC Publicity Committee 7 Nov. and 14 Dec. 1939, 25 Nov. 1940 and 11 Jan. 1945.

104 Nuffield College Social Reconstruction Survey (1944) *The Devon Tourist Trade*: 6–7.

105 *TT* 22 Feb. 1946.

106 *TT* 18 April 1947.

107 *TT* 10 June 1949; TMBC Publicity Committee 21 June 1949.

108 Kotler P. *et al.* (1994) *Marketing Places. Attracting Investment, Industry and Tourism to Cities, States, and Nations*, The Free Press, New York: 21.

109 *TT* 3 Mar. and 29 Sept. 1950 and April 1951.

110 *TT* 14 Mar. 1952, 18 May 1956 and 17 Aug. 1960; TMBC Publicity Committee 15 Dec. 1960.

111 TMBC Publicity Committee, 10 Nov. 1949 and 16 Feb. 1950.

112 *TT* 24 Sept. 1953 and 31 Dec. 1954.

113 *TT* 22 June and 28 Sept. 1951, and 2 May and 1 and 8 Feb. 1952.

114 TMBC Publicity Committee 19 Sept. 1950 and 14 April 1956.

115 SUDC Publicity Committee 17 Jan. 1951.

116 SUDC Publicity Committee 22 June 1951, 11 Feb. 1952 and 28 July 1952.

117 SUDC Publicity Committee 15 Oct. 1952.

118 *WT* 28 July and 8 Sept. 1950.

119 SUDC Publicity Committee 15 Oct. 1952.

120 SUDC Publicity Committee, 9 Mar. 1953 and 7 Jan. and 1 Feb. 1956.

121 *IC* 18 Jan. 1946, quoting Mr Knill of the JAC.

122 *IC* 20 Dec. 1946.

123 *IC* 20 Dec. 1946, 14 Nov. 1947, and 23 Dec. and 1 Oct. 1948.

124 *IC* 27 Feb. and 1 Oct. 1948.

125 *IC* 20 Dec. 1946 and 16 Dec. 1949.

126 *IC* 23 Dec. 1948, 28 July 1950, 13 June 1952 and 28 Aug. 1953.

127 *IC* editorial 10 July 1953.

128 IUDC General Purposes Committee 12 Nov. 1957.

129 Ilfracombe guides, 1950–65.

130 See, for instance, Chase, 'Social tone in Clacton and Frinton': 167.

131 Ilfracombe guides, 1960–79.

132 SUDC Publicity Committee 6 Dec. 1954 and 23 Sept. 1953.

133 SUDC Publicity Committee 21 April 1955.

134 SUDC Publicity Committee 17 Sept. and 17 Dec. 1957 and 25 Jan. and 25 Mar. 1958.

135 SUDC Publicity Committee 14 Sept. 1960.

136 SUDC Publicity Committee 19 April and 14 Sept. 1960 and 23 Oct. 1961.

137 *WMN* 12 Feb. 1962.

138 *Sidmouth Herald* 27 Mar. 1971; *Country Life* 2 May 1968; and Lewes F.M.M. (1970) *et al.*, *The Holiday Industry of Devon and Cornwall*, HMSO, London: 164.

139 *Sidmouth Official Guide*, 1950.

140 *Sidmouth Official Guide*, 1971; and *Devon Life*, June 1971: 28.

141 IUDC Finance Committee 16 Mar. 1954; 18 Mar. 1955, 1 Oct. 1956; 19 Mar. 1957; and TMBC Publicity Committee, 12 Jan. 1956 and 17 Jan. 1957.

142 *TT* 1 Nov. 1957.

143 *TT* 1 Jan. 1960.

144 *TT* 22 Jan. 1960 and *WMN* 20 Jan. 1960.

145 *TT* 19 Aug. 1960.

146 TMBC Publicity Committee 14 June 1962.

147 TMBC Publicity Committee 12 July 1962.

148 TMBC Publicity Committee 18 Feb. 1963 and *TT* 10 July 1964.

149 *WMN* 1 April 1968.

150 TMBC Publicity Committee 11 Nov. 1965 and 14 April 1966 and *TT* 5 June 1966.

151 TMBC Publicity Committee 13 Jan. 1966; and *TT* 16 Feb. and 19 April 1968.

152 Pritchard A. and Morgan N.J. (1995) 'Evaluating vacation destination brochure images: the case of local authorities in Wales', *Journal of Vacation Marketing* 2 (1) 23–38.

153 *WMN* 1 April 1968 and Lewes *et al.*, *The Holiday Industry of Devon and Cornwall*: 241.

154 ETB (1982) *Torbay Tourism Study*, ETB, London.

155 Pritchard and Morgan, 'Mood marketing'.

156 Torbay Tourist Board (1985) *An Integrated Tourism Strategy for Torquay, Paignton and Brixham*, Torbay; and *Herald Express* 26 Nov. 1987 and 1 Mar. 1988. Also material from interview in 1989 with Neil Whitehead, Director of the TTB.

157 Yates, 'Selling the seaside', and Chase, 'Social tone in Clacton and Frinton': 168.

158 Yates, 'Selling the seaside': 27.

159 'Torbay "mystery" promotion sweeps up award', *Leisure News* (32) 24 May 1990: 12; European Tourism Year 1990 newsletter, winter 1990: 7; and 'Tide turns for holidays at home', *Radio Times*, 6–12 Jan. 1990: 56–9.

160 Vernon M. (1998) 'Get ready for the electronic billboard', *Independent* 31 Mar.

161 *Sidmouth Guide*, 1988.

CHAPTER 6

1   Councillor Ely, Torquay Alderman, quoted in *TT* 5 Aug. 1949.

2   Huggins M.J. (1997) 'Sport and the English seaside resort, 1880–1914', *International Journal of Maritime History* 9 (1) 213–32: 227.

3   Brown G.P. and Essex S.J. (1989) 'Tourism policies in the public sector', 543–39 in Witt S. and Moutinho L. (eds) *Tourism Marketing and Management Handbook*, Prentice Hall, Hemel Hempstead: 533.

4   Heeley J. (1981) 'Planning for tourism in Britain: an historical perspective', *Town Planning Review* 52 (1) 61–79.

5   Wanhill S. (1989) 'Development and investment policy in tourism', 193–5 in Witt and Moutinho (eds) *Tourism Marketing*: 103. See also Gill I. (1988) 'Tourism and entertainment services in local government', 155–77 in Bennington J. and White J. (eds) *The Future of Leisure Services*, ILAM/Longman, Harlow.

6   Lewes F.M.M. *et al.* (1970) *The Holiday Industry of Devon and Cornwall*, HMSO,

London: 161.

7   TMBC Entertainments Committee 22 Nov. 1911.

8   SUDC Entertainments Committee 24 Jan. 1947.

9   *WT* 20 Dec. 1946.

10 *Sidmouth Herald* 18 May 1957; and SUDC Minutes 16 May, 16 June and 18 Sept. 1958.

11 EUDC Foreshore and Pleasure Grounds Committee 20 Jan., 2 Feb., 3 May and 27 Sept. 1920, 21 Jan. 1921, and 25 Sept. 1922.

12 EUDC Foreshore and Pleasure Grounds Committee Minutes, 1911–34, and Nuffield College (1944) *Devon Tourist Trade*.

13 EUDC Foreshore and Pleasure Grounds Committee, 18 May 1936, and Entertainments Committee, 7 Nov. 1933.

14 *The Times* 24 and 31 July and 7 Aug. 1920.

15 EUDC Foreshore and Pleasure Grounds Committee, 27 Jan. 1936, and IUDC Minutes 5 Feb. 1929.

16 Papers of the Rev. Dr McIntyre, compiler of the 1944 Nuffield Survey.

17 Morgan N.J. (1992) 'Perceptions, patterns and policies of tourism. The development of the Devon seaside resorts in the twentieth century with special reference to Torquay and Ilfracombe', unpublished University of Exeter PhD: 300–4.

18 Nuffield College *The Devon Tourist Trade*.

19 Nuffield College *The Devon Tourist Trade*: 8.

20 *The Times* 24 July 1921.

21 Nuffield College *The Devon Tourist Trade*.

22 Sidmouth 1950 brochure: *Sidmouth, South Devon: The Gem of that Fair Galaxy*: 28.

23 SUDC Entertainments and Publicity Committee, 18 June 1957, quoting BTA figures.

24 Nuffield College *The Devon Tourist Trade*.

25 Papers of the Rev. Dr McIntyre.

26 British Rail (1947) *Holiday Guide*: 211.

27 See , for instance, IUDC Minutes 5 July and 4 Oct. 1910; 7 Feb., 4 April and 4 July 1911, 20 and 29 July 1920, 7 June 1922, and 31 Mar. 1931.

28 Chase L. (1997) 'Modern images and social tone in Clacton and Frinton in the interwar years', *International Journal of Maritime History* 9 (1) 149–69: 161–2.

29 IUDC Harbour Committee 27 April 1910 and EUDC Minutes 28 May 1912, 24 June 1913, 7 and 27 June and 26 Sept. 1911

30 Much of this information is drawn from Pike J., unpublished and undated material on Torquay, held in Torquay Library: 11 and from a personal conversation with John Pike in 1989.

31 *TT* 17 May 1912.

32 TMBC Harbour Sub-Committee 7 June 1911; Ward Locke & Co., *Sidmouth Guide* (1923–4 edn): 5; and SUDC Pleasure Grounds Committee, 25 April 1923, 18 Feb. 1924, and 6 May 1927.

33 EUDC Foreshore and Pleasure Grounds Committee 24 Mar. 1924, 2 Feb. 1920, 25 Aug. 1925, 25 June 1928, 27 Aug. 1934 and 21 June 1937.

34 Hern A. (1967) *The Seaside Holiday: The History of the English Seaside Resort*, Cresset, London: 26–8.

35 Ward Lock & Co., *Sidmouth Guide*: 28; and *WMN* 15 June 1956.

36 EUDC Foreshore and Pleasure Grounds Committee 29 Oct. 1935 and 12 Mar. 1937.

37 IUDC Minutes 3 May 1910 and Finance Committee 16 Feb. 1971.

38 IUDC Harbour Committee 18 June 1914.

39 IUDC Minutes 4 June 1919, and *IC* 31 and 17 May, and 7 June 1919.

40 *The Times*, 20 July 1920; and *TT* 12 Sept., 6 June and 11 July 1919.

41 *The Times*, 5 July 1923.

42 EUDC Foreshore and Pleasure Grounds Committee, 25 May 1920, and Band Committee, 28 May 1926.

43 *TT* 29 Oct. 1937; and EUDC Foreshore and Pleasure Grounds Committee, 24 June 1929, 29 June 1931, and 24 July and 5 Sept. 1933.

44 Morgan, 'Perceptions, patterns and policies': 282–3.

45 *TT* editorial 4 Aug. 1933, and 30 July and 29 Oct. 1937.

46 *IC* 16 Aug. and 27 Dec. 1940.

47 EUDC Finance and General Purposes Committee 30 April and 29 Oct. 1946; and *WT* 29 Aug. 1947.

48 IUDC Minutes 6 July and 3 Aug. 1948; *IC* 9 July 1948; IUDC Minutes 5 April 1949; and *IC* 8 April 1949.

49 *WT* 25 May 1951.

50 *TT* 2 July and 5 Nov. 1948; and *WT* 14 Jan. 1949.

51 Morgan, 'Perceptions, patterns and policies': 283.

52 *TT* 22 April and 6 May 1955.

53 *TT* 5 April, 3 May and 5 July 1957; and TMBC Minutes 2 July 1957.

54 *TT* 14 July 1967.

55 EUDC Foreshore and Pleasure Grounds Committee 27 Oct. and 5 Nov. 1919.

56 Good A. (1980) 'The coastal resort', 87–95 in DCC, *Coastlines of Devon*, DCC, Exeter: 90; *WT* 4 Feb. 1949; and SUDC Minutes 29 April 1946.

57 IUDC purchase and lease of foreshore, 1926–36; IUDC Minutes 6 April and 29 July 1926 and 3 Jan. 1928; and *WT* 25 Jan. 1929 and 10 Dec. 1937.

58 TMBC Minutes, 3 April 1962; Improvement Committee 22 Sept. 1962; Beaches Committee 18 July 1963; and Finance Committee 26 July 1963.

59 Lewes *et al.*, *The Holiday Industry of Devon and Cornwall*: 157.

60 Lewes *et al.*, *The Holiday Industry of Devon and Cornwall*: 149 and 168.

61 Lewes *et al.*, *The Holiday Industry of Devon and Cornwall*: 131.

62 Lewes *et al.*, *The Holiday Industry of Devon and Cornwall*: 139.

63 DCC (1981) *Devon Structure Plan* DCC, Exeter: 108; and Hughes H.L. (1989) 'Entertainment', 125–30 in Witt and Mouthino (eds) *Tourism Marketing*: 125.

64 Lindley K. (1973) *Seaside Architecture*; Bainbridge C. (1986) *Pavilions on the Sea*;

and Mickleburgh T. (1991) 'Piers—adapting for survival', *Leisure Manager* 9 (3) 17–19.

65 Russell P. (1960) *A History of Torquay and the Famous Anchorage of Torbay*, Torquay: 142–3, 147 and 18; and *Herald Express* 7 Feb. 1980.

66 IUDC Harbour Committee 18 May 1939 and 1 Jan. 1941; and *IC* 1 Jan. and 1 June 1945.

67 Deane and Mason, engineers to the IUDC, letter to the Ministry of Transport, 12 July 1948.

68 IUDC Minutes 13 Feb. 1948.

69 *IC* 8 Oct. and 31 Dec. 1948.

70 Russell, *A History of Torbay*: 141.

71 Russell, *A History of Torbay*: 139–40.

72 TMBC, Chamber of Commerce 1903 Annual Report: 4

73 TMBC General Purposes Committee 11 Mar. 1910; *WMN* 19 Aug. 1912; and *TT* 16 Aug. 1912.

74 *The Times* 5 and 19 Aug. 1912; *WMN* 19 Aug. 1912; and *TT* 16 Aug. 1912.

75 Morgan, 'Perceptions, patterns and policies': 293.

76 TMBC Special Meeting 20 Sept. 191; Harbour Beaches and Piers Committee 2 and 6 Oct. 191; Entertainments Committee, 20 Dec. 1911 and 12 Dec. 1912.

77 Morgan, 'Perceptions, patterns and policies': chapters 4 and 7.

78 *TT* 14 Feb., 25 April, 3 Oct. and 20 Oct. and 7 Nov. 1911; and TMBC Entertainments Committee, 20 Jan. 1919.

79 TMBC Entertainments Committee, 11 Nov. and 23 Oct. 1923; *TT* 31 Oct. 1924; TMBC Special Meeting 28 Oct. 1924 and *TT* 14 Nov. 1924.

80 *TT* 26 Feb. 1926 and 2 April 1926.

81 *TT* 5 and 26 Mar., and 2 and 9 April 1926; and TMBC Monthly and Special Meeting 7 April 1926.

82 Morgan, 'Perceptions, patterns and policies': 297.

83 TMBC Baths Committee 17 Jan. 1947 and Entertainments Committee 29 Oct. 1947.

84 TMBC Entertainments and Marine Spa Committees 22 Dec. 1950.

85 *TT* 5 Jan. and 9 Feb. 1951; and *TT* 23 Mar. and 6 April 1951, and 4 Jan. 1952.

86 TMBC Special Meeting 16 Feb. 1965 and 18 Jan. 1966; *TT* 5 Mar. and 2 July 1965; and *WMN* 8 Feb. 1966.

87 *TT* 29 June 1969.

88 TMBC, Development of the Pavilion, Torquay: brief and terms of reference, 1967; and Russell, *A History of Torquay*: 147–8.

89 Torbay District Council, The Pavilion, Torquay, undated, *c.* 1971.

90 Morgan, 'Perceptions, patterns and policies': chapter 5.

91 IUDC Minutes, 22 and 29 Dec. 1921; and Pleasure Grounds and Entertainments Committee 2 Sept. 1921.

92 IUDC Minutes 5 Sept. 1922 and 28 Aug. 1923.

93 *IC* 6 Oct. 1923 and 25 Oct. 1924.

94 *IC* 27 Oct. 1927.

95 IUDC Minutes 18 Mar. 1924; and *IC* 22 Mar. 19224.

96 IUDC Works Committee 28 April 1926.

97 Nuffield College *Devon Tourist Trade*, and *The Times* 10 Nov. 1921; TMBC Entertainments Committee 22 Mar. 1922. See Morgan, 'Perceptions, patterns and policies': 278.

98 TMBC Entertainments Committee 1927–28.

99 *TT* editorial 29 June 1928.

100 Morgan, 'Perceptions, patterns and policies': 306.

101 TMBC Monthly Committee 1 Dec. 1931.

102 *TT* 14 Feb. 1936.

103 *TT* 2 Oct. and 6 Nov. 1936, 1 and 15 Jan. and editorial 8 Jan. 1937.

104 Morgan, 'Perceptions, patterns and policies': 308.

105 Morgan, 'Perceptions, patterns and policies': 308.

106 *TT* 29 Jan. 1937, and 7 Oct. and Dec. 1938.

107 *TT* 18 Dec., 6 May, 22 July, and 18 Nov. 1938.

108 EUDC Foreshore and Pleasure Grounds Committee 31 Dec. 1924, 10 March 1932.

109 *TT* 14 Feb. 1919; TMBC Harbour and Beaches 13 Feb. 1925; and *TT* 9 Sept. and editorial 7 Oct. 1932.

110 TMBC Finance Committee 22 Feb. 1918, and *The Times* 22 April 1919.

111 TMBC Baths Committee 27 June 1918; and *TT* 6 Aug. 1920.

112 TMBC Baths Sub-Committee 2 June 1921.

113 *TT* 21 Oct. and 4 Nov. 1921.

114 *TT* 19 Aug. and 28 Oct. 1921.

115 TMBC Baths Committee, 2 Dec. 1921, and monthly and Special Committee 3 Jan. 1922, and *TT* 31 Mar. 1922.

116 Ward Locke & Co., *Torquay*, *c.* 1924.

117 *TT* 11 April 1930.

118 TMBC Baths Committee 13 Sept. 1934; and 16 May and 10 Jan. 1935; and *TT* 7 Feb. and 3 July 1936.

119 TMBC, Torquay Official Guides 1956 and 1961.

120 TMBC Entertainment and Marine Spa Committee 24 June 1955.

121 TMBC Entertainment and Marine Spa Committee Minutes 1955–58.

122 Special re-development of the Pavilion and Spa Committee, 5 July 1967; and Entertainment and Marine Spa Committee, 3 Mar. 1966.

123 *WMN* 15 Oct. and 28 Sept. 1971; and *Herald Express* 15 Aug. 1988.

124 *Leisureweek*, Friday 15 Mar. 1991: 2.

125 Goodrich J.N. (1994) 'Health tourism: a new positioning strategy for tourist destinations', 227–38 in Uysal M. (ed.) *Global Tourism Behaviour*, Haworth Press, London.

126 Colin Buchanan Partners and Industrial Market Research Ltd (1979) *A Tourism Study for the West Country: Main Report to English Tourist Board*, English Tourist

Board, London: iii.

127 Martin B. and Mason S. (1990) 'Water leisure riding a wave', *Leisure Management* 10 (4) 28–32; and Channon J. *et al.* (1994) 'Towards the twenty-first century', 258–67 in Duffy *et al.*, *The New Maritime History of Devon*, Vol. II, Conway Maritime Press and University of Exeter Press.

128 NDDC Planning Department (1979) *Officer Working Party on Ilfracombe Harbour*, NDDC, Barnstaple: 4.

129 Swansea City Council (1987) *Swansea Maritime Quarter: Survey of Residents and Tourists*, Swansea City Council, Swansea.

130 NDDC Planning Department *Officer Working Party on Ilfracombe Harbour*. 4.

131 DCC *Tourism Review* 1985 edn: 27 and 1987 edn.: 33.

132 Selby M. and Morgan N.J. (1996) 'Reconstruing place image: a case study of its role in destination market research', *Tourism Management* 17 (4 June) 287–94; and work in progress by Tim Gale for a PhD on the development of Rhyl.

133 Burton I. (1989) 'All eyes on Ilfracombe', *Planning* 841 (20 October) 30–1.

134 *WMN* 1 Aug. 1989; and *Herald Express* 8 and 14 April 1988.

135 *Herald Express* 9 May 1988.

136 Martin and Mason, 'Water leisure riding a wave': 31.

137 *Planning* 860 (16 Mar. 1990). See also Channon *et al.*, (1994) 'Towards the twenty-first century'.

138 Ahmed Z.A. (1996) 'An international marketing perspective of Canadian tourists' shopping behaviour', *Journal of Vacation Marketing* 2 (3) 207–14.

139 DCC, *Structure Plan*: 149.

140 Selby and Morgan, 'Reconstruing place image'.

CHAPTER 7

1   Walton J.K. (1983), *The English Seaside Resort: A Social History 1750–1914*, Leicester University Press, Leicester: 25, original emphasis.

2   Morgan N.J. (1992) 'Perceptions, patterns and policies of tourism: the development of the Devon seaside resorts during the twentieth century with special reference to Torquay and Ilfracombe', unpublished University of Exeter PhD.

3   Lewes F.M.M., *et al.*, (1970) *The Holiday Industry of Devon and Cornwall*, HMSO, London: 200–1.

4   DCC (1958) *Teignmouth: A Survey of Holidaymakers, 1957*, DCC, Exeter; and Teignbridge District Council (1987) *Teignmouth, Shaldon and Dawlish Structure Plan*: 19–20.

5   Lewes *et al.*, *The Holiday Industry of Devon and Cornwall*: 200.

6   East Devon Action Project (1987) *Tourism in East Devon: A Report of a Set of Surveys Conducted in East Devon, June 1986–June 1987*, Totnes: 4 and 15.

7   *Herald Express*, 9 May 1988.

8   Councillor Stephens of the IUDC, quoted in *IC* 17 Mar. 1931.

9   DCC Minutes 1910–60; Coastal Preservation Committee 1950–60; and

Planning Committee 1960–65.

10 Morgan, 'Perceptions, patterns and policies': 343.

11 Heeley J. (1988), 'Planning for tourism: what should be the role of the local authorities?', 7–17 in McDowell L.D. (ed.) *Planning for Tourism and Leisure*, Proceedings of the First International Conference, held at the University of Ulster at Jordonstown, Ulster.

12 Letter to the editor of *Leisure Management* 9 (2) 1989: 7.

13 Morgan N.J. and Pritchard A. (1996) 'Welsh seaside resort strategies', paper presented to the third Urban History Conference, Budapest.

14 Morgan N.J. (1998) 'Welsh seaside resort strategies: changing times, changing needs at the end of the twentieth century', 193–216 in Starkey D.J. and Jamieson A.G. (eds) *Exploiting the Sea. Aspects of Britain's Maritime Economy Since 1870*, University of Exeter Press, Exeter.

15 Morgan N.J and Pritchard A. (1998) *Tourism Promotion and Power: Creating Images, Creating Identities*, John Wiley & Sons, Chichester: Chapter 5.

16 Sports Council for Wales (1991) *A Strategy Review. Changing Times, Changing Needs*, Sports Council for Wales, Cardiff: chapter 2.

17 Hay B. (1998) 'Tourism futures', paper presented at University of Wales Institute, Cardiff research seminar, February.

Bibliography

COLLECTIONS OF PRIMARY SOURCES
Public Record Office (Kew)

Nuffield College, Devon Industries (with special reference to South Devon), Nuffield College Social Reconstruction Survey, May 1941, and The Devon Tourist Trade: Nuffield College Social Reconstruction Survey, May 1944. HLG 82/49 and 82/46.

Files on Cornwall County Council National Parks Policy, 1945–51, and on Coastal Preservation (Cornwall), 1942–7. HLG 791121–2.

DCC Development Plan Inspector's Report, 1954–6. HLG 7911028.

Reports by J.A. Steers for the Minister of Town and Country Planning on the South and South-West Coasts. Minehead to Lands End to Helford River; River Helford to the River Erme, and Padstow to Bideford, 1944. HLG 9216, 92/10 and 92112.

National Parks Administration. Representations by the Standing Committee on National Parks and notes for the Minister's response, 1952. HLG 92/19.

National Parks. Amenity and Coastal Areas Development Control Directions to the South-West, 1946–7. HLG 92158.

National Parks Committee. Potential National Park Areas on Dartmoor, Exmoor and North Devon Coast, 1945–7. HLG 93/12.

National Parks Committee. Purpose and Requirements of National Parks. HLG 93/16.

Recreational Facilities, 1945–6. HLG 93/28.

National Parks Committee Correspondence, 1945–6. HLG 93/34.

National Parks Committee. The Authority and Organisation of National Parks. General Interim Development Order, 1945. HLG 93/35.

National Parks Commission: Advertisements, 1945–6. HLG 93/30. National Parks Commission: Evidence from Voluntary Organisations, 1945–6. HLG 93/44.

British Transport Records, RAIL 268/130–1, 134, 146, 152, 160 and 198; and 653/17.

Traffic at GWR Stations 1903–38. RAIL 266/45.

British Rail Holiday Guide Posters, 1949–58. AN 14/43, 49, 50–4 and 57.

British Railways Western Region Holiday Guide, 1949, and British Railways Holiday Haunts, West of England and South and Central Wales, 1958 and 1960 edns. AN 17/2, 17/52 and 62.

Devon County Record Office, Exeter

IUDC, Minutes, 1910–63, R2458A/ (2/3) C22–37.

IUDC, Committees, Minutes, 1908–27, R2458A/ (2/3) C57–63.

IUDC, Committees (General) Minutes, 1927–74, R2458A/(2/3) C64–85A and C321–32.

IUDC, Surveyor's Letter Books, 1908–39, R2458A/ (2/3) S7–16.

IUDC, Treasurer's Accounts Books, 1926–52, R2458A/(2/3) T1A-25.

IUDC, Treasurer's Rate Books, 1935–70, R2458A/(2/3) T70–119.

IUDC, Letter Books, 1910–51, R2458A/(2/3) C107–19.

IUDC, Rating Committee, 1927–58, R2458A/(2/3) C52.

IUDC, Pier Tolls Accounts Books, 1928–40, and Pier Tickets Register, 1935–43, R2458A/(2/3) R1–10.

IUDC, Rapparee Bathing Cove Collection Book, 1925–39, Bicclescombe Pleasure Grounds Collection Book, 1938–44, and file on deck chair payments, 1954. R2458A/(2/3) R11–22.

IUDC, Expenditure Journal, 1925–35, Cash Collection Account Book, 1925–39, Wages Book, 1925–31, and Miscellaneous Sales Book, 1938–44, R2458A/(2/3) R13–17.

Various agreements and contracts between IUDC and artistes, leasees and entertainment staff etc., 1946–70, R2458A/(213) R18–43, C190 and C193.

Copies of Provisional Orders for IUDC entertainments 1914–31 under the Public Health Acts, R2458A/ (2/3) C276–8.

File on unsuccessful IUDC bid for the Ilfracombe Sea Bathing Company, 1938, R248A/(2/3) C290.

IUDC, Weather Record Books, 1910–49, R2458A/ (2/3) S77–88.

IUDC, Medical Officer of Health Reports, 1910–49, R2458A/ (2/3) M01.

IUDC Act of 1936: files and general correspondence, 1935–6, and IUDC Act of 1936 and Parliamentary Papers, 1935–6, R2458A/(2/3) C202–8.

IUDC, Files on the Royal Commission on Common Land, 1956–8, and Rights of Way and Public Footpaths, 1891–1958, R2458A/(2/3) C142–3.

IUDC, Purchase and Lease of the Foreshore, 1926–36, R2458A/(2/3) H22.

IUDC, Speedboat Licences, 1928–38, R2458A/(2/3) H33–7, H39–40 and C223.

IUDC, Pier Repairs: tenders, papers and plans, 1940 and 1948–50, R2458A/ (2/3) H42–3.

IUDC, Pier: reconstruction and re-opening, 1946–53, R2458A/(2/3) H23–7.

IUDC, Pier: correspondence with Campbells Ltd, 1956–8, R2458A/(2/3) H38.

IUDC, file: possible sites for municipal airport, 1930–9 and 1951, R2458A/ (2/3) C287.

IUDC, files: by-laws on lodging houses, 1872, and hackney carriages, 1920–57, R2458A/(2/3) C136 and C153–4.

IUDC, files: reduced fares for resorts, 1956; and the closure of Barnstaple–Ilfracombe railway line, 1966–8, R2458A/(2/3) C134–5.

IUDC, files: evacuees and evacuation schemes, 1939–45, R2458A/(2/3) C155, C231 and C250–8.

IUDC, files: requisitioning, training and defence, 1940–8, R2458A/ (2/3) C227.

IUDC, files: the British Restaurant, rationing, and the administration of permits, 1942–6, R2458A/(2/3) C240–9.

Copies of Circulars from various Ministries re. IUDC war damage compensation etc. 1938–42, R2458A/(2/3) C260.

IUDC, files: the Ilfracombe Hotel, 1930–55, R2458A/(2/3) C139, C173 and C291.

IUDC, file: industrial development, 1950–7, R2458A/(2/3) C146.

Devon Draft Development Plan; Agreement between IUDC and DCC, claims and enforcement notices, 1941–54, R2458A/(2/3) C126–33.

EUDC, Finance and General Purpose Committee, 1906–57, R7/41 C69–81.

EUDC, Roads and General Purposes Committee, 1911–32, R7/4/C82–3.

EUDC, Foreshore and Pleasure Grounds Committee, 1919–38, R7/4/C92–6.

EUDC Act, 1920, R7/4110613 Box 1.

SUDC, Pleasure Grounds Committee, 1923–35, R7/7/C137.

SUDC, Publicity Committee, 1928–57, R7/7/C139.

SUDC, Entertainments and Publicity Committee, 1957–62, R7/7/C140.

Papers of the Rev. Dr J. McIntyre, compiler of Nuffield College Social Reconstruction Surveys on Devon Industries and Tourism, 1941–3, 4369M/O 1–9.

TMBC Medical Officer of Health Reports, 1934 and 1936; and Weston-Super-Mare Medical Officer of Health Report, 1936, R2458A/ (213) N02.

Torquay Central Library

TMBC, Committees' Minutes, 1910–68.

Box files containing miscellaneous pamphlets, guides and Torquay local government documents, D981, Files A–C, DES–DEV, DIR–HA, HI–LI, LO–X, and N–Z.

Box in Torquay Archives labelled Torquay Board of Health, Bath Saloons and Misc. Documents.

Copy of Charter of Incorporation with the Order of the Privy Council and Scheme, September 1893 and papers relating to Torquay's Incorporation, D981 Box File A–C.

Local Acts and Orders 1900–37, D981.

Tor Abbey Sands: report to the Town Council by W.T. Douglass, June 1912, D981 Box File N–Z.

Torquay Pavilion Wages Books: July 1914–December 1916; July 1920–May 1924;

221

June 1928–July 1930; and July 1930–October 1931.

Torquay Princess Pier Wages Book: May 1915–February 1920; and August 1930–October 1931.

Provisional Order for Torquay Harbour Plan Proposal (Plan by P.W. Ladmore, Borough Engineer, dated 1932–3).

Box in Torquay Archives labelled 'Publicity', includes misc. undated guides.

Four boxes of Torquay Pavilion and Princess Theatres Programmes 1936–88.

Proposed Post-War Development Scheme, prepared by P.W. Ladmore, May 1945, D981 Box File DFS–DEV.

'Torquay today—new amenities. The Princess Gardens Development Scheme' by J. Robinson, *The Municipal Review Special Supplement* December 1961, D981 Box File I–Z.

Report to the Council on corporation publicity and information services, April 1966–March 1967, prepared by the Torquay Publicity Committee, D981 Box File N–Z.

Re-Development of the Pavilion, Torquay: brief and terms of reference, 1967, and undated pamphlet on the Pavilion, D981 Box File N–Z.

Torquay Marine Spa Re-Development: report and drawings of Sir Basil Spence Bannington and Collins, consultant architects, 1968, D981 Box File DES–DEV.

Holiday Study, chalets, caravans and camping, Report to the Chairman and members of the Policy Advisory Committee and the Planning Committee, 10 November 1969; and untitled notes on Torbay Tourism *c.*1971.

The Beacon Leisure and Entertainiment Centre: lease and prospectus, 1977, D981 Box File DES–DEV.

Civic and Regional Survey of Brixham, *c.*1936, D983.

Teignbridge District Council, Teignmouth, Dawlish and Shaldon Local Plan, March 1987.

Ilfracombe Town Council, pamphlet an industrial development, *c.*1979.

East Devon Action Project, Tourism in East Devon: a report of a set of surveys conducted in East Devon, June 1986–June 1987 (Totnes, 1987).

Torbay Tourism and development newspaper cuttings books, D981, numbers 1–2.

Torquay Library's collection of photographs and postcards of the Torbay resorts.

J.M. Scott (ed.), Torquay Marine Spa, an official invitation to Torquay issued by the Baths Committee (1922).

Torquay Official Guides: *c.*1913, *c.*1918, *c.*1922, 1926, 1928, *c.*1930, 1932–5 and 1947–80.

Torquay Official Handbooks: 1937–8, 1940–1 and *c.*1947.

Lynton and Lynmouth Official Guides: 1963–88.

Sidmouth Official Guides: 1950 and 1966–88.

Woolacombe and Mortehoe Official Guides, 1964, 1966–75, 1983 and 1985–8.

Torquay Chamber of Commerce Annual Reports 1903–12.

Torquay Chamber of Trade and Commerce (Torquay, 1986).

Torquay Hotels' Association Year Book 1955–6, D981 Box File DES–DEV.

J.R. Pike, 'Studies in local history' (1984), material on Torquay held in Torquay Library.

Four box files containing A.C. Ellis's material compiled 1934–52 for a supplement to his Historical survey of Torquay.

Ilfracombe Museum

NDDC, Ilfracombe District Plan (Barnstaple, 1979).

NDDC, Ilfracombe District Plan, policy options report (Barnstaple, 1979).

Report of NDDC Officer Working Party on Ilfracombe Harbour (Barnstaple, 1979).

Ilfracombe Official Guides: *c.*1965, 1970, 1974, 1975, 1977, 1979 and 1986.

Miscellaneous Guides and Programmes etc.

Ilfracombe Museum collection of visual material on the development of Ilfracombe as a resort, including postcards and photographs.

West Country Studies Library (Exeter)

DCC, Quarterly Committee, 1910–74.

DCC, Finance Committee, 1910–74

DCC, General Purposes and Legal and General Purposes Committee, 1910–74.

DCC, Town and Country Planning Committee, 1936–9.

DCC, Planning Committee, 1944–74.

DCC, Dartmoor Forest Preservation Committee, 1919–31.

DCC, National Parks Committee, 1944–74.

DCC, Dartmoor National Park Committee, 1952–74.

DCC, Coastal Protection Committee, 1950–74.

Devon and Exeter Institution (Exeter)

Files compiled by Mrs Lamb containing newspaper cuttings, postcards, programmes, etc. from the mid-1950s to the early-1970s relating to various Devon towns.

Collection of postcards of Devon resorts.

Kelly's Directory of Devonshire, 1910, 1919, 1930 and 1939.

Council for the Preservation of Rural England Annual Reports, 1937–9 and 1955–8.

University of Exeter Library

Census Reports, 1911–91.

Hansard Parliamentary Debates (Commons) 5th series, vols 139–141, 144 and 145, 1921.

Newspapers

Daily Telegraph
Guardian
Herald Express
Ilfracombe Chronicle
Independent
South Wales Daily Post
The Times
Torquay Times
Western Morning News

CONTEMPORARY PUBLICATIONS

Astor J.J. (1922) *The Third Winter of Unemployment*, London.

Beales H.L. and Lambert R.S. (1934). *Memoirs of the Unemployed*, London.

Bewley A.L. and Hogg C. (1925) *Has Poverty Diminished?*, London.

Brunner E. (1945) *Holiday Making and the Holiday Trades*, Nuffield College, Oxford.

BTA (1967) *South Western Counties Tourist Study: Interim Report*, BTA, London.

Buchanan, Colin and Partners (1979) Industrial Market Research Ltd. *A Tourism Study for the West Country: Main Report to the English Tourist Board*.

Burton I. (1989) 'All eyes on Ilfracombe', *Planning* 841 (20 October) 30–1.

Burton T.L. (1965) 'Holiday movements in Britain', *Town and Country Planning* 33, 118–23.

Central Office of Information (1978) *The English Regions: The South West*, London.

Central Statistical Office (1985) *Regional Trends* 20, London.

Countryside Commission (1970) *The Planning of the Coastline*, Countryside Commission, Cheltenham.

Countryside Commission (1980) *Trends in Tourism and Recreation 1968–78*, Countryside Commission, Cheltenham.

Dartington Amenity Research Trust (1980) *North Devon: A Brief Appraisal of Problems and Opportunities*, Dartington.

DCC (1958) *Teignmouth: A Survey of Holidaymakers*, Exeter.

DCC (1958) *A Survey of Holiday Hiring Static Caravans in Devon*, Exeter.

DCC (1959) *A Survey of Mobile Caravaninng and Tented Camping in Devon*, Exeter.

DCC (1960) *A Survey of Roadside Parking, Caravaning and Camping*, Exeter.

DCC, (1960) *A Social Survey of the Holidaymakers in Devon*, 1960, Exeter.

DCC (1961) *A Survey of the Holiday Industry of Devon*, Exeter.

DCC, *Background: An Information Summary of Devon County Council*, Exeter, 1965–1987 issues.

DCC (1975), *Town Trails in Devon*, Exeter.

DCC (1977), *Devon in Figures*, Exeter.

DCC (1980), *Coastlines of Devon*, Exeter.

DCC (1981) *Devon County Structure Plan*, Exeter.

DCC, *Recreation Topic Reports*, Exeter, 1981–4 edns.

DCC (1983) *A Discussion Paper on Tourism: The First Alteration to the Devon County Structure Plan*, Exeter.

DCC, *Devon Tourism Reviews*, Exeter, 1984–7 edns.

DCC (1983) *Landscape Policy Areas Local Plan: Written Statement and Proposals Map*, Exeter.

DCC, (1985) *Employment In Devon: Policies and Programmes*, Exeter.

DCC, (1985), *Devon in Figures*, Exeter.

DCC (1988) *Landscape Policy Areas Local Plan: Written Statement and Proposals Map, First Alternation*, Exeter.

DCC (1988) *Devon in 2001: A Review of County Planning Policies*, Exeter.

DCC, (1988) *Integrated Conservation, Recreation and Tourism Strategy for North Devon*, Exeter.

Delisle Burns C. (1932) *Leisure in the Modern World*, Allen and Unwin, London.

Devon Alliance of Amenity Societies (1978) *Report of a Survey on the Effects of Tourism in Devon*, Exeter.

Dougill W. (1935) 'The British coast and its holiday resorts', *Town and Country Planning Review* 9 (4) 265–78.

Durant H. (1938) *The Problem of Leisure*, G. Routledge & Sons, London.

East Devon Action Project (1987) *Tourism in East Devon: A Report of a Set of Surveys Conducted in East Devon, June 1986–June 1987*, Totnes.

ETB (1981) *Tourism Fact Sheets: West Country*, ETB, London.

ETB (1982) *Torbay Tourism Study*, ETB, London.

ETB (1983) *Tourism and Leisure: A Statement of Development Intent*, ETB, London.

ETB, *European Tourism Year Newsletter*, autumn 1989 and winter 1990 edns.

ETB (1991) *The Future for England's Smaller Resorts*, ETB, London.

The English Tourist Board, the Northern Ireland Tourist Board, the Scottish Tourist Board and the Wales Tourist Board (1994) *The UK Tourist*, Edinburgh.

Farley R. (1967) 'The British seaside resort—can it survive? Part one: the facts', *Hotel and Catering Review*, July, 12–15.

Farley R. (1967) 'The British seaside resort—can it survive? Part two: the problems', *Hotel and Catering Review*, August, 13–25.

Federation of British Health and Holiday Resorts (1915) Annual Report.

Harding Thompson V. (1932) *Devon: A Survey of its Coasts, Moors and Rivers with some Suggestions for their Preservation*.

Graves R. and Hodge A. (1940) *The Long Weekend: A Social History of Great Britain 1918–1939*, Faber and Faber, London.

Hoggart R. (1969) *The Uses of Literacy*, Penguin, Harmondsworth.

Lewes F.M.M. *et al.* (1969) 'The holiday industry', 244–58 in Barlow, F. (ed.) *Exeter and its Region*, University of Exeter Press, Exeter.

Lewes, F.M.M. *et al.* (1970) *The Holiday Industry of Devon and Cornwall*, HMSO, London.

Lickorish L.J and Kershaw A.G. (1958) *The Travel Trade*, Practical Press Ltd., London.

National Parks Commission (1967) 'The coasts of south-west England: report of the regional coastal conference held in Exeter, July 22 1966'.

NDDC (1982) *A Fair Share for North Devon: A Plea for Assisted Area Status*, Barnstaple.

Office of Population Censuses and Surveys (1985) *Regional Profiles: the South West*.

Office of Population Censuses and Surveys (1989) *General Household Survey, 1986*.

P.A. Cambridge Economic Consultants (1992) *Prospects for Coastal Resorts*, Wales Tourist Board, Cardiff.

Paignton UDC (1929) *Paignton Official Guide*, Paignton.

Pember Reeves M. (1913) *Round About a Pound a Week*, Penguin, Harmondsworth.

Pilcher, D. (1938) 'Leisure as an architectural problem', *Architectural Review*, 84 (505), July–December.

Pimlott J.A.R. (1947) *The Englishman's Holiday: A Social History*, Faber and Faber, London.

Torbay Borough Council (1985) *The English Riviera 2000: An Integrated Tourism Strategy for Torquay, Paignton and Brixham*, Torbay.

Torbay Borough Council (1986) *The English Riviera 2000: Tourism Development Action Programme for Torquay, Paignton and Brixham*, Torbay.

Torbay Borough Council (1986) *The English Riviera 2000: Tourism Development Action Tourism Position Statement*, Torbay.

Torbay Borough Council, *The English Riviera: Torquay, Paignton and Brixham* brochures, Torbay, 1984–98.

SWEPC (1967) *A Region with a Future*, SWEPC, London.

SWEPC (1976) *Economic Survey of the Tourist Industry in the South West*, SWEPC, London.

Swansea City Council (1987) *Swansea Maritime Quarter: A Survey of Residents and Tourists*, Swansea.

Smith M., Parker S. and Smith C. (eds) (1973), *Leisure and Society in Britain*, Allen Lane, London.

Spring Rice M. (1939) *Working Class Wives. Their Health and Conditions*, Penguin, Harmondsworth.

Teignmouth Advertising Committee (1931) *Teignmouth Official Guide*, Teignmouth.

The Pilgrim Trust (1938) *Men Without Work*, Cambridge University Press, Cambridge.

Ventures Consultancy (1989) *Seaside Resorts in England Market Profile*, ETB, London

Ward Lock & Company, *Sidmouth Guide* (1915, 1923–24 and 1949 edns), London.

Ward Lock & Company (*c.* 1920) *A Pictorial and Descriptive Guide to Exmouth and the South Devon Coast from the Axe to the Teign*, London.

Ward Lock & Company (*c.* 1906–7) *Ilfracombe, Barnstaple, Clovelly* etc, London.

Ward Lock & Company (*c.* 1920) *Ilfracombe, Barnstaple, Clovelly and North Devon*, London.

Ward Lock & Company, *Ilfracombe, Barnstaple, Clovelly and North West Devon* (1931–2 and *c.* 1946 edns), London.

Ward Lock & Company, (*c.* 1935) *Ilfracombe*, London.

WCTB (1989) *Towards a Strategy for the 1990s and Beyond: A Review and Key Issues Report Consultation Document*, Exeter.

SECONDARY PUBLICATIONS

Agarwal S. (1994) 'The life cycle approach and south coast resorts', 194–208 in Cooper C. and Lockwood A. (eds) *Progress in Tourism Recreation and Hospitality Management*, Vol. 5, John Wiley & Sons, Chichester.

Agarwal S. (1997) 'The public sector: planning for renewal?', 137–58 in Shaw G. and Williams A. (eds) *The Rise and Fall of British Coastal Resort. Cultural and Economic Perspectives*, Cassell, London.

Ahmed Z.A. (1996) 'An international marketing perspective of Canadian tourists' shopping behaviour', *Journal of Vacation Marketing* 2 (3) 207–14.

Aitchison C. (1997) Book review of Apostolopoulos Y *et al.* (eds) (1996) *The Sociology of Tourism: Theoretical and Empirical Investigations*, Routledge, in *Leisure Studies* 16, 53–4: 53.

Ashplant T.G. (1981), 'London working men's clubs, 1875–1914', 241–70 in Yeo I. and Yeo S. (eds) *Popular Culture and Class Conflict 1590–1914: Explorations in the History of Labour and Leisure*, The Harvester Press Ltd., Brighton.

Ashworth G.J. and Goodall B. (1990) *Marketing Tourism Places*, Routledge, London.

Bailey P. (1987) *Leisure and Class in Victorian England: Rational Recreation and the Contest for Control 1830–1885*, 2nd edn, Methuen, London.

Bainbridge C. (1986) *Pavilions on the Sea*, London.

Barker T. (1985) 'The international history of motor transport', *Journal of Contemporary History* 20, 3–19.

Barlow F. (ed.) (1969) *Exeter and its Region*, University of Exeter Press, Exeter.

Briggs A. (1960) *Mass Entertainment: The Origins of a Modern Industry*, Griffin Press, Adelaide.

Brown G.P. and Essex S.J. (1989) 'Tourism policies in the public sector', 543–39 in Witt S. and Moutinho L. (eds) *Tourism Marketing and Management Handbook*, Prentice Hall, Hemel Hempstead.

Burdett Wilson R. (1970) *Go Great Western: A History of GWR Publicity*, David and Charles, Newton Abbot.

Cannadine D. (ed.) (1982) *Patricians, Power and Politics*, University of Leicester, Leicester.

Channon J. *et al.* (1994) 'Towards the twenty-first century', 258–67 in M. Duffy *et al. The New Maritime History of Devon,* vol. II, Conway Maritime Press and University of Exeter Press, London/Exeter.

Chase L. (1997) 'Modern images and social tone in Clacton and Frinton in the interwar years', *International Journal of Maritime History* 9 (1) 149–69.

227

Clarke J. and Critcher C. (1985) *The Devil Makes Work: Leisure in Capitalist Britain*, University of Illinois Press, Champaign.

Clegg S.R. (1989) *Frameworks of Power*, Sage, London.

Cohen E. (1972) 'Towards a sociology of international tourism' *Social Research* 39, 164–82.

Cohen C. (1995) 'Marketing paradise, making nation', *Annals of Tourism Research* 22, 404–21.

Cooke P. (ed.) (1989) *Localities*, Unwin Hyman, London.

Cooper C. (1992) 'The life cycle concept and strategic planning for coastal resorts', *Built Environment* 18 (1) 57–66.

Crick M. (1989) 'Representations of international tourism in the social sciences: sun, sex, sights and servility', *Annual Review of Anthropology* 18, 307–44.

Cross G. (1993) *Time and Money. The Making of Consumer Culture*, Routledge, London.

Cunningham H. (1980) *Leisure in the Industrial Revolution 1780–1880*, Croom Helm, London.

D'Abbs P. (1975) *North Devon 1966–1974: Aspects of Social and Economic Change*, Exeter.

Dann G. (1996), *The Language of Tourism: A Sociolinguistic Perspective*, CAB International, Oxford.

Davies K.M. (1993) 'For health and pleasure in the British fashion: Bray, Co. Wicklow, as a tourist resort, 1750–1914', in O'Connor B. and Cronin M. (eds) *Tourism in Ireland: A Critical Analysis*, University of Cork, Cork.

Demetriadi J. (1997) 'The golden years: English seaside resorts 1950–74', 49–78 in Shaw G. and Williams A. (eds) *The Rise and Fall of British Coastal Resorts. Cultural and Economic Perspectives*, Cassell, London.

Denman R. (1994) *A Record of Achievement*, WTB, Cardiff.

Dumazedier J. (1974), *The Sociology of Leisure*, translated by MacKenzie M.A., Amsterdam.

Duncan N. (1996) 'Sexuality in public and private spaces', 127–45 in Duncan N. (ed.) *Bodyspace: Destabilizing Geographies of Gender and Sexuality*, Routledge, London.

Durie A. (1994) 'The development of the Scottish coastal resorts in the central Lowlands, c. 1770–1880', *Local Historian* 24, 206–16.

Durie A. (1997) 'The Scottish seaside resort in peace and war, c. 1880–1960', *International Journal of Maritime History* 9 (1) 171–86.

Ellis A.C. (1930) *An Historical Survey of Torquay*, 2nd edn, Torquay.

Enloe C. (1989) *Bananas, Beaches and Bases. Making Feminist Sense of International Politics*, Pandora, London.

Evans M., McDonagh P. and Moutinho L. (1992) 'The coastal hotel sector: performance and perception analysis', *Built Environment* 18 (1) 67–78.

Foucault M. (1977) *Discipline and Punishment*, Tavistock, London.

Foucault M. (1980) *Power/Knowledge*, Harvester, Brighton.

Foucault M. (1980) *Power/Knowledge: Selected Interviews and Other Writings 1972–1977*, ed. Gordon C., Random House, New York.

Gale T., Botterill D., Morgan N.J. and Shaw G. (1995) 'Cultural change and the British seaside resort—implications for the quality and integrity of resort environments', 129–33 in Healy M.G. and Doody J.P. (eds), *Directions in European Coastal Management*, Samara Publishing Ltd., Dyfed.

Gardiner V. *et al.* (1977) 'Scenic qualities of the south east Devon coast', *Transactions of the Devonshire Association* 109, 171–8.

Gill I. (1988) 'Tourism and entertainment services in local government', 155–77 in Bennington J. and White J. (eds) *The Future of Leisure Services*, ILAM/Longman, Harlow.

Gold J.R. and Ward S.V. (eds) (1994) *Place Promotion: The Use of Publicity and Marketing to Sell Towns and Regions*, John Wiley & Sons, Chichester.

Good A. (1980) 'The coastal resort', 87–95 in DCC, *Coastlines of Devon*, DCC, Exeter.

Goodall B. and Ashworth G.J. (1988) *Marketing Tourism Places—The Promotion of Destination Regions*, Croom-Helm, London.

Goodall B. (1992) 'Coastal resorts: development and redevelopment', *Built Environment* 18 (1) 5–11.

Goodrich J.N. (1994) 'Health tourism: a new positioning strategy for tourist destinations', 227–38 in Uysal M. (ed.) *Global Tourism Behaviour*, Haworth Press, London.

Grafton D.J. and Bolton N. (1986) 'Planning policy and economic development in Devon and Cornwall 1945–1984', in Gripaios P. (ed.) *The Economy of Devon and Cornwall*, Occasional Papers Series, No. 9, South West Papers in Geography, Plymouth Polytechnic, Plymouth.

Green E., Woodward D. and Hebron S. (1988) *Women's Leisure: Constraints and Opportunities*, Leisure Studies Association Newsletter Supplement.

Greenwood J., Williams A. M. and Shaw G. (1990) 'Policy implementation and tourism in the UK: Implications from recent research in Cornwall', *Tourism Management* 11 (1) 53–62.

Hall D. (1998) 'Reconstruction, modernization and sustainability: prospects for the role of tourism in Albania', 321–30 in Hahrstedt W. and Kombol T.P. (eds) *Leisure, Culture and Tourism in Europe*, Bielefeld, Germany.

Hall S. (1997) 'The work of representation', 13–74 in Hall S. (ed.) *Representation: Cultural Representations and Signifying Practices*, Sage and the Open University, London.

Hargreaves J. (1982) 'Sport, culture and ideology', 30–61 in Hargreaves J. (ed.) *Sport, Culture and Ideology*, Routledge & Kegan Paul, London.

Hargreaves J. (1986) *Sport, Power and Culture*, Polity Press, Cambridge.

Harrison B. (1967) 'Religion and recreation in nineteenth-century England', *Past and Present*, 38, 98–125.

Heeley J. (1981) 'Planning for tourism in Britain: an historical perspective', *Town Planning Review* 52 (1) 61–79.

Heeley J. (1988) 'Planning for tourism: what should be the role of the local authorities?', 7–17 in McDowell L.D. (ed.) *Planning for Tourism and Leisure*, Proceedings

229

of the First International Conference, held at the University of Ulster at Jordonstown, Ulster.

Henley Centre (1989) 'The discerning consumer', *Leisure Management* 9 (5) 34–6.

Hern A. (1967) *The Seaside Holiday: The History of the English Seaside Resort*, Cresset, London.

Heuston J. (1993) 'Kilkee: the origins and development of a west coast resort', in O'Connor B. and Cronin M. (eds) *Tourism in Ireland: A Critical Analysis*, University of Cork, Cork.

Hoskins W.G. (1959) *Devon and its People*, University of Exeter Press, Exeter.

Howkins A. (1981) 'The taming of Whitsun. the changing face of a nineteenth century rural holiday', 187–208 in Yeo I. and Yeo S. (eds) *Popular Culture and Class Conflict 1590–1914: Explorations in the History of Labour and Leisure*, The Harvester Press Ltd., Brighton.

Hudson R. and Williams A.M. (1995) *Divided Britain*, 2nd edn, John Wiley & Sons, Chichester.

Huggins M. (1984) 'Social tone and resort development in North East England: Victorian seaside resorts around the mouth of the Tees', *Northern History* 20, 187–206.

Huggins M.J. (1997) 'Sport and the English seaside resort 1800–1914', *International Journal of Maritime History* 9 (1) 213–32.

Hughes H.L. (1989) 'Entertainment', 125–30 in Witt S. and Mouthino L. (eds) *Tourism Marketing and Management Handbook*, Prentice Hall, Hemel Hempstead.

Humphries S. (1981) *Hooligans or Rebels? An Oral History of Childhood and Youth 1880–1939*, Basil Blackwell, Oxford.

Humphries S. (1981) 'Steal to survive: the social crime of working class children 1890–19401, *Oral History* 9 (6) 24–33.

Jones S. (1986) *Workers at Play: A Social and Economic History of Leisure 1918–1939*, Routledge & Kegan Paul, London.

Joyce P. (1991) *Visions of the People. Industrial England and the Question of Class, 1848–1914*, Cambridge University Press, Cambridge.

Kinnaird V. and Hall D. (eds) (1994) *Tourism: A Gender Analysis*, John Wiley & Sons, Chichester.

Kotler P. *et al.* (1994) *Marketing Places. Attracting Investment, Industry and Tourism to Cities, States, and Nations*, The Free Press, New York

Lamplugh L. (1984) *A History of Ilfracombe*, Harvester Sussex.

Lewis R. (1980) 'Seaside holiday resorts in the United States and Britain: a review', *Urban History Yearbook*, 44–52.

Lindley K. (1980), *Seaside Architecture*.

Lowerson J. and Myerscough J. (1977) *Time to Spare in Victorian England*, Harvester Press, Hassocks.

MacCannell D. (1976 and 1989) *The Tourist. A New Theory of the Leisure Class*, 2nd edn, Schocken Books, New York.

Martin B. and Mason S. (1990) 'Water leisure riding a wave', *Leisure Management* 10

(4) 30–3.

Marquand D. (1986) 'Sir Stafford Cripps' 155–77 in Sissons M. and French P. (eds) *Age of Austerity 1945–51*, Oxford University Press, Oxford.

Marwick A. (1982) *British Society Since 1945*, Penguin, Harmondsworth.

May F.B. (1980) 'The rise of Ilfracombe as a seaside resort in the nineteenth century', 137–59 in Fisher H.E.S. (ed.) *West Country Maritime and Social History*: Exeter Papers in Economic History 13, University of Exeter, Exeter.

May F.B. (1983) 'Victorian and Edwardian Ilfracombe', 186–205 in Walton J.K. and Walvin J. (eds) *Leisure in Britain 1780–1939*, Manchester University Press, Manchester

Mickleburgh T. (1991) 'Piers—adapting for survival', *Leisure Manager* 9 (3): 17–19.

Middleton V.T.C. (1989) 'Seaside resorts', *Insights*, B5–13, ETB

Middleton V.T.C. (1994) *Marketing in Travel and Tourism*, 2nd edn, Butterworth Heinemann, Oxford.

Mintel International Group Ltd (1995) *Targeting the Rich and Poor. Executive Summary.*

Morgan M. (1991) 'Majorca: dressing up to survive', *Tourism Management* 12 (1) March.

Morgan N.J. (1989) 'Twentieth century Devon seaside tourism: some aspects of the holiday industry of Ilfracombe', 60–71 in Botterill D. (ed.) *Tourism and Leisure (Part Two): Markets, Users and Sites,* Leisure Studies Association.

Morgan N.J. (1994) 'Devon seaside tourism since 1900', 250–8 in M. Duffy *et al.* (eds), *The New Maritime History of Devon*, vol. II, Conway Maritime Press and University of Exeter Press, London/Exeter.

Morgan N.J. (1996) 'Resort social tone in Torquay in the 'twenties', 129–31 in Gray T. (ed.) *Devon Documents,* Devon and Cornwall Notes & Queries.

Morgan N.J. (1997) 'Seaside resort strategies: the case of inter-war Torquay', 84–100 in Fisher S. (ed.) *Recreation and the Sea,* University of Exeter Press, Exeter.

Morgan N.J. (1998) 'Welsh seaside resort regeneration strategies: changing times, changing needs at the end of the twentieth century', 193–216 in Starkey D.J. and Jamieson A.G. (eds) *Exploiting the Sea. Aspects of Britain's Maritime Economy Since 1870*, University of Exeter Press, Exeter.

Morgan N.J. and Pritchard A. (1998) *Tourism Promotion and Power: Creating Images, Creating Identities,* John Wiley & Sons, Chichester.

Parker S. (1981), 'Change, flexibility, spontaneity, and self-determination in leisure', *Social Forces* 60 (2): 323–31.

Parry K. (1983) *The Resorts of the Lancashire Coast,* David and Charles, Newton Abbot.

Perkin H.J. (1975) 'The social tone of Victorian seaside resorts in the North West', *Northern History* 11, 187–94.

Porter M. (1994) 'Devon's port industry since 1914', 235–242 in M. Duffy *et al.* (eds), *The New Maritime History of Devon*, vol. II Conway Maritime Press and University of Exeter Press, London/Exeter.

Pritchard A. and Morgan N.J. (1995) 'Evaluating vacation destination brochure images: the case of local authorities in Wales', *Journal of Vacation Marketing* 2 (1)

23–38.

Pritchard A. and Morgan N.J. (1998) '"Mood Marketing". The new destination branding strategy. A case study of "Wales" the brand', *Journal of Vacation Marketing* 3 (4): 215–29.

Pritchard A., Morgan N.J., Sedgley D. and Jenkins, A. (1998) 'Reaching out to the gay tourist: opportunities and threats in an emerging market segment', *Tourism Management* 19 (3).

Reid D. (1976) 'The decline of Saint Monday 1776–1876', *Past and Present*, 71, 76–101.

Richards J. (1983) 'The cinema and cinema-going in Birmingham in the 1930s', 31–52 in Walton J.K. and Walvin J. (eds) *Leisure in Britain 1780–1939*, Manchester University Press, Manchester.

Roberts R. (1983) 'The corporation as impresario: the municipal provision of entertainment in Victorian and Edwardian Bournemouth', 137–58 in Walton J.K. and Walvin J. (eds) *Leisure in Britain 1780–1939*, Manchester University Press, Manchester.

Rojek C. (1985) *Leisure and Capitalist Theory*, Tavistock, New York.

Rojek C. (1989) 'Leisure time and leisure space', 191–204 in Rojek C. (ed.) *Leisure for Leisure*, Sage, London.

Russell P. (1960) *A History of Torquay and the Famous Anchorage of Torbay*, Torquay.

Said E. (1991) *Orientalism. Western Concepts of the Orient*, Penguin, London.

Selby M. and Morgan, N.J. (1996) 'Reconstruing place image: a case study of its role in destination market research', *Tourism Management* 17 (4 June) 287–94.

Selwyn T. (ed.) (1996) *The Tourist Image: Myths and Myth Making in Tourism*, Wiley & Sons, Chichester.

Shaw G. and Williams A. (eds) (1997) *The Rise and Fall of the British Coastal Resort. Cultural and Economic Perspectives*, Cassell, London.

Shaw G. and Williams A. (1997) 'The private sector: tourism entrepreneurship—a constraint or resource?', 117–36 in Shaw G. and Williams A. (eds) *The Rise and Fall of British Coastal Resort. Cultural and Economic Perspectives*, Cassell, London

Shields R. (1991) *Places on the Margin. Alternative Geographies of Modernity*, Routledge, London.

Simmons J. (1982) 'The railway in Cornwall 1835–1914', *Journal of the Royal Institution of Cornwall*: 11–29.

Simmons J. (1984) 'Railways, hotels and tourism in Britain, 1839–1914', *Journal of Contemporary History* 19 (2) 201–22.

Sigsworth E.M. (ed.) (1980) *Ports and Resorts in the Regions*, Proceedings of the Conference of Regional History Tutors, held at Hull College of Higher Education, Hull.

Snelling A. (1997) 'Letter from America: marketing Wales in the USA', *Leisure Monitor*, 3.

Sports Council for Wales (1991) *A Strategy Review. Changing Times, Changing Needs*, Sports Council for Wales, Cardiff.

BIBLIOGRAPHY

Stanes R. (1978) *A History of Devon*, Harvester Press, Sussex.

Starkey D.J. (1994) 'The ports, sea-borne trade and shipping industry of South Devon, 1786–1914', 32–47 in M. Duffy *et al.* (eds), *The New Maritime History of Devon*, vol. II, Conway Maritime Press and University of Exeter Press, London/Exeter.

-Stedman Jones G. (1977) 'Class expression versus social control? A critique of recent trends in the social history of leisure', *History Workshop* 4, 162–70.

Thomas K. (1983) 'No passion for the brute creation', *History Today* 33, 5–10.

Thompson E.P. (1967) 'Time, work-discipline, and industrial capitalism', *Past and Present* 38, 56–97.

Thompson F.M.L. (1990) *The Cambridge Social History of Britain 1750–1950, Vol. 2, People and their Environment*, Cambridge University Press, Cambridge.

Towner J. (1996) *An Historical Geography of Recreation and Tourism in the Western World 1540–1940*, John Wiley & Sons, Chichester.

Travis J.F. 'Lynton in the nineteenth century: an isolated and exclusive resort', 152–67 in Sigsworth E.M. (ed.) *Ports and Resorts in the Regions*, Proceedings of the Conference of Regional History Tutors, Hull College of Higher Education, Hull.

Travis J.F. (1993) *The Rise of the Devon Seaside Resorts 1750–1900*, University of Exeter Press, Exeter.

Urry J. (1990) *The Tourist Gaze. Travel and Leisure in Contemporary Societies*, Sage, London.

Urry J. (1991) 'The sociology of tourism', 48–57 in Cooper C. (ed.) *Progress in Tourism, Recreation and Hospitality Management*, vol. III, Belhaven Press, London.

Urry J. (1997) 'Cultural change and the seaside resort', 102–16 in Shaw G. and Williams A. (eds) *The Rise and Fall of British Coastal Resorts. Cultural and Economic Perspectives*, Cassell, London.

Vamplew W. (1976) *The Turf: A Social and Economic History of Horse Racing*, Allen Lane, London.

Vernon, M. (1998) 'Get ready for the electronic billboard', *Independent* 31 Mar.

Vincent D. (1983), 'Reading in the working-class home', 207–12 in Walton J.K. and Walvin J. (eds), *Leisure in Britain 1780–1914*, Manchester University Press, Manchester.

Walton J.K. (1978) *The Blackpool Landlady: A Social History*, Manchester University Press, Manchester

Walton J.K. and McGloin P.R. (1979) 'Holiday resorts and their visitors', *Local Historian* 13, 323–31.

Walton J.K. (1980) 'Railways and resort development in North West England 1830–1914', 120–37 in Sigsworth E.M. (ed.) *Ports and Resorts in the Regions*, Proceedings of the Conference of Regional History Tutors, Hull College of Higher Education, Hull.

Walton J.K. (1981) 'The demand for working class seaside holidays in Victorian England', *Economic History Review* 34, 253–8.

Walton J.K. and McGloin P.R. (1981) 'The tourist trade in Victorian lakeland',

233

Northern History 17, 153–82.

Walton J.K. (1983) 'Municipal government and the holiday industry in Blackpool 1876–1914', 158–85 in Walton J.K. and Walvin J. (eds) *Leisure in Britain 1780–1939*, Manchester University Press, Manchester.

Walton J.K. (1983), *The English Seaside Resort: A Social History 1750–1914*, Leicester University Press, Leicester.

Walton J.K. and O'Neill C. (1993) 'Numbering the holidaymakers: the problems and possibilities of the June census of 1921 for historians of resorts', *Local Historian* 23 (4) 205–16.

Walton J.K. (1994) 'The re-making of a popular resort: Blackpool Tower and the boom of the 1890s', *Local Historian* 24, 194–205.

Walton J.K. (1996) 'Leisure towns in wartime: the impact of the First World War in Blackpool and San Sebastian', *Journal of Contemporary History*, 31, 603–18.

Walton J.K. (1997) 'Seaside resorts and maritime history', *International Journal of Maritime History* 9, (1) 125–47.

Walton J.K. (1997) 'The seaside resorts of Western Europe 1750–1939', 24–38 in Fisher H.E.S. (ed.) *Recreation and the Sea*, University of Exeter Press, Exeter.

Walton J.K. (1997) 'The seaside resorts of England and Wales, 1900–1950: growth, diffusion and the emergence of new forms of coastal tourism', 21–48 in Shaw G. and Williams A. (eds) *The Rise and Fall of British Coastal Resorts. Cultural and Economic Perspectives*, Cassell, London.

Walvin J. (1975) *The People's Game: A Social History of Football*, Allen Lane, London.

Walvin J. (1978) *Leisure and Society 1830–1950*, Longman, London.

Walvin J. (1978) *Beside the Seaside: A Social History of the Popular Seaside Holiday*, Allen Lane, London.

Wanhill S. (1989) 'Development and investment policy in tourism', 103–5 in Witt S. and Moutinho L. (eds) *Tourism Marketing and Management Handbook*, Prentice Hall, Hemel Hempstead.

Ward C. (1984) 'The end of an era', *Town and Country Planning* 53 (4) 107.

Ward S.V. (1988) *The Geography of Inter-War Britain: The State and Uneven Development*, Routledge, London.

Waterman D. (1984) 'Seaside resorts to a theme for a dream', *Town and Country Planning* 53 (4) 104–6.

Watts H.D. (1965) 'Industry in a coastal resort', *Town and Country Planning* 33 (4) 169–74.

Webster C. (1982) 'Healthy or hungry thirties?', *History Workshop* 13, 110–29.

Whyman J. (1972) 'Visitors to Margate in the 1841 census returns', *Local Population Studies*, 7, 19–38.

Whyman J. (1980) 'Water communications and their direct effect on the growth and character of Margate c.1750–1840', 138–51 in Sigsworth E.M. (ed.) *Ports and Resorts in the Regions*, Proceedings of the Conference of Regional History Tutors, Hull College of Higher Education, Hull.

Williams A. and Shaw G. (1988) 'Tourism: candy floss industry or job generator',

BIBLIOGRAPHY

Town Planning Review 59, 81–104.

Williams A and Shaw G. (1997) 'Riding the big dipper: the rise and decline of the British seaside resort in the twentieth century', 1–20 in Shaw G. and Williams A. (eds) *The Rise and Fall of British Coastal Resorts. Cultural and Economic Perspectives*, Cassell, London.

Williams G. (1985) 'Community, class and rugby in Wales 1880–1914', *Society for the Study of Labour History Bulletin*, 50 (Spring) 10–11.

Williams R. (1966) *Communications*, Penguin, Harmondsworth.

Williams R. (1983) 'Culture', 15–55 in McLellan D. (ed.) *Marx: The First 100 Years*, Oxford University Press, Oxford.

Wilson J. (1988) *Politics and Leisure*, Unwin Hyman, London.

Wright H. (1989) 'At home or abroad?', *Leisure Management* 9, 29–30.

Wrightson K. (1981) 'Alehouses, order and reformation in rural England 1590–1660', 1–27 in Yeo I. and Yeo S. (eds) *Popular Culture and Class Conflict 1590–1914: Explorations in the History of Labour and Leisure*, The Harvester Press Ltd., Brighton.

Yates N. (1988) 'Selling the Seaside', *History Today*, 38, 20–7.

Yeo I. and Yeo S. (eds) (1981) *Popular Culture and Class Conflict 1590–1914: Explorations in the History of Labour and Leisure*, The Harvester Press Ltd., Brighton.

Young R.C. (1977) 'The structural context of the Caribbean tourist industry. A comparative study', *Economic Development and Cultural Change* 25, 657–71.

UNPUBLISHED THESES AND PAPERS

Bolton N. (1988) 'The rural population turnaround: a case study of north Devon', unpublished Plymouth Polytechnic PhD.

Brown B.J.H. (1971) 'A survey of the development of the leisure industries of the Bristol region, with special reference to the history of the seaside resorts', unpublished University of Bath PhD.

Demetriadi J. (1995) 'English and Welsh seaside resorts—with special reference to Blackpool and Margate', University of Lancaster unpublished PhD.

Eisenschitz A. (1988) 'The politicisation of Leisure', paper presented to the Leisure Studies Association International Conference, Brighton.

Hay B. (1998) 'Tourism futures', paper presented to the University of Wales Institute, Cardiff research seminar, February.

Martin G.C. (1968) 'Some aspects of the provision of annual holidays for the working classes down to 1947', unpublished University of Leicester MA.

May F.B. (1978), 'The development of Ilfracombe as a resort in the nineteenth century', unpublished University of Wales MA.

Morgan N.J. (1992) 'Perceptions, patterns and policies of tourism: the development of the Devon seaside resorts during the twentieth century with special reference to Torquay and Ilfracombe', unpublished University of Exeter PhD.

Morgan N.J. and Pritchard A. (1996) 'Welsh resort strategies: creating a viable seaside industry for the next century?', paper presented to the Third International Urban History Conference, Budapest.

Pearson, R.E. (1965) 'The Lincolnshire holiday region', unpublished University of Nottingham MA.

Redfern A. (1982) 'The development of leisure in Crewe, 1880–1914', unpublished University of York M.Phil.

Travis J.F. (1988) 'The rise of holidaymaking on the Devon coast with special reference to health and entertainment', unpublished University of Exeter PhD.

Walton J.K. (1974) 'The social development of Blackpool 1788–1914', unpublished University of Lancaster PhD.

WTB (1994) unpublished qualitative findings for the Quality Assurance Schemes Report (1994), WTB, Cardiff.

Index

Aberystwyth 60, 174
abilism 14, 189
advertising 8, 23, 33, 92
  agencies 109, 127
  on buses 111–112
  committees 100, 103, 104, 105, 106, 109, 113, 119, 123, 127–128, 131–132, 141
  funding of 100, 101, 104–105, 107–113, 119–120, 122–128, 132, 134, 136–137
  and local government 28, 36, 52, 100–142, 179
  organisation of 101, 104–105, 108–110, 112–113, 120, 122–123, 125–127, 134
  on posters 102, 104–110, 120, 127, 128, 134, 141
  in press 103–105, 107, 108, 110, 113, 118–119, 122, 124, 127–129, 132, 134, 141
  and sexual themes 107, 132–133, 137
  strategies 8, 102, 103, 114–115, 120, 122–123, 129–132, 134, 136–7, 140–141
  see also imagery, marketing; promotional films; public relations activities
Agarwal, Sheila 25, 51, 54
age 14, 48, 79
Association of British Travel Agents 140
bands 147, 148, 149, 155
  facilities for 166, 168–170
Barry Island 32, 35, 41, 49, 54, 55, 143,

170
bathing 33, 151
  facilities 108, 132, 138, 151, 155, 156
  machines 108, 150, 151
  mixed sex 149–150
bathing beauty contests 59, 107
beach management 147, 148, 150–151, 154–156, 170, 188
Beeching Report 75
Bigbury 67
Blackpool 17, 45
  and advertising 100, 101, 109
  development of 27, 32, 33, 36, 50, 51, 57, 60, 61, 78, 98, 184
  and entertainment 55, 60
  facilities of 33, 35
  social tone of 91, 95, 96, 97, 142, 143, 153, 182
  see also Walton, John
boarding houses 33, 37, 40, 49, 124, 149, 159
  see also hotels
Bournemouth 27, 36, 38, 42, 49, 50, 57, 78, 84, 94, 120, 143, 169, 184
Brighton 27, 50, 57, 60, 78, 95, 97, 137, 143, 170, 184
Bristol 174
British Health Resorts Association 117
British Rail 126, 127, 130, 134
British Resorts Association 117, 188
  see also British Health Resorts Association; Federation of British Health and Holiday Resorts; Health and Pleasure Resorts Association

237

British Tourist Authority 140
British Travel Association 76
Brixham 68, 72, 80–81, 134, 155
  marina 175–6
brochures 101–102, 106, 109, 111, 116,
122–123, 126, 127, 130, 131–141
  production of 103, 107, 108, 125,
  136–141
  see also Holiday Haunts guide
Brunner, Elizabeth 36
  see also Nuffield Survey
Budleigh Salterton 67, 68, 70, 75, 92, 183
  demographics of 80, 81
  entertainment in 145, 148
  marketing of 131, 136
  social tone of 92, 143, 180, 181
Butlins 55
by-laws 27, 28, 149–155, 182
camping 121
campsites 41, 62, 72, 92, 121, 182, 183
Cannes 114, 115
  see also French Riviera
Cardiff 174
census data 33, 50, 69, 70
central government 44, 188
  and 1931 crisis 115–119
  and resort development 7, 32, 37–39,
  50–51
  and tourism funding 37, 39, 50–51,
  105, 126, 143, 187
Chambers of Commerce 109, 153, 168,
179
  of Ilfracombe 28, 84, 86
  of Sidmouth 131
  of Torquay 28, 87–88, 94, 104, 153,
  154, 159, 160
charabancs 10, 17, 62, 72–73, 82, 90, 149,
150, 182
  see also motor transport
Chase, Laura 25, 27, 35, 100, 150
Christie, Agatha 140
cinemas 33, 37, 47
Clacton 27, 60, 109, 140, 143, 150
Colwyn Bay 60
Combe Martin 65
commuters 49
  and resort growth 49–50, 78

conferences 43, 52, 60, 98, 99, 130, 190
content analysis 118–119
Cornish Riviera Express 106
Cornwall 80, 188
Cross, Gary 18, 24, 32
Dartmouth 67, 81
  and yachting 176, 183
Dawlish 77, 81, 153, 155
  social tone of 67, 70, 71
Dawlish Warren 67, 79, 71
day-tripper traffic 62, 89, 91, 92, 149, 180,
190
  of Devon 67, 70, 72, 90
  of Exmouth 69, 70, 147
  of Ilfracombe 90, 186
  of Torquay 94–95, 96, 106
Demetriadi, Julian 25, 39, 41
Development of Tourism Act 50, 136,
143, 187
Devon 4, 25, 64–78, 67–68
  and day-trippers 67, 70, 72, 90
  demographics of 78, 79–81
  economy of 65, 68, 74, 78
  employment patterns of 65, 74, 77
  and fishing industry 65, 175
  geography of 62, 64–65, 67, 72, 78,
  90, 180, 181, 182
  hotels in 56, 75
  and social tone 7, 19, 29, 62–63, 67,
  70–71, 180
  and transport 64, 68, 70–75, 78,
  90–91, 181
Devon County Council 185
  and resort planning 65, 77, 88, 187
Durie, Alaistair 4, 25, 33
Eastbourne 38, 42, 140, 184
English Riviera 114–115, 118, 132, 133,
137, 140
  see also Torquay
English Tourist Board 51, 56, 57, 98, 136,
184, 185
entertainment 35, 59, 61, 84, 86,
  facilities 17, 8, 21, 29, 33, 36, 40,
  42–43, 52, 55, 87–88, 108, 142–179
  funding of 143–146, 151, 155–157
  and local government 29, 82,
  108–110, 142–179

and social tone 142–155, 161
entertainment committees 143, 145
    of Ilfracombe 103, 145
    of Sidmouth 103, 127, 145–146
    of Torquay 103, 145–146, 168
entertainment officers 145
ethical tourists 58–59, 89
European Union 175
Exeter 69
Exmouth 68, 69, 75, 81, 150, 151, 170
    and day-trip market 70, 90
    entertainment in 145, 147–148, 152,
    153, 156
    marketing of 123, 131
    marina 174, 176
    social tone of 67, 69, 147, 180, 184
family life cycle 48
fashion 197, 150
Federation of British Health and Holiday
Resorts 108
    see also British Resorts Association;
Health and Pleasure Resorts Association
Felixstowe 33
feminist thought 14, 63
First Leisure 55
fishing industry 65, 175
Fleet Walk development 140, 176
Foucault, Michael 10, 12, 14, 17, 18
French Riviera 114–115, 117, 118, 135
Frinton 27, 102, 109, 150
gender 5, 14, 18, 48
    see also women; sexuality
General Strike (The) 161
golf 53, 89
    see also sport
Goodrington Sands 64
Great Western Railway 71, 114
    and advertising 106, 108, 110–113,
    115, 118–121
    and Torquay 103, 10, 112–113, 120
Great Yarmouth 57, 60
Hastings 36, 53, 170
Health and Pleasure Resorts Association
112
Health and Pleasure Resorts Acts 36, 52,
108–110, 120, 124
holiday camps *see* Butlins; campsites

Holiday Haunts guide 106, 108, 111, 115,
121
hoteliers associations 28, 119, 123, 127,
130, 131
    of Torquay 28, 85, 104–106, 108, 112,
    120–122, 125–126, 132, 137, 153,
    160, 168, 179
    see also hotels
hotels 33, 37, 41–42, 75, 77, 94, 98, 117,
124, 131, 149, 154, 183, 185
    and advertising 92, 103, 106, 112,
    118–119, 122, 136
    and investment 43, 51, 55, 56, 159
    and war 68, 72
    see also boarding houses; hoteliers
associations
Hove 27, 78
Huggins, Mike 142
Ilfracombe 35, 37–38, 43, 60, 65, 74,
80–84, 127, 144
    catchment areas of 26, 90–92
    council 82, 84, 86, 108, 119, 163–166,
    185–187
    entertainment in 92, 145, 151–153,
    182
    facilities of 75–76, 82–84, 87–88, 148,
    156, 165–167, 170, 174–175, 186
    guide 123, 128–129, 136–137
    investment in 163–166
    marketing of 100–104, 108–110,
    113–115, 119, 123–124, 128–129,
    136–137, 141, 186
    pavilion 82–84, 113, 148, 163–167
    pier 82, 113, 158
    politics of 28, 82, 86, 123, 128, 163,
    166
    and railways 68, 75, 185
    social tone of 67, 89–93, 119, 141,
    143, 148, 151, 180, 184, 186
    visitor profile of 69–70, 90–92, 186
Ilfracombe Chronicle 110, 119, 128
imagery 11, 99, 140
    and advertising 100, 124, 131, 134,
    136–141
    and repositioning 53, 98, 136–137,
    176
    of resorts 27, 43, 101, 102, 146, 150

inequality
in leisure 13, 14, 18–19, 21, 46
in society 14–16, 18–19, 21, 48, 189–190
in tourism 11–12, 14, 15, 45, 46, 189–190
see also social class and social tone
information bureaux 104–105, 112, 126, 128, 130, 136, 162
Internet 140
investment 51–58, 96, 140, 155, 156, 164, 169, 170, 173–175, 187–189
failure of 56, 76, 88, 175, 176, 177
and hotels 43, 51, 55, 56, 159
see also central government; European Union; local government; national lottery; private sector
Ireland 4
Isle of Wight 184
joint advertising committees *see* advertising
Joyce, Patrick, 17, 22, 27
Kingswear 176
landladies 33
leisure 15–17, 20–24
choices 13, 14, 18, 45, 48, 74, 189–190
meaning of 13–15, 18, 22
and power 6, 8, 15, 17, 18, 29, 180–181
and social class 46–48
and space 8, 18–19, 29, 180, 190
theory 1, 6, 10, 12–13, 15–16, 20
Lewes F.M.M. 71, 182
Llandudno 58, 184
local government 42, 44, 49, 50
and advertising 28, 36, 52, 100–142, 179, 187
and entertainment 3, 8, 29, 82, 86, 109, 142–179
and facilities 155–179, 187
and investment 52–56, 82, 86, 88, 142–145, 155–157, 173, 175
and marketing 8, 28, 36, 52, 86, 100–142
and resort development 3, 7, 8, 19, 26–28, 31, 51–54, 92, 100, 109, 179, 187–190

and reorganisation of 1974 53, 87, 156–157
and social tone 25–26, 100, 142, 150–155, 181
see also Urban District Councils Association; municipal conservatism
Lyme Regis 67
Lynton/Lynmouth 65, 67, 69, 70, 81, 145, 148, 180
MacDonald, Ramsey 115
Margate 55
marinas 52, 98, 99, 157, 173–176
see also yachting
market segmentation 3, 180, 182–183, 189
marketing
of destinations 3, 8, 100–101, 106–107, 112, 114
politics of 105, 134
of resorts 3, 5, 8, 36, 57, 59, 86, 100–142, 189
strategies 8, 52, 101, 112, 114
see also advertising; imagery, promotional films; public relations activities
Marxist thought 14, 15, 16, 17
May, Bruce 89
Metropolitan Railway 105
Ministry of Health 38, 166
Ministry of Transport 38, 39, 158
motor transport 33, 41, 68, 75, 121, 128
and motorcar ownership 40, 45, 72, 74
and petrol rationing 37–38
and road network 40, 71, 73, 76
see also charabancs
Mumbles 42
municipal conservatism 52
Newport (Gwent) 174
Newquay 33, 57, 184
niche marketing 120
Northern Ireland 44
Nuffield Survey 62, 72, 149
see also Brunner, Elizabeth
oil crisis 40–42
paid holidays 36, 40, 45, 47
Paid Holidays Act 36, 45
Paignton 38, 69, 70, 88, 114, 118, 150

demographics of 80–81
entertainment in 145, 152–153, 155, 166
marketing of 124, 134
social tone of 67–68, 97, 184
pavilions 33, 35, 155, 158–166, 170
Penarth 42
Perkin, Harold 25, 26
piers 140, 143–144, 152, 157–158, 170
decline of 156, 157
rise of 157
in wartime 37, 158
Pimlott, J.A.R. 25, 103
Plymouth 67, 156
politics 28, 79, 86, 179
and leisure 13, 20, 29
and power 10, 13, 14, 17, 28, 44, 100, 180
and space 10, 13
Porthcawl 32, 170
posters see advertising
poverty 46, 49, 61
power 3, 44
and leisure 8, 13–15, 17, 154, 181
and society 5–6, 13–15, 17–18, 91, 180, 181
and space 6, 8, 19, 91
and tourism 5–6, 13–15, 17–18, 91, 180–181
see also politics; Foucault, Michael
Prestatyn 33
private sector
and advertising 104, 106, 107, 122, 132
and investment 32, 38, 41, 52, 54–58, 143–144, 175, 177–178, 187–189
and resort development 7, 26–27, 52, 143–144
promotional films 105, 121, 122, 124
public relations activities 107, 11–112, 122, 125
Public Works Loan Board 158
publicity managers 109, 112, 124, 126, 134, 141
punch and judy shows 147
race 5, 14, 18
railways 36, 41, 42, 71, 75, 89, 113–114, 121
and advertising 102, 105–111, 116–118, 121–123, 126–127, 134
in Devon 68, 70–72, 90, 111
nationalisation of 103, 126
see also Beeching Report; British Rail
Redcar 36
residents 53
and advertising debates 105–106, 109–110, 120
and resort development 26, 49, 62, 179
and resort politics 5, 7, 8, 49, 62, 81–88, 84, 99, 105, 143
and social tone 28, 62–63, 90, 91, 113–114
and tourism facilities 159–170
resorts 24, 26–27, 30, 43–44, 51, 52, 189–190
and cultural change 6, 7, 32, 35, 44, 58–61, 152–153
in decline 2–4, 31, 41, 44, 50, 59, 177
and demographics 49–50, 53, 60–61, 69, 78–81
in Europe 2, 51, 56, 59
and European Union funding 175
future of 32, 51, 57, 86, 176–178, 187–190
life cycle of 54
and national lottery funding 166
rise of 24–44, 56
and social class 13, 19, 24–25, 101
social graduation of 7, 13, 19, 27, 29, 32, 44, 59, 89
specialisation 182–183, 186, 189
of USA 2, 60
see also social tone
retailing 98, 140, 162, 163, 173, 174, 185
see also Fleet Walk development
retirees 49, 53, 61, 78, 131, 154, 183,
and resort development 48, 50, 78–79, 80–81, 144
and resort ethos 50, 55, 79, 81, 86–87
and social tone 67, 88
Rhyl 35, 36, 42, 43, 49, 55, 58, 143, 175, 184
Rojek, Chris 13, 14

Salcombe 67, 81, 183
Scarborough 10, 27, 53, 57, 170, 184
Scotland 4, 16, 33, 44
seaside architecture 60
Seaton 67, 68, 70, 72, 75, 80, 81
    social tone of 180
self-catering 41, 48, 75, 77
sexuality 5, 14, 18
    see also gender; women
Shaw, Gareth 31, 44, 51, 54, 60
Shields, Rob 6, 60
Sidmouth 49, 67–68, 70, 75, 77, 79, 92,
123, 124, 128, 151, 180, 182
    and entertainment 130–131
    facilities of 92, 146, 155; 183
    local government of 92, 102, 122,
    127, 131
    marketing of 102–103, 109, 117, 119,
    122–123, 126–127, 129–131, 136,
    141, 183
    official guide of 131, 136–137
    social tone of 67, 91–92, 97, 102–103,
    109, 123, 129–131, 141, 143, 149,
    151, 180–184,
Skegness 33, 122
social class 27, 33, 46–48, 90, 101, 115,
130–131
    and leisure 12, 16–17, 20–21, 23
    and resort development 24–25, 27,
    29, 45, 62–3, 90, 180, 186
    and space 6–7, 13, 19, 22, 45, 49,
    62–3, 180
    and society 18, 21, 23, 45, 46, 60, 181
    and tourism 5, 8, 12–14, 45–49,
    142–143, 153–154
    see also inequality and social tone
social tone 7, 8, 44, 61, 88, 141, 162, 179
    and advertising 100, 102–103,
    109–110, 113, 130–131
    'debate' 27–29, 63, 89, 91, 180, 190
    in Devon 7, 62–63, 67, 89, 90, 146,
    180–182
    and entertainment 8, 142, 145–155
    and local government 25–26, 27
    see also inequality and social class
Southend 36, 50, 78
Southern Railway 82, 113, 128

Southport 36, 78
space 6, 60–61
    conflict over 7, 13, 22–23, 88, 175
    and leisure 18–19, 180, 181, 190
    and politics 10, 13, 14
    and power 5, 6, 180–181
    and social class 45, 49, 63, 180
    and tourism 63, 88, 150, 175
sport 3, 6, 20–23, 35, 46, 53, 89, 102
    and social tone 142–3, 151–155
    see also golf; water sports; yachting
St Annes 27
steamer traffic 89, 90, 91, 93, 148, 158
steamship companies 112, 128
Stedman Jones, Gareth 16, 20, 22, 24
sunbathing 33, 35–36, 59, 64, 107, 137
Sunday entertainments 82, 142, 151–155,
182
Sunday excursions 113
Swansea 42, 174
swimming pools 33, 35, 53, 69, 145, 148,
169–173
Teignmouth 75, 77, 81, 136, 151, 153, 156,
174
    and railways 68, 71
    social tone of 67
    visitor profile of 70, 182
Tenby 54, 58, 184
tennis courts 53, 89, 130, 147, 149, 153,
154, 170
The Times 114, 117, 118, 119, 148, 152
Torbay *see* Brixham; English Riviera;
Paignton; Torquay
Torbay Tourist Board 136–137, 140
Torquay 32, 38, 42, 49, 55, 57, 60, 67,
74–75, 80–81, 87, 120, 123, 127–129, 134,
155, 159, 166, 168, 184, 188
    baths 120, 149, 170–173
    as conference town 112, 120,
    125–126
    council 51, 84–86, 94, 97, 108, 112,
    155, 184
    and entertainment policies 97, 145,
    152–155, 160–161
    facilities of 85, 92, 94, 146–147,
    155–163, 166–176
    guide book 63, 107, 114–116, 126,

132–140, 172

investment in 76, 84–85, 96, 155, 168–174, 184

marketing of 77, 98–99, 101–103, 106, 108–116, 119–126, 132–141, 172, 185

as medicinal spa 172–173

orchestra 160–162, 166

pavilion 115, 145–146, 149, 154, 158–163, 166, 169, 176

pier 145–149, 157–158

politics of 28, 84–87, 105, 106, 109–110, 120, 160–161, 168–169, 184–185

and railways 68, 71, 96, 108, 114

rejuvenation of 54, 98, 130, 136–137, 163

social tone of 63, 67, 85, 88–91, 109, 94–98, 113–114, 142–143, 149, 153–154, 161–162, 180–182

visitor profile of 70, 94–98, 105, 112, 149, 182, 185

see also English Riviera; Fleet Walk development

Torquay Times 95, 96, 97, 108, 109, 110, 114, 118, 120, 153, 168, 172

tourism 1, 2, 15, 143

employment 3, 12, 28, 38, 43, 50, 55, 65, 74, 77

and holidays abroad 37–42, 47, 59, 75, 88, 118, 126, 129, 141

and power 14–15, 180–181

and social class 46–48

studies 1–3, 8, 14, 54

surveys 36, 39, 48, 54–55, 74

theory 5–6, 10–14

value of 39, 43, 44, 50, 57, 65, 74, 76, 77

volume 38–40, 42–44, 46, 57, 74, 77

Tourism Development Action Programme 185

'Tourism For All' 189

traffic management 175, 188

transport 19, 75, 90, 106

in Devon 64, 68, 71–73, 91, 181

see also charabancs; motor transport; railways

Travel and Industrial Development Association of Great Britain and Ireland 121

travel and tourist agencies 112, 120

Travel Association of Great Britain 37

Travis, John 89–90

Urban District Councils Association 37, 108

Urry, John 12, 58, 60, 89

Wales 4, 16, 32, 44, 51, 58, 89, 178, 188

Wales Tourist Board 4, 48, 117

Walton John 35, 40, 45, 49, 55, 60, 61, 69, 78, 89

and Blackpool 26, 30, 36

and resort studies 3, 4, 25, 26, 29, 181

Walvin, James 25, 46, 48

water sports 176

see also yachting

West Country Tourist Board 136

Western Morning News 75, 131, 151

Western Times 95

Weston-Super-Mare 78, 90, 148

Williams, Allan 31, 44, 51, 54, 60

Williams, Raymond 20, 21

'Winter in Britain' campaign 117–118

women 3, 47

and leisure choices 19, 35, 48

social position of 33, 35, 107

see also gender

Woolacombe 64, 65, 67, 91

World War One 32, 33, 68, 72

and advertising 101, 107, 108

and post-war boom 155

World War Two 33, 36, 37, 72, 153

and advertising 107, 124–125, 128

and post-war boom 38, 74

and rationing 37–38, 74

and reconstruction 37, 72, 74, 128, 158

World Wide Web 140

yachting 67, 89, 173, 175, 183

see also marinas

Yates, Nigel 109, 140

Margin + Probationd   on lists (2ed) ?, p4
which T. B— too.
Shields: Places @ margin

Coros, Time and Money.   20th C man lecturer

Perkin } on social time   Northern History 20 (1984
Huggins }

Walton. — English Seaside Resort

    \ municipal etc in Blackpool
     \ in Shaw + Williams (ed), Rise + Fall

Selby + Morgan + (Barry lists (20th))

Barry: lists ith develop
Role of Windsor?
    Why Barry Co so slow
    to develop lister
    valley1?
Already a thing
market for B.S dev
difficulties of getting
there.
What was 'Barrys
'product' in 1890s?